Religious Experience

In this book, Phillip H. Wiebe examines religious, spiritual, and mystical experiences, assessing how these experiences appear to implicate a spiritual order. Despite the current prevalence of naturalism and atheism, he argues that experiences purporting to have a religious or spiritual significance deserve close empirical investigation. Wiebe surveys the broad scope of religious experience and considers different types of evidence that might give rise to a belief in phenomena such as spirits, paranormal events, God, and an afterlife. He demonstrates that there are different explanations and interpretations of religious experiences, both because they are typically personal accounts and they suggest a reality that is often unobservable. Wiebe also addresses how to evaluate evidence for theories that postulate unobservables in general and a Theory of Spirits in particular. Calling for more rigorous investigation of these phenomena, Wiebe frames the study of religious experience among other accepted social sciences that seek to understand religion.

Phillip H. Wiebe[†] (1945–2018) was Professor of Philosophy and former Dean of Arts and Religious Studies at Trinity Western University, Canada. He was the author of *Vision and Jesus* (Leafwood Publishers, 2014), *God and Other Spirits* (Oxford University Press, 2014), and *Intuitive Knowing as Spiritual Experience* (Palgrave Macmillan, 2015).

CAMBRIDGE STUDIES IN RELIGION, PHILOSOPHY, AND SOCIETY

Series Editors

Paul K. Moser, Loyola University, Chicago
Chad Meister, Bethel College, Indiana

This is a series of interdisciplinary texts devoted to major-level courses in religion, philosophy, and related fields. It includes original, current, and wide-spanning contributions by leading scholars from various disciplines that (a) focus on the central academic topics in religion and philosophy, (b) are seminal and up-to-date regarding recent developments in scholarship on the various key topics, and (c) incorporate, with needed precision and depth, the major differing perspectives and backgrounds – the central voices on the major religions and the religious, philosophical, and sociological viewpoints that cover the intellectual landscape today. Cambridge Studies in Religion, Philosophy, and Society is a direct response to this recent and widespread interest and need.

Recent Books in the Series

Roger Trigg *Religious Diversity: Philosophical and Political Dimensions*

John Cottingham *Philosophy of Religion: Towards a More Humane Approach*

William J. Wainwright *Reason, Revelation, and Devotion: Inference and Argument in Religion*

Harry J. Gensler *Ethics and Religion*

Fraser Watts *Psychology, Religion, and Spirituality: Concepts and Applications*

Gordon Graham *Philosophy, Art, and Religion: Understanding Faith and Creativity*

Keith Ward *The Christian Idea of God: A Philosophical Foundation for Faith*

Timothy Samuel Shah and Jack Friedman *Homo Religiosus? Exploring the Roots of Religion and Religious Freedom in Human Experience*

Sylvia Walsh *Kierkegaard and Religion: Personality, Character, and Virtue*

Roger S. Gottlieb *Morality and the Environmental Crisis*

J. L. Schellenberg *Religion after Science: The Cultural Consequences of Religious Immaturity*

Clifford Williams *Religion and the Meaning of Life: An Existential Approach*

Allen W. Wood *Kant and Religion*

Michael McGhee *Spirituality for the Godless: Buddhism, Humanism, and Religion*

William B. Parsons *Freud and Religion*

Charles Taliaferro and Jil Evans *Is God Invisible?: An Essay on Religion and Aesthetics*

David Wenham *Jesus in Context: Making Sense of the Historical Figure*

Paul W. Gooch *Paul and Religion: Unfinished Conversations*

Herman Philipse *Reason and Religion: Evaluating and Explaining Belief in Gods*

Religious Experience

Implications for What Is Real

PHILLIP H. WIEBE[†]
Trinity Western University

Shaftesbury Road, Cambridge CB2 8EA, United Kingdom

One Liberty Plaza, 20th Floor, New York, NY 10006, USA

477 Williamstown Road, Port Melbourne, VIC 3207, Australia

314–321, 3rd Floor, Plot 3, Splendor Forum, Jasola District Centre, New Delhi – 110025, India

103 Penang Road, #05–06/07, Visioncrest Commercial, Singapore 238467

Cambridge University Press is part of Cambridge University Press & Assessment, a department of the University of Cambridge.

We share the University's mission to contribute to society through the pursuit of education, learning and research at the highest international levels of excellence.

www.cambridge.org
Information on this title: www.cambridge.org/9781108423717

DOI: 10.1017/9781108529228

© Phillip H. Wiebe 2025

This publication is in copyright. Subject to statutory exception and to the provisions of relevant collective licensing agreements, no reproduction of any part may take place without the written permission of Cambridge University Press & Assessment.

First published 2025

A catalogue record for this publication is available from the British Library

Library of Congress Cataloging-in-Publication Data
NAMES: Wiebe, Phillip H., 1945–2018.
TITLE: Religious experience : implications for what is real / Phillip H. Wiebe, Trinity Western University, British Columbia.
DESCRIPTION: Cambridge, United Kingdom ; New York, NY, USA : Cambridge University Press, 2025. | Series: Cambridge studies in religion, philosophy, and society | Includes bibliographical references and index.
IDENTIFIERS: LCCN 2022027028 | ISBN 9781108423717 (hardback) | ISBN 9781108529228 (ebook) | ISBN 9781108438292 (paperback)
SUBJECTS: LCSH: Experience (Religion)
CLASSIFICATION: LCC BL53 .R44445 2025 | DDC 204/.2–dc23/eng20221128
LC record available at https://lccn.loc.gov/2022027028

ISBN 978-1-108-42371-7 Hardback
ISBN 978-1-108-43829-2 Paperback

Cambridge University Press & Assessment has no responsibility for the persistence or accuracy of URLs for external or third-party internet websites referred to in this publication and does not guarantee that any content on such websites is, or will remain, accurate or appropriate.

Contents

Preface		*page* vii
1	The Scope of "Religious Experience"	1
	Plato (or Socrates)	2
	St. Paul's Nine Gifts of the Spirit (First Century CE)	5
	St. Augustine's Tripartite View of "Vision"	8
	St. Teresa of Avila	12
	Augustin Poulain (cf. Thomas Merton, *Inner Experience*, 2003)	14
	William James	16
	Psychical Phenomena	20
	Roland Fischer	23
	Richard Swinburne	25
	Caroline Franks Davis	26
	Robert Zaehner	27
	Near-Death Experiences (NDEs)	28
	Sir Alister Hardy	29
	Emma Heathcote-James	30
	Digression on Levitation	31
2	The General Theory of Spirits	34
	Intelligibility	36
	Defining "Spirit"	47
	Lambda-Baryon Particles	53
	Western Origins of Human Soul (Spirit?)	58
3	Testability and Evidence	72
	God	80
	Testability	84
	Angels and Elves	92
	Principles of Evidence	96

4	**Phenomenological Evidence**	107
	Apparitions	110
	Hallucinations	118
	St. Teresa of Avila (1515–82)	129
	Catholic Constraints	134
5	**Evidence for the World of Spirits**	137
	"Decisive" Cases	141
	The Lincoln College Case	143
	The Hertfordshire Angel Case	151
	The Rhineland Case	154
	The Case of Adeline	159
	Postmortem Existence	164
	Resurrection	164
	Marian Apparitions	168
	Near-Death Experiences (NDEs)	173
6	**The Future of Religious Experience**	177
	The Fukushima Phenomena	177
	Spirit Possession and Attachment	183
	Is the Theory of Spirits Dispensable?	188
	The Future for RSM Experience	192
Bibliography		201
Index		211

Preface

Experiences that are deemed to have religious significance are found in every culture on Earth. As empirical dogmas and methodologies become increasingly important in society, science is viewed as having the ideology that will give us knowledge of religious matters, as surely as it has given us knowledge of the mundane material world we live in. Rationalist instincts that people have around religion have not disappeared, to be sure, but empirical measures are seen as needing to be exhausted before we turn to the powers of the human intellect itself. As atheism has become progressively more prevalent in Western culture, religious believers of every stripe are increasingly put on the defensive over their religious beliefs and practices and earnestly want reasons for thinking that the cosmos must "have more to it" than is suggested by the naturalism and earthly pursuits with which we tend to fill our lives. This "more" is seemingly behind many of the reasons for investigating experience, as though this "more" might be attainable by anyone at all.

The existence of God has been a particular object of interest in Western culture, influenced by Hebrew and Christian faith, and increasingly by Islam. These Abrahamic religions profess belief in one supreme God, creator of all, but they differ on the number and kind of Divine interventions in human history, interventions that obviously have experiential features to them. This is a point where controversy begins, of course, but part of the mystery of religion is whether the Deity has entered human history, and if so, how often and exactly where. This is one topic that I will discuss, in addition to other questions arising from religious, spiritual, and mystical experiences – a nondiscrete collection which I will generally refer to as RSM experience (Religious, Spiritual, Mystical). Sometimes God is said to be sensed directly, as though we have an inbuilt *sensus deitatis* (or *sensus divinitatis*) capable of giving us direct knowledge, much as our physical senses have been considered as giving us direct knowledge of common physical objects; I will consider this claim as well.

For some the existence of God is an issue that arises from the definition of God. When God is defined as a Being having more excellences that any other being (and no deficiencies), the existence of God seems an immediate inference, for if God has only excellences then God must exist necessarily, since a Being that has only contingent existence – its nonexistence is possible – is not as great as one that exists necessarily. Even a Being that can create from nothing, whether or not it exists necessarily, seems to be greater (in some sense) than anything that is created. Rationalism is perfectly at home in this environment, and some prefer using our rational powers rather than our empirical ones on RSM issues.

One issue that traditional discussion of theism has not given much attention to is the possible existence of beings – spirits – other than God. Philosophy of religion that is strongly influenced by Christian religion seems particularly inclined to consider God alone, as though human spirits (or souls) of the departed, angels, and evil spirits were not part of Christianity's history. Here the empirical method obviously triumphs, although some efforts have occasionally been expended to defend the reality of Satan by construing this being as one who is the worst possible (or perhaps conceivable). The argument that is advanced is more or less a mirror image of St. Anselm's famous argument for God's existence that defines God is that than which nothing greater can be conceived. This being who is worse than anything conceivable allows a continuum from the best possible to the worst possible to be postulated, which moves the beings who are central to religion away from empirical methods. This makes central the features by which such beings can be identified as the best or the worst possible, and agnosticism about religious realities seems guaranteed. Philosophy is naturally attracted to what appears to be a logical puzzle, at least a semantic one, and the curiosities of *human thought*, not *possible beings* implicated in human experience, come into focus. We are immediately stopped on this slide to agnosticism, however, by some religious experience related by a trusted friend, or an experience that we ourselves might have had.

Religious experience is intensely personal, which places such phenomena in an awkward position, since genuine evidence is deemed to be beyond personal preference. In every domain in which philosophy functions it encounters expectations that rise above personal preferences: In logic we discover that, although a line of arguing might tempt us, we realize upon calmer reflection that this line is *fallacious*; in epistemology we discover that while some item of information might momentarily impress us, upon reflection we realize that this information has *little evidential weight* for an issue under consideration; in the study of ontology we might discover that some population widely considers fairies to be real, but upon closer examination we find this claim to have *much less support* than the people in question are apt to adduce; and so on. Although philosophic views are now found, commonly known as postmodern, that deny a critical stance for evaluating competing epistemic and ontological claims, a similar position cannot be coherently adduced for logic. To suggest such a stance concerning logic *without* argument is simply to impose the stance, and to suggest such a stance *using* argument is to presuppose the value of the argument, and to depart from the relativism implicit in the postmodern view. Logic becomes the obstacle around which the relativity of philosophy collapses. Logic must be making some claim to objectivity, to an impersonal perspective from which some argument is being evaluated. Moreover, if logic must be objective in order to be useful at all, we can plausibly construe ontology and epistemology to have a similar perspective implicit in them. While similar arguments can be mounted concerning the study of ethics, value theory, and even aesthetics, perhaps, which seemingly reflects values "in the eye of the beholder" more than any other area of philosophy, I will not address this issue here. I do not think that finding this perspective in epistemology or ontology is an easy matter, or devoid of significant controversy, but I do consider this perspective to relate directly and profoundly to the assessment of religious experience.

The term "religion" is so rich in meaning that its contents can only be incompletely sketched. Here I generally follow Daniel Pals who reviews the Victorian anthropology of E. B. Tylor and J. G. Frazer, the social science of Sigmund Freud, Émile Durkheim, and Karl Marx, and the approaches of Max Weber, William James, Mircea Eliade, E. E. Evans-Pritchard, and Clifford Geertz. Pals holds that "Religion consists of belief and behavior associated in some way with a supernatural realm of divine or spiritual beings."[1] In another comprehensive review of religion, Ninian Smart (1927–2001), past President of the American Academy of Religion (2000), and author of many books on religion, identifies the experiential and emotional as one dimension among seven prominent features

---

[1] Pals, *Nine Theories*, p. 338.

of religion.[2] The six others consist of (1) the practical and ritual dimension; (2) the narrative and mythic dimension, which offers a systematic interpretation of the universe; (3) social and institutional structures; (4) ethical and legal teachings; (5) doctrinal and philosophic features; and (6) the material dimension, consisting of objects or places deemed to exhibit the sacred. Religious experience is clearly in a class of its own when we consider the ontological implications of the various fields in Smart's list. The topic of this book is implications for what is real in RSM experience.

[2] Smart, *The World's Religions*, pp. 11–21.

I

The Scope of "Religious Experience"

The term "Religious Experience" exists alongside such terms as "Mystical Experience" and "Spiritual Experience," perhaps overlapping with them in important ways, to denote a broad set of very important experiences. Using the rubric "RSM Experience" (Religious, Spiritual, Mystical) I will survey phenomena that seemingly implicate "a Spiritual Order," or, more likely, several such Orders, including paranormal ones.[1] We live in an age in which religion is curiously fading from view, an age now widely considered to be secular,[2] although the scope of secularity is uneven in Western culture, once decidedly Christian. We are not in a position to describe the full scope of RSM experience with confidence because the details of these experiences are insufficiently known. This claim will be supported by surveying the experiences we know about, for they point to variations on which our evidence is incomplete.

Former President of the American Academy of Religion (2010), Ann Taves, suggests that scholarly focus be directed to the experiences that subjects *deem* to be religious, rather than adopt a contrary model of research that assumes that religious things exist, and are causally active in peoples' lives.[3] This is a helpful approach to the subject of this book, since RSM experiences are ones that their subjects assess from a personal standpoint, primarily. I will not make ontological *assumptions*;

---

[1] Cf. David Griffin, *Parapsychology, Philosophy, and Spirituality*. He asserts: "Parapsychology offers evidence against the intellectual adequacy of late modern worldview" (p. 3), and I agree.
[2] Cf. Charles Taylor, *A Secular Age*.
[3] Taves, *Religious Experience*, p. 19.

rather experiential domains that are religious, spiritual, or mystical need to advance arguments for any objectivity to them. Since my interests here are overtly ontological (or metaphysical), I will be giving close attention to any evidence proffered by RSM experience. Some of these experiences have been the object of explicit attention in Western history, and so I turn to efforts to bring some order into the study of RSM experience, beginning with a philosopher who is universally known and also widely considered, correctly in my view, to have been "intoxicated" by RSM matters.

PLATO (OR SOCRATES)

Socrates is widely credited with giving to Western civilization its notion of soul. Oxford classicist, John Burnet (1836–1928) advanced this view in 1916 and was joined by other prominent twentieth-century Plato scholars, A. E. Taylor and Francis Cornford,[4] in making it. Although the historical Socrates is difficult to extract from the literary figure bearing that name, I will refer here to the writings of Plato, assuming that he elucidates the views of Socrates at least some of the time. A most significant feature of soul in the Socratic sense is that soul (a) is distinct from the body and (b) is immortal, which implies that it does not merely survive the death of the body but lives on continually in some way, possibly animating some (living) nonhuman animal or other. The Socratic concept of soul was embraced by Christian faith during its long hegemony over Western thought, and so is familiar everywhere.

Plato describes Socrates as referring to various RSM experiences that he either has had or knows about from observation or reports of others. In *The Laws* the major figure is an Athenian stranger, probably not the historical figure known widely as Socrates, so the views are evidently those of Plato. They accord with earlier dialogues in which the historical Socrates is seemingly represented. Xenophon (430–354 BCE), a contemporary of Socrates and Plato, says this of Socrates: "[he was] so religious that he did nothing without counsel from the gods; so just that he did no injury, however small, to any man, but conferred the greatest benefits on all who dealt with him."[5]

The references in Plato's *Dialogues* to RSM experiences include the following:

---

[4] A. E. Taylor, *Socrates*, p. 132; Cornford, *Before and after Socrates*, p. 50.
[5] Xenophon, *Memorabilia*, bk. 4, chap. 8, *sec.* 11.

1. *Possession or inspiration*: "God takes away the minds of poets" ... [and] "also uses diviners and holy prophets in order that we who hear them may know them to be speaking not of themselves ... who utter these priceless words in a state of unconsciousness, but that God himself is the speaker...; poets are only the interpreters of the God by whom they are severally possessed."[6] Possession is also said to be a state in which one is "taken hold of."[7] In his discussion with Cratylus over knowledge in general, including the meaning of names, Socrates accepts that he might be an oracle, perhaps inspired by some Muse.[8] In a discussion with Phaedrus, he poses the question whether he might be inspired as he speaks, to which Phaedrus replies: "Yes, Socrates, you seem to have an unusual flow of words."[9] He describes his state as ecstasy, since he is unable to remember some of what he said.[10]

2. *Prophecy*: This category merges with the previous one, but Socrates speaks generally of the human soul as being prophetic.[11] Here he also mentions that while he is a diviner, he is not a good one. The feature of his experience that he singles out for comment is the presence of "the sign" that only forbids, never bids. In this conversation with Phaedrus, he mentions the voice telling him that he was guilty of impiety: "buying honour from men at the price of sinning against the gods."[12] Prophecy is described as the "blessing of divine madness."[13] He also mentions that he had been exposed to the Nymphs when describing the demands of a lover: "Do you not perceive that I am already overtaken by the Nymphs to which you [Phaedrus] have mischievously exposed me?"[14] When the Muses take hold of "a delicate and virgin soul," they inspire frenzy.[15]

3. *Prescient Dream*: As Socrates is preparing for his execution, he converses with Crito about his vision (in sleep) that he views as predicting

---

[6] Plato, *Ion* 534. Quotations are from Jowett's translation, which gives the Stephanus pagination as shown here.
[7] Plato, *Ion*, p. 536.
[8] Plato, *Cratylus*, p. 428.
[9] Plato, *Phaedrus*, p. 238.
[10] Ibid., p. 263.
[11] Ibid., p. 242.
[12] Ibid., p. 242; cf. *Alcibiades* I, p. 105.
[13] Plato, *Phaedrus*, p. 265.
[14] Ibid., p. 241.
[15] Ibid., p. 245. Rohde describes the dismembering of living victims at the height of religious frenzy in *Psyche: The Cult of Souls and Belief in Immortality among the Greeks*.

the date of his death: "There appeared to me the likeness of a woman, fair and comely, clothed in bright raiment, who called to me and said, 'O Socrates, The third day hence to fertile Phthia shalt thou go'."[16] He and Crito take this as knowledge from the gods.

4. *Waking Vision*: In a discourse about the insights, as well as misleading descriptions, found in poets, Socrates speaks of God as incapable of deceit: "He deceives not, either by sign or word, by dream or waking vision."[17] The waking vision is not illustrated, but the reference could be to apparition, of which he speaks in connection with reciting an account of an apparition that creates the greatest effect upon an audience: "Are you not carried out of yourself, and does not your soul in ecstasy seem to be among the persons or places of which you are speaking, whether they are in Ithaca or in Troy or whatever may be the scene of the poem?"[18] He speaks of a chain of inspirations, beginning with Homer, for instance, but then devolving upon those who use the words of Homer.[19]

5. *Apparitions*: Socrates speaks about the condition that follows those who have craved after immoral and material things, and cannot bear to part with their bodies: "These must be the souls, not of the good, but of the evil, which are compelled to wander about such places [tombs and sepulchers] in payment of their former evil way of life."[20] Moreover, "the souls of the dead have the power after death of taking an interest in human affairs."[21] Consequently legislators for a state must take care to order correctly "the repositories of the dead, and the rites which have to be observed by him who would propitiate the inhabitants of the world below."[22] Legislators should also prevent the erection of private shrines at places where apparitions are seen, for secret attempts to propitiate the God will only multiply crimes infinitely, "bringing guilt from heaven upon themselves, and also upon those who permit them ... and the consequence is that the whole state reaps the fruit of their impiety."[23]

---

[16] Plato, *Crito*, p. 44.
[17] Plato, *Republic* II, p. 382.
[18] Plato, *Ion*, p. 535.
[19] Ibid., pp. 535–36.
[20] Plato, *Phaedo*, p. 81; cf. *Laws* V, p. 738, where apparitions are said to have determined where temples should be built.
[21] Plato, *Laws* IX, p. 927.
[22] Plato, *Republic* IV, p. 427.
[23] Plato, *Laws* X, p. 910.

6. *Witchcraft and Conjuring*: *The Laws* orders that any diviner or prophet who uses incantations or enchantments to injure another, and the cause is deemed to be the diviner's actions, that prophet or diviner must die; if such (successful) enchantment is performed by someone who is not a prophet, a court can try the case and administer punishment or a fine.[24] Moreover, those who claim to be able to conjure the dead and charm the Gods will overthrow individuals and families and must be severely punished.[25]
7. *Efficacious Sacrifice:* Diotoma of Mantineia, said to be wise in many ways, supposedly delayed the onset of a plague upon Athens when the Athenians offered sacrifice. Significant injunctions are given for performing proper sacrifices. Consistent with this is the injunction not to slander Proteus and Thetis, known to be wizards.[26]

Plato's Myth of Er in his *Republic* provides us with a classic account of souls of the dead receiving justice in their afterlife. I do not include it here based on an actual experience, although it is possible that Plato intended it to be such. It is anticipatory of what has become known in the twentieth century as a Near-death Experience (NDE), discussed in the following text.

ST. PAUL'S NINE GIFTS OF THE SPIRIT (FIRST CENTURY CE)

Paul is the next major figure in Western history in which RSM experience is mentioned significantly. He shows evidence of knowledge of the writings found in Greek antiquity, such as those of Epimenides, but the influence upon him of Hebrew literature and Christian experience is greater. Numerous experiences are mentioned in which spirits of various kinds are said to have been implicated, but no effort to classify them is included, apart from Paul's efforts to identify gifts of "the Holy Spirit;" that is, the Presence deemed to derive from the Creator-God. If we add apparitions and exorcism, as well as the enigmatic event described by St. Luke as "the giving of the Spirit" on the Feast of Pentecost – a special event in the Hebrew calendar – we have twelve phenomena:[27]

---

[24] Plato, *Laws* XI, p. 933.
[25] Plato, *Laws* X, p. 909.
[26] Plato, *Republic* II, p. 381.
[27] *I Corinthians* 12 is the source for most of these.

1. *The word of wisdom*: This gift is evidentially meant to signify awareness of how to deal with a difficult situation, although distinguishing Divine wisdom from enhanced human wisdom would be difficult without some other indication that God was its source. This is a gift that Socrates would have recognized, also the next one.
2. *The word of knowledge*: An example of extraordinary knowledge, evidently from a Divine source, is given in the life of the early Christian Church when St. Peter is said to have known that Ananias and Sapphira, a married couple in the first Church in Jerusalem, were deceptive about the size of their gift from the sale of their land. He says that "Satan filled their hearts to lie to the Holy Spirit," whereupon each of them, at separate times in one day, fell down dead.[28]
3. *Faith*: This is evidently extraordinary confidence that something of significance will occur. Jesus, said to be the Christ, is described by St. John as having assured his disciples that he would rise from death to live again.[29] This particular RSM experience is close to prophecy.
4. *The gifts of healing*: This gift is evidently the power to cause the sick and diseased to become well and is frequently mentioned in the New Testament (NT), and sometimes in the Old Testament. It perhaps belongs with the next one.
5. *The working of miracles*: In this book, I am not giving particular attention to events in which the natural order is interrupted or altered. The Hebrew-Christian scriptures are full of marvels, and the allegation of these continues throughout the history of Christendom.
6. *Prophecy*: Agabus, known to be a prophet from Judea, went to Caesarea, where Paul was staying, to prophesy that Paul would be bound and "delivered into the hands of the Gentiles" by the Jews at Jerusalem.[30] This evidently happened, according to Luke's account.
7. *Discerning of spirits*: In conventional Christian theology, the domain of Divine beings is challenged by Satan and his demonic hordes; Socrates and his Greek compatriots seemingly did not recognize this order of being. So prophets and diviners could be

---

[28] *Acts of the Apostles* 5:1–11.
[29] *The Gospel of St. John* 10:17–18.
[30] *Acts of the Apostles* 21:10–11.

influenced, in Christian views, by either the Divine or the diabolical, making discernment about the source of insight vital. Gordon Fee, noted scholar of Christian charismata, says that little agreement exists on the meaning of the phrase that Paul uses.[31]

8. *Speaking in various kinds of tongues* (glossolalia): This still-controversial gift among Christians is said to have been exhibited on several occasions, most notably when "the Holy Spirit was given." Gordon Fee says that Paul understands those who exhibit this gift to be neither "out of control" nor "in ecstasy."[32]

9. *The interpretation of glossolalia*: No precise example of where this occurred is given in the NT, but Paul seems to have been familiar with it, seemingly involving giving the sense of some instance of glossolalia occurring in Christian worship. It is likely not a *translation* of what was said.

10. *Baptism in the Spirit*: Paul mentions this phenomenon, but Luke gives the paradigmatic description of it "on the day of Pentecost": when a powerful wind was heard, flames of fire were seen resting on the heads of the Christ's disciples, and Jewish Christians spoke a dozen or so known languages, evidently without having learned them.[33] The Christ himself said that baptism in the Spirit would be an experience that would leave his followers empowered.[34] Extraordinary controversy still exists in the Church over the meaning of NT texts that speak to this issue.

11. *Exorcism*: Luke describes several exorcisms by Paul, including one in Philippi where he exorcised "a spirit of divination" from a damsel.[35] Luke also describes an unsuccessful attempt at exorcism, when some Jewish vagabonds tried to exorcize on the authority of the Christ, although they seemingly were not his disciples, "and the man in whom the evil spirit was leaped on them [seven exorcists] and prevailed against them, so that they left the house naked and wounded."[36]

12. *Visions and Apparitions*: Paul reports that his apostolic authority rested in part on the fact that he had seen the Risen Christ.[37] The

---

[31] Gordon Fee, *God's Empowering Presence*, p. 171.
[32] Ibid., p. 173.
[33] Acts 2:1–12.
[34] Acts 1:8.
[35] Acts 16:16–18.
[36] Acts 19:16.
[37] I Corinthians 9:1.

nature of his experience is widely debated, especially in view of the three descriptions of it in *Acts*, not all parts of which concur with one another. When St. Stephen was being stoned, he reported: "Behold, I see the heavens opened, and the Son of man standing at the right hand of God." This is just one of several RSM experiences that appear to involve conventional human perception. The nature of these experiences remains debatable, as my discussion of Christic visions in Chapter 5 will show.

Biblical scholarship is now so extensive that every term and phrase in the Hebrew-Christian Bible is subject to searching scrutiny, so that discussion of these dozen RSM experiences could perhaps fill several books. Because some of them are evidently illustrated in the NT, they are not as obscure as they might seem.

ST. AUGUSTINE'S TRIPARTITE VIEW OF "VISION"

The work of St. Augustine of Hippo on RSM experience from approximately 400 CE remains a starting point for virtually all Western discussion of experience variously known as religious, spiritual, mystical, or comparable designations. Mystics such as St. Teresa of Avila and St. John of the Cross illustrate this fact, for not only these mystics but also their critics who discuss their experience do so in Augustinian categories. Augustine's influence extends right to the present time. He illustrates: In reading a text such as "Love your neighbor as yourself," he observes that "the letters are seen *corporeally*, the neighbor is thought of *spiritually*, and love is beheld *intellectually*."[38] He says that when a body is seen corporeally, an image of it is produced "in the spirit," and if "the spirit is irrational, as in the beasts, the announcement made by the eyes goes just as far as the spirit."[39] With creatures having a rational soul, however, "the announcement is made also to the intellect, which presides over the spirit."[40] Augustine identifies:

1. the body (*corpus*),
2. the imagination *(spiritus)*, and
3. the intellect

as the human faculties involved in ordinary perception and knowledge, but they are also involved in experiences that have RSM significance.

[38] Augustine, *The Literal Meaning of Genesis* (*Lit. Gen.*) 12.11.22; my italics.
[39] Ibid.
[40] Ibid.

The Scope of "Religious Experience"

Augustine considers perception in humans to occur as a result of rays *from* our bodies grasping earthly objects; in this he exhibits his tie to antiquity.[41] This phenomenon of having rays encounter common objects makes an impression upon the body, which the soul notices, but Augustine does not consider anything corporeal to be able to act directly upon the soul, for "only spirit acts on spirit."[42] The principle that "like can only act upon like" was prevalent in the ancient world,[43] and is still discussed.[44] Augustine holds that corporeal vision never "oversees" another operation in a human being, but when an object is imagined, the "spirit" functions as an overseer of the body. When the intellect reflects on matters that are neither seen nor imagined, such as love, it exercises its unique powers of overseeing both the perceptual senses and the imagination (spirit). He does allow for the possibility that "a progression of revelation" might also be found in each one of the three categories, and speaks about intellectual vision varying in its clarity;[45] he also says, however, that he cannot "recognize or maintain any objects or visions other than the three kinds perceived by the body and spirit and the mind."[46]

In order to elucidate the notion of spiritual vision and to distinguish it from intellectual vision, Augustine turns to St. Paul where he makes a distinction between the human spirit and the human mind:[47] "If I pray in a tongue (*glossolalia* in Greek), my spirit (*pneuma*) prays but my understanding (*nous*) is unfruitful." Paul is contrasting glossolalia with the normal exercise of one's intellectual powers in speech. Paul elaborates on the distinction between the human spirit and the human mind in the same passage, writing: "One who prays in a tongue speaks not to men but to God, for no one understands him, but he utters mysteries in the Spirit,"

---

[41] *Lit. Gen.* 7.13.20; the front part of the brain is said to be particularly significant (7.17.23).

[42] J. H. Taylor, *Lit. Gen.*, Vol. 2, notes on bk. 12, p. 306, n. 53. "Spirit" and "soul" are often used interchangeably.

[43] Cornford, *From Religion*, p. 86. We still see a trace of it in the twentieth century where theorists wonder whether mind can act on body, or vice versa, since they are such different substances. Homeopathic medicine, widely known in Europe and now undergoing a renaissance in North America, also clings to this ancient adage.

[44] For example, see Nadler, *Occasionalism*, pp. 7–11.

[45] *Lit. Gen.* 12.6.15. In *On the Quantity of the Soul* (*De Quantitate Animae*), he speaks about the seven degrees of the soul, the last of which is contemplation of God (33.76), but earlier degrees are animation, sensation, art, virtue, tranquility, and entrance into intellectual vision; cf. John Peter Kenney, *The Mysticism of Saint Augustine*, pp. 91–92. This list evidently describes something different than the three kinds of vision.

[46] *Lit. Gen.* 12.29.57.

[47] *Lit. Gen.* 12.8.19; see I Corinthians 14:14f.

and "He who speaks in tongues edifies [only] himself."[48] The Greek word *pneuma* in these texts is generally translated as "spirit," not as "imagination," so the expression "spiritual vision" more accurately carries the connotation of Augustine's thought than "imaginative vision." His explanation of spiritual vision demonstrates that this Pauline passage was not peripheral in his understanding.

Augustine accepts the reality of divination, and speculates on the mechanism by which the soul can exercise such a power. He rejects not only the notion that the soul has the power of divination in itself, but also the possibility that the soul might be assisted by an inferior corporeal object, and then conjectures that divination is the result of another spirit (besides one's own) aiding the human soul. He asks a long series of questions, including the following: "Are images produced in the soul which were not previously there? Or are they in some spirit into which the soul rushes and enters to see them? ... Or does the soul see the objects sometimes in itself and at other times by means of *mingling with another spirit*?"[49] Augustine observes that both evil and good spirits might be implicated in such events, which makes the discernment of their source difficult. He understands the human spirit as having ontological integrity in a way that modernity no longer accepts, and any suggestion that "spirit" and "imagination" are interchangeable (without confusion) in his discussion of divination is impossible to maintain. His speculation about the possibility that spirits might mingle, for instance, could hardly be expressed without elaborate explanation as the mingling of imaginations.[50]

Augustine obviously considers the human spirit to be implicated in ordinary experiences, but his primary interest in "visions" is related to his conviction that in them "the transcendent world" is encountered. Augustine claims that some people have knowledge about events that are beyond the reach of their senses by virtue of being possessed by a devil; on the other hand, "when a good spirit *seizes or ravishes* the spirit of a man to direct it to an extraordinary vision, there can be no doubt that the images are signs of other things which it is useful to know, for this is a

---

[48] *I Corinthians* 14:2, 4, respectively.
[49] *Lit. Gen.* 12.13.28; my italics.
[50] We might wonder how spirits could mingle or impenetrate one another; cf. Russell, *Logical Atomism* (1924) on impenetrability: "Matter is impenetrable because it is easier to state the laws of physics if we make our constructions so as to secure impenetrability. Impenetrability is a logically necessary result of definition, though the fact that such a definition is convenient is empirical" (p. 134).

gift of God."[51] He does not explain how a person could recognize being "ravished" or "seized" by a good spirit, or by being possessed by a devil, for that matter, but he is clearly thinking of extraordinary experiences, which some might now call "altered states of conscious awareness."[52] As Augustine understands the phenomenon, the human spirit can be involved in both ordinary and extraordinary experience, and because the term "imagination" is the most appropriate term to describe the ordinary experience, the expression "imaginative vision" has become widely used to describe this visionary experience. Augustine considers spiritual vision to include human insights into spiritual realities, not merely the mundane experience of imagining an object or an event, so using "imaginative vision" to identify Augustine's spiritual vision is to tame it, so to speak, for the term "imagination" has no obvious connotations of a transcendent form of reality to those of a modern mind-set. Moreover, the term "imaginative vision" is not generally associated now with those extraordinary gifts of the Spirit featured in Augustine's original explication.

Augustine argues that several kinds of objects exist for each kind of human experience of reality: At the corporeal level we find luminous bodies and stars, as well as the objects that these lights illuminate; at the spiritual level are angels and the objects that they reveal; finally, at the intellectual level are objects seen in the soul itself, such as virtues, and also "the Light by which the soul is illumined, in order that it may see and truly understand everything, either in itself or in the light. For the Light is God Himself." He adds that "when [the soul] tries to behold the Light, it trembles in its weakness and finds itself unable to do so."[53] However, when the soul is withdrawn from the senses of the body and is appropriately fitted for a (noncorporeal) vision of the Light, it "sees above itself that Light in whose illumination it is enabled to see all the objects that it sees and understands in itself."[54] Augustine's respect for the Hebrew-Christian Scriptures *and* for Platonic (or Socratic) categories in the theory

---

[51] *Lit. Gen.* 12.13.28; my italics.
[52] See Pilch, "Visions in Revelation and Alternate Consciousness," "The Transfiguration of Jesus," and "Appearances of the Risen Jesus in Cultural Context," for an interpretation of appearances of Jesus and other visions using the category of altered states of consciousness. Pilch includes the effects of alcohol, and so he offers yet another list of curious experiences having possible religious significance; drunkenness, however, is rarely seen as having RSM significance.
[53] *Lit. Gen.* 12.31.59. The annotator, Taylor, thinks that this remark demonstrates that Augustine is not an ontologist, which is often interpreted as a heretical doctrine, n. 159, pp. 317–18.
[54] Ibid.

of knowledge links him to two significant thought-structures in Western history; moreover, continued respect for him brings Plato and Paul into our time.

ST. TERESA OF AVILA

St. Teresa is perhaps best known for her autobiography, in which her RSM experiences are prominently featured. In her *Interior Castle*, written in 1577, she brings (her) order into various experiences. This book reflects theology in the Christian tradition in which experience is "generally divided into three parts, respectively called the purgative,[55] the illuminative, and the unitive life. In the first, man is cleansed from sin and habitual imperfection by the use of the sacraments and by voluntary mortification of the passions."[56] This is described in the first three Mansions. In the fourth Mansion (of seven), Teresa begins to describe the experiences that would generally be described as mystical, but they could possibly fall into other categories arising from a person's active pursuit of God, or at least being open to his favors. She says that progress is made by love: "Love does not consist in great sweetness of devotion, but in a fervent determination to strive to please God in all things, in avoiding, as far as possible, all that would offend Him."[57] She describes its effects: "These feelings of devotion produce fits of sobbing; I have even heard that sometimes they cause a compression of the chest, and uncontrollable exterior motions violent enough to cause bleeding at the nose and other painful effects."[58] I suppose that some might include this as RSM experience, but I will not comment further on it. Dramatic changes that occur to our perceptual-emotive-cognitive fields of experience are apt to be construed as originating in Divine–human interaction.

Teresa speaks about the *prayer of recollection*, which she considers supernatural: "There is no occasion to retire nor to shut the eyes, nor does it depend on anything exterior; involuntarily the eyes suddenly close and solitude is found. Without any labour of one's own, the temple of which I spoke is reared for the soul in which to pray: the senses and exterior surroundings appear to lose their hold, while the spirit gradually regains

---

[55] St. John of the Cross's *The Ascent of Mount Carmel* is a substantial catalog of the evils that we subject to, both before beginning a contemplative life and then after it has advanced some distance.
[56] Teresa, "Introduction to" *Interior Castle*.
[57] Teresa, *Mansions*, p. 4, chap. 1, para. 7.
[58] Ibid., 4.2.1.

its lost sovereignty. Some say the soul enters into itself; others, that it rises above itself."[59] This is a kind of mystical experience that others have noted, as I shall indicate in the following text. In the *prayer of union*

God then deprives the soul of all its senses that He may the better imprint in it true wisdom: it neither sees, hears, nor understands anything while this state lasts, which is never more than a very brief time; it appears to the soul to be much shorter than it really is. God visits the soul in a manner which prevents its doubting, on returning to itself, that it dwelt in Him and that He was within it, and so firmly is it convinced of this truth that, although years may pass before this favour recurs, the soul can never forget it nor doubt the fact.[60]

These forms of prayer that Teresa is describing are quite different from the usual meditative prayers that might characterize the life of an average person.

In *spiritual espousal* "the soul in a secret manner sees to what a Bridegroom it is betrothed; the senses and faculties could not, in a thousand years, gain the knowledge thus imparted in a very short time. The Spouse, being Who He is, leaves the soul far more deserving of completing the espousals, as we may call them."[61] Here the soul is "resolved to fulfil the will of her Spouse in all things and to do all she can to please Him."[62] In the sixth Mansion, God arouses the soul "by means of words addressed to the soul in many different ways; sometimes they appear to come from without; at other times from the inner depths of the soul; or again, from its superior part; while other speeches are so exterior as to be heard by the ears like a real voice."[63]

Teresa speaks of *raptures* of several kinds in the sixth Mansion: "In one sort of rapture the soul, although perhaps not engaged in prayer at the time, is struck by some word of God which it either remembers or hears. His Majesty, touched with pity by what He has seen it suffer for so long past in its longing for Him, appears to increase the spark I described in the interior of the spirit until it entirely inflames the soul which rises with new life like a phoenix from the flames."[64] Another experience in the sixth Mansion is described in these terms:

Sometimes the person is at once deprived of all the senses, the hands and body becoming as cold as if the soul had fled; occasionally no breathing can be

---

[59] *Ibid.*, 4.3.1.
[60] *Ibid.*, 5.1.8.
[61] *Ibid.*, 5.4.2.
[62] *Ibid.*
[63] *Ibid.*, 6.1.3. St. John of the Cross speaks of this in *The Ascent*, bk. 2, chaps. 28–31.
[64] Teresa, *Ibid.*, 6.4.2–6.4.3.

detected. This condition lasts but a short while; I mean in the same degree, for when this profound suspension diminishes the body seems to come to itself and gain strength to return again to this death which gives more vigorous life to the soul. This supreme state of ecstasy never lasts long, but although it ceases, it leaves the will so inebriated, and the mind so transported out of itself that for a day, or sometimes for several days, such a person is incapable of attending to anything but what excites the will to the love of God; although wide awake enough to this, she seems asleep as regards all earthly matters.[65]

Some of the forms of prayer Teresa has in mind are likely experienced only by those in monastic vocations in which meditative prayer is made the focus of a person's attention.

She next treats of *imaginary (or imaginative, or spiritual) visions* "whereby it is held that the devil is more liable to deceive people than by the other visions I have already described. This is probably true. Yet when imaginary visions are Divine, they seem, in a certain manner, more profitable for us than the others, as being more suited to our nature – with the exception of the visions sent by our Lord in the seventh mansion which far surpass all others." Moreover, in imaginary visions the favor of Divine and spiritual nuptials is bestowed. She writes:

after having received Holy Communion [she] beheld our Lord, full of splendour, beauty, and majesty, as He was after His resurrection. He told her that henceforth she was to care for His affairs as though they were her own and He would care for hers: He spoke other words which she understood better than she can repeat them. This may seem nothing new, for our Lord had thus revealed Himself to her at other times; yet this was so different that it left her bewildered and amazed, both on account of the vividness of what she saw and of the words heard at the time, also because it took place in the interior of the soul where, with the exception of the one last mentioned, no other vision had been seen.[66]

Teresa accepts the Augustinian categories of "visions" that I mentioned earlier, including *intellectual visions*, deemed to be devoid of deception.

AUGUSTIN POULAIN (CF. THOMAS MERTON, *INNER EXPERIENCE*, 2003)

Augustin Poulain published a study of the eight distinct states of consciousness of those who have practiced mysticism in Christian contexts, calling them kinds of *prayer*.[67] Poulain considers these distinctions largely

---

[65] Ibid., 6.4.17–6.4.18.
[66] Ibid., 7.2.1.
[67] Poulain, *The Graces of Interior Prayer*, in 1901. This is no longer a customary way of speaking of mystical states.

artificial ones, for "[n]ature does not proceed by sudden bounds."[68] Poulain's study went into ten editions, the fifth of which was endorsed by the Pope at the time, so it garnered significant interest and influence. Poulain supplements his detailed discussion with references to more than 150 writers in the Christian tradition, demonstrating that he is attempting to do justice to a large literary legacy. "Mystical state" is hard to define, but we can go along with the definition proposed in the *Stanford Encyclopedia of Philosophy*: "A (purportedly) super sense-perceptual or sub sense-perceptual experience granting acquaintance of realities or states of affairs that are of a kind not accessible by way of sense perception, somatosensory modalities, or standard introspection."[69] Poulain considers a person's natural dispositions, intellectual abilities, and vocation as having an influence on how quickly one can reach these states.[70] His classification sheds light on the categories treated by St. Teresa in the *Mansions*, indeed, on all her other writing.

In construing mysticism as capable of participating in that "forward movement which is to be seen in all the descriptive sciences,"[71] Poulain expresses his belief that mystical experience might be made the subject of an *exact study*, although mysticism might not now belong to science as this is conventionally interpreted. Exact and critical forms of inquiry will increasingly have a significant role in the future study of RSM experience, so studies tending in this direction are worthy of note. The eight kinds of prayer recognized by Poulain illuminate the categories discussed by Teresa of Avila:

1. *Recitation* and
2. *Meditation*.

These two are not of interest to Poulain, since we initiate these kinds of prayer. The prayers he recognized as mystical are:

3. *Affective prayer*, which involves a dominant idea that is accompanied with "very ardent affections," perhaps love or praise or gratitude, etc. Then he adds, "The *deduction* of truths is partly replaced by *intuition*. From the intellectual point of view the soul becomes simplified."[72]

---

[68] Poulain, *Graces* 2.11. William James also remarks that generation and regeneration are matters of degree and that "here as elsewhere, nature shows continuous differences," *Varieties*, lect. 10.
[69] Gellman, "Mysticism."
[70] Poulain, *Graces* 2.18.
[71] Ibid., Preface to 1st ed., p. xiv (5th ed.).
[72] Ibid., 2.2.

4. *The prayer of simplicity* (or the prayer of simple regard) occurs when our will becomes involved, and when our affections vary little and can be expressed with very few words.[73] He does not think that we can generate this state by an act of the will.
5. *The prayer of quiet.*
6. *The prayer of union.*

In the prayer of quiet, the Divine action is said to be insufficiently strong to hinder distractions, but in the prayer of union the Divine influence is so great that "the soul is fully occupied with the divine object."[74]

7. *Ecstatic union*, and
8. *Deifying union* (or "spiritual marriage").

In his discussion of the effects of mystic union upon the human body, he mentions the immobility of limbs, and then cites the reported levitations of Catherine Emmerich (1774–1824), who often "climbed" the columns of her church without a ladder in order to clean or decorate cornices that were humanly inaccessible.[75] Poulain does not question the veracity of these reports, and I will not go into the miraculous claims made.

He sums up the object of prayer as follows: "Sometimes, when entering into prayer or some other exercise, with dryness and disgust, after suffering this pain, she [the soul] suddenly perceives that the Bridegroom is *present*, and this presence, with regard to which she feels great certainty, causes a loving and reverent trembling.... This presence (whether transient or not) operates in such wise as to make us *perceive*, *feel*, and know with certainty that *God is in the soul* and that the soul is in God."[76] The list that Poulain offers illuminates features of Teresa and perhaps even Augustine, who might not have viewed as plausible the continuum that we find in Poulain.

WILLIAM JAMES

William James (1842–1910), Professor of Psychology at Harvard University for many years, is well known for his examination of RSM experience in his Gifford Lectures for 1901–2, and in the subsequent

---

[73] Ibid., 2.3.
[74] Ibid., 3.8.
[75] Ibid., 13.2; he drops this remark on levitation as though the phenomenon was uncontroversial. The article on her in *The Catholic Encyclopedia* omits any mention of her levitation.
[76] Ibid., 5.28; italics original. He quotes and translates from Le P. Nouet, *La conduite de l'homme d'Oraison* (1674), bk. 4, chap. 6.

book, *The Varieties of Religious Experience*. This book signals an interest in RSM experience in Western culture not beginning from religious assumptions, and is valuable for that reason alone. He does not attempt an obvious catalog of recognized kinds of RSM experience, but his review of the topic, which includes many detailed accounts of experience from those who themselves underwent it, provides a reader with some sense of its scope. He notes that his interest is not institutional religion,[77] but rather the experiences that experiencers themselves consider religious. He construes religion as pertaining to that which is Divine[78] but does not focus on a definition of "religion." I will say more about definitions in Chapter 2. James is particularly taken with self-description, but he does not confine his attention to just this category of experience. The following list of RSM experience shows his range of interests:

1. *The sense of God*, or of the Spirit of God.[79] This is reminiscent of John Calvin's *sensus divinitatis* ("sense of divinity"): "That there exists in the human minds and indeed by natural instinct, some sense of Deity, we hold to be beyond dispute, since God himself, to prevent any man from pretending ignorance, has endued all men with some idea of his Godhead."[80]
2. *The place of strong emotions*, including joy, fear, and laughter, often considered to be evoked by God.[81]
3. *The sense of being "born anew"* or "born again," which is an experience reported by those James describes as "twice-born" rather than "once-born."[82] The twice-born often have a melancholic disposition; the "once-born" are healthy-minded[83] and do not feel a need for a substantial change in outlook, and the accompanying behaviors.
4. *Mind-cures* are possible, and "miracles" of healing can occur as a consequence of relaxation, rather than preoccupation with fear-driven religion and morbid-mindedness.[84]

---

[77] James, *Varieties*, p. 31f.
[78] Ibid., p. 32.
[79] Ibid., p. 60f.
[80] Calvin, *Institutes*, bk. 1, chap. 3, para. 1. This view is shared by John Baillie in *The Sense of the Presence of God* (Gifford Lectures 1961–62), Alvin Plantinga in *Warranted Christian Belief*, chap. 6, and also by William Alston in *Perceiving God*.
[81] James, *Varieties*, pp. 74–76.
[82] Ibid., p. 79ff.
[83] Ibid., p. 86.
[84] Ibid., p. 104ff.

5. *Conversion* is an experience for which James is well known. In general, conversion signifies the unification of a divided self, resulting in firmer convictions on religious matters.[85] Many examples are adduced, largely from Christianity, especially Protestantism. Some involve rapid changes, but others more subtle and gradual ones. He collects very different kinds of experience under "conversion," such as visions, Spirit-baptism, illumination, and striking emotions. James sees the source of change to derive from a person's unconscious or subconscious life.[86]
   a. *Conversion in adolescence* follows a sense of incompleteness, imperfection, brooding, depression, morbid introspection, and a sense of sin; the resulting conversion brings happy relief, confidence within oneself, objectivity, and a movement into adulthood.[87]
   b. In the *conversion of drunkards*, emphasis is upon the moral aspect of religion, and doctrinal matters are virtually nonexistent.[88]
   c. *Redemption to another universe* was the experience of St. Paul, John Bunyan, and Leo Tolstoy; their melancholy seems never to have disappeared.[89]
6. *Mystical states* of consciousness are considered, including some that might simulate them, such as the effects of alcohol and nitrous oxide.[90] Here cosmic consciousness, Hindu Samadhi, and hypnosis are also discussed.[91]

James does not attempt to penetrate the metaphysical realm that might be implicated in RSM experience but highlights the subconscious domain that exists beyond the conscious and wants to intrude upon our conscious life.[92] He writes: "If there be higher powers able to impress us, they may get access to us only through the subliminal door."[93] The worth of an experience cannot be decided by its origin, he says, but only by its fruits. But when we examine fruits, we find that no significance attaches to sudden changes, for people who have not had such

---

[85] Ibid., p. 180ff.
[86] Ibid., p. 201.
[87] Ibid., p. 203.
[88] Ibid., p. 207.
[89] Ibid., p. 146.
[90] Ibid., p. 376f.
[91] Ibid., p. 389f.
[92] Ibid., p. 234.
[93] Ibid.

experiences often exhibit as much goodness as those who do. He devotes two chapters to saintliness.

A curious feature of James's treatment of RSM experience is his failure to mention its occasional intersubjective features. He writes of Paul's conversion with considerable interest, for example, but he overlooks aspects of Paul's alleged experience that are intersubjective. Our main source for Paul's conversion is Luke's *Acts of the Apostles*, although Paul makes brief reference to it also in his letters. We find three accounts in *Acts* of this conversion, two of which appear to be quotations from Paul, whereas Luke speaks in the other. In the first account Luke says that the men who were with Saul (later Paul) heard the voice that spoke to him, but saw no one.[94] The being that appeared in great light spoke to Paul, an experience he considers an encounter with the Risen Christ. In the second account he says that "they that were with me saw indeed the light, and were afraid; but they heard not the voice of him that spake to me."[95] In the third account Paul says: "At midday, O king, I saw in the way a light from heaven, above the brightness of the sun, shining round about me and them which journeyed with me. And when we were all fallen to the earth...."[96]

In discussing Paul's conversion experience James says: "There is one form of sensory automatism which possibly deserves special notice on account of its frequency. I refer to hallucinatory or pseudo-hallucinatory luminous phenomena, *photisms*, to use the term of the psychologists. Saint Paul's blinding heavenly vision seems to have been a phenomenon of this sort."[97] A striking feature of all three accounts of Paul's experience is that, while they might not agree precisely on details, they all mention some intersubjectively observable causal effect or concomitant. I shall discuss this feature of (some) RSM experience in the following text, for it speaks to something independent of Paul's own phenomenological impressions. James does not discuss this, and I cannot understand exactly why that is. A researcher would be indisputably biased if s/he dealt with those parts of a report for which one already has an explanation, and ignored another part of the same report for which no explanation is readily at hand.

Another telling feature of James's discussion of "Religious Experience" is that he considers psychical phenomena to be in the general domain of

---

[94] *Acts* 9:7.
[95] *Acts* 22:9.
[96] *Acts* 26:13–14.
[97] James, *Varieties*, pp. 136–67.

such experience. In this respect he has the outlook of Augustine who also discusses phenomena that would often be deemed as psychical, not religious, *per se*. In view of my interest here in not eliding over any experience that might be deemed religious, or spiritual, or mystical – problematic terms all – I will include a rough overview of psychical phenomena. I have drawn them from a study that purports to be encyclopedic.[98]

PSYCHICAL PHENOMENA

Phenomena conventionally viewed as "psychical" or "spiritual" are not always included in phenomena deemed religious, but Socrates, Paul, Augustine, Teresa, and James all allude to some, so it is fitting to include them in my broad view of RSM experiences. Here is a partial list on the subject drawn from *The Encyclopedia of Ghosts and Spirits*, by Rosemary Guiley, for which I will only offer minimal descriptions when the phenomena seem poorly known:

1. *Apparitions.*
2. *Automatisms and automatic writing*: These are peculiar, often rapid, human behaviors deemed to be caused by a spirit.
3. *Bilocation*: The phenomenon of someone being (or seeming to be) in two locations at one and the same time; this is alleged, for example, of the monk, St. Padre Pio of Pietrelcina, Italy (1887–1968).
4. *Clairvoyance & extra-sensory perception*: Perceptual insights into matters beyond normal perceptual powers.
5. *Death omen*: Predicting the time of someone's death, with the connotation that death is thereby ensured.[99]
6. *Conjuration of the dead*: To call upon the spirit of one who is dead to appear and to do one's bidding.[100]
7. *Deathbed visions*: Experiences of the dying, mostly "apparitions of the dead or mythical or religious figures."[101]
8. *Divination*: Foretelling or divining of the future, seemingly because of the causal powers of spirits acting upon the foreteller.
9. *Doppelgänger apparition*: An apparition of oneself.
10. *Exorcism*: The act(s) of removing influence(s) of spirits.

---

[98] Guiley, *Encyclopedia of Ghosts and Spirits* ("*EGS*").
[99] Acts 5:1–11.
[100] *Oxford English Dictionary*, "Conjure."
[101] Guiley, *EGS*, "Deathbed visions."

11. *Hyperacuity*: Specially enhanced perceptual senses, supposedly caused by the power of spirits acting in or upon a person.
12. *Hypnosis*: An altered state of consciousness in which openness to suggestions is enhanced, once thought to be brought about by spiritual forces.
13. *Levitation*: Rising into the air and maintaining such a position without material aids, sometimes considered to be the effect of a spirit acting on that body.
14. *Materialization*: A phenomenon in which a ghost, spirit, or similar entity appears in bodily form.
15. *Mirror writing*: The producing of script seen to be normal when viewed in a mirror, which is a phenomenon supposedly caused by a spirit.
16. *Moving coffins*: The movement of coffins, apparently by supernatural forces.
17. *Necromancy*: The summoning of spirits of the dead, presupposing "belief in the survival of the soul after death, the possession of a superior knowledge by the disembodied spirit, and the possibility of communication between the living and the dead."[102]
18. *Demonic possession or obsession (Western)*: These supposed effects of evil spirits are distinguished by the fact that the demon acts from an external position upon humans in obsession, but from an internal one in possession.
19. *Planchette (or Ouija board) messages*: Using a small wooden or plastic piece on a board with letters and numbers to communicate with the dead or predict the future.
20. *Prophetic dreams*: Having dreams that are an accurate portent of future events.
21. *Psychokinesis*: The (supposed) ability to move objects by mental efforts alone, for example, the acts of Uri Geller in bending spoons, which were alleged to be instances of psychokinesis.[103]
22. *Retrocognition*: The (supposed) ability to reconstruct events of the past without normal methods of gleaning information.
23. *Séance experiences*: "A sitting organized for the purpose of receiving spirit communications or paranormal manifestations via the services of a human medium."[104]

---

[102] *The Catholic Encyclopedia*, "Necromancy."
[103] Cf. https://en.wikipedia.org/wiki/Uri_Geller (accessed August 9, 2018).
[104] Guiley, *EGS*, "Séance."

24. *Sense of reincarnation*: The sense, often in children, that one has lived another life in another time, place, and body. The researches by psychiatrist Ian Stevenson (1918–2007) on reincarnation are very widely known, especially his first book on the subject, *Twenty Cases Suggestive of Reincarnation*, first published in 1966. He worked at the University of Virginia School of Medicine for fifty years.
25. *Shamanism*: Medical-religious practices in which communication with totem spirits and spirits of the dead takes place and in which supernatural feats are performed.[105] "[This is] a vague term used by explorers of Siberia in the eighteenth and nineteenth centuries to designate not a specific religion but a form of savage magic or science, by which physical nature was believed to be brought under the control of man."[106]
26. *Soul loss*: The temporary departure of the soul, hypothesized to explain sickness; permanent departure results in death.[107]
27. *Spirit attachment*: "A type of possession in which a discarnate entity becomes attached to a living person ... it does not carry demonic associations."[108] Frederick Smith offers examples of such attachment from South Asian religious literature and ongoing experience.[109]
28. *Stone throwing*: The phenomenon of stones being thrown at someone or something, seemingly from a supernatural agent or cause. A deceased brother-in-law from southern India once told me about an incident near his Indian home in which "bricks" thrown at a Christian worker by a fakir "dissolved into nothing" as they hit the ground. Diabolical forces were thought to be at work.
29. *Telepathy*: The transmission of thought from one person to another without any conventional methods of conveying information.
30. *Teleportation*: The movement of an object from one place to another without occupying the places in between, thought by some to be effected by spiritual powers.
31. *Totemism*: "The intimate relation supposed to exist between an individual or a group of individuals and a class of natural objects, that is, the totem, by which the former regard the latter as identified with them in a mystical manner."[110]

[105] Adapted from Guiley, *EGS*, "Shamanism."
[106] *The Catholic Encyclopedia*, "Shamanism."
[107] Adapted from Guiley, *EGS*, "Soul loss."
[108] Guiley, *EGS*, "Spirit attachment."
[109] Smith, *The Self Possessed*.
[110] *The Catholic Encyclopedia*, "Totemism."

32. *Trance-state*: A state of awareness other than that which occurs during waking consciousness, often occurring involuntarily.
33. *Waking dreams*: The sensation of dreaming while one is awake, also known as a hypnagogic hallucination.

The variety exhibited by this list could be a research project in its own right, which I cannot undertake here. However, I do not want to ignore this (possibly) sizeable body of RSM evidence.

ROLAND FISCHER

Roland Fischer has developed two continua for representing human experience. He offers a "cartography of inner space" in which various conscious states are mapped onto two perception-hallucination continua, both of them beginning with ordinary perception and ending with hallucinatory states.[111] These states are often considered RSM experiences, but some items in the continua are not. The first of these continua is marked by increasing levels of ergotropic arousal, that is, arousal characterized by increased activity of the sympathetic nervous system and an activated psychic state. The state of arousal found in ordinary perception marks the low end of the first arousal continuum, and points along that continuum include the increasing arousal found in states of:

1. *Sensitivity.*
2. *Creativity.*
3. *Anxiety.*
4. *Acute schizophrenia*: The American Psychiatric Association summarizes prominent features of schizophrenia as follows:[112]
    a. Positive psychotic symptoms: Hallucinations, such as hearing voices, paranoid delusions, and exaggerated or distorted perceptions, beliefs, and behaviors.
    b. Negative symptoms: A loss or a decrease in the ability to initiate plans, speak, express emotion, or find pleasure.
    c. Disorganization symptoms: Confused and disordered thinking and speech, trouble with logical thinking, and, sometimes, bizarre behavior or abnormal movements.

---
[111] Fischer, "Cartography," p. 204f.
[112] "What is schizophrenia?" www.psychiatry.org/patients-families/schizophrenia/what-is-schizophrenia (accessed April 13, 2018).

5. *Impaired cognition*: Problems with attention, concentration, memory, and declining educational performance.
6. *Catatonia*: "Catatonic schizophrenia is dominated by prominent psychomotor disturbances that may alternate between extremes such as hyperkinesis and stupor, or automatic obedience and negativism. Constrained attitudes and postures may be maintained for long periods. Episodes of violent excitement may be a striking feature of the condition."[113]
7. *Mystical rapture*.

Fischer's second continuum is marked by trophotropic arousal, that is, arousal characterized by the integration of parasympathetic with somatomotor activities resulting in behavior that reflects decreasing sensitivity to external stimuli. Here the state of arousal found in ordinary perception is at the high end of the spectrum, while the points along the second continuum include states of increasing tranquility such as the following:

1. *Zazen*: We experience everything "on the same low level of subcortical arousal but nevertheless are receptive and appreciating."[114]
2. *Dharna*: "The practice of concentrating and holding the mind on a fixed center, within or without, to the exclusion of all others; for example, one may discern only the tip of the nose or the color of a flower without associating or noting any other parts or properties. The concentration is uninterrupted."[115]
3. *Dhyan*: "Meditation, such that a continuous flow of only one thought (i.e., of the subject matter of concentration in the preceding step) is constantly maintained, much like the motion of water at a constant rate of flow."[116]
4. *Savichar Samadhi*: "Samādhi is the stage in which meditation deepens and the mind by projection may assume the form of (and thus become) the object itself on which it was meditating in the previous step. This complete union and identity of the mind with the object reveals to the yogi the real and true nature of things. Just as there is no alternative but to taste an apple to know how an apple tastes or to bear a child and be a mother to know what

---

[113] World Health Organization, "Catatonic schizophrenia," 294, https://apps.who.int/iris/bitstream/handle/10665/246208/9789241549165-V1-eng.pdf (accessed October 12, 2022).
[114] Fischer, "Cartography," p. 209.
[115] Jain and Jain, "The Science of Yoga," p. 99.
[116] *Ibid.*

motherhood is, so also there is no alternative to true knowledge other than to be what one wants to know. In other words, to know = to be. This is exactly what a yogi accomplishes through complete identity of the mind with the subject matter in savikalpa (substantive) samādhi (*vide infra*). That is why he claims direct and total knowledge and perception. Since at this stage the mind is still occupied, even though with only one thought process, it is called 'substantive'."

5. *Nirvichar Samadhi*: "In the next and final phase, the vestiges of 'substantive' samādhi are also wiped out by the yogi so that there are no thought waves at all in the mind and the true samādhi, that is, the union between the chitta (mind) and the chaitanya (consciousness) takes place. Since in this state the mind is contentless or unsubstantive, devoid of all desires, volitions, thoughts, etc., it is called 'sheer' or 'absolute'." Fischer calls this: "An emptiness where there is 'no form, no perception, no name, no concepts, no knowledge, [n]o eye, no ear, no nose, no tongue, no body, no mind ... no sound, no smell, no taste, no touch, no objects ... no knowledge, no ignorance, no decay nor death. It is the Self'."[117]

The focused meditative states along this second perception-meditation continuum, identified by Sanskrit words, are indicative of the cultural context in which these have been most assiduously cultivated and studied. Fischer then correlates these states with beta, alpha, and theta EEG waves. The end points of the two continua, that is, the ecstasy of mystical rapture of the first and *samadhi* of the second, are described by Fischer as "the two most hallucinatory states" known in human experience.[118]

RICHARD SWINBURNE

Notable among the descriptions and classifications of RSM experiences is that offered by Richard Swinburne, who, in his (former) position as Nolloth Professor of the Philosophy of the Christian Religion at Oriel College in the University of Oxford, advanced Christian faith in an prolific way.[119] In his efforts to appraise the significance of religious

---

[117] Fischer, "Cartography," p. 209.
[118] *Ibid.*, p. 205.
[119] He has published more than a dozen books on Christian themes and other books on philosophical topics.

experience for belief in God he has offered a classification scheme that he deems complete:[120]

1. *Unusual public events/objects*, such as the post-Resurrection appearances of Jesus,
2. *Seeing something as Divine* by virtue of certain sensations, such as a dream,
3. *Seeing something as Divine by virtue of certain sensations that are private* but not describable in normal vocabulary, which applies to various experiences widely considered to be mystical,
4. *Having religious experience without having sensations at all*, such as states of consciousness in which a person feels immersed in that which is Eternal or Absolute, and
5. *Seeing something as the work of God.*

Swinburne curiously claims that he has advanced a complete classification. I observe that he is considering RSM experiences in relation to *God*, which is a restriction that I shall not make while discussing phenomena that include alleged diabolical and angelic encounters.

CAROLINE FRANKS DAVIS

Another classification based on a variety of religions is offered by Caroline Franks Davis, whose study formed the basis for her doctoral dissertation at Oxford University under the supervision of Richard Swinburne. Her six main classes are:[121]

1. *Interpretive experiences*, in which an ordinary experience is interpreted within a religious framework,
2. *Quasi-sensory experiences*, including "visions and dreams, voices and other sounds, smells, tastes, the feeling of being touched, heat, pain, and the sensation of rising up (levitation),"[122]
3. *Revelatory experiences*, such as flashes of insight, enlightenment, sudden convictions, and inspirations that descend unannounced,
4. *Regenerative experiences*, such as the phenomena reported by John Wesley, and made famous by William James,

---

[120] Swinburne, *Existence of God*, 2nd ed., chap. 13.
[121] Davis, *Evidential Force*, chap. 2.
[122] *Ibid.*, p. 36.

5. *Numinous experiences*, such as those described by Rudolf Otto in *The Idea of the Holy*,[123] and
6. *Mystical experiences*, strictly interpreted as involving:
   a. the sense of having apprehended an ultimate reality,
   b. the sense of freedom from the limitations of time, space, and the individual ego,
   c. a sense of "oneness", and
   d. bliss or serenity.

Davis canvasses experiences in religions that extend beyond Christianity, which gives her classification greater scope than that found in Swinburne.

ROBERT ZAEHNER

Davis's classification of mystical experiences is shaped in part by Professor Robert Zaehner, who, in the Gifford lectures for 1967–69 as Spalding Professor of Eastern Religion and Ethics at Oxford University, advanced a tripartite classification of mysticism, based upon his extensive experience with various kinds of consciousness reported in various religious traditions:[124]

1. *Nature mysticism*: An experience in which the "I" is merged into the cosmic All, and where subject and object are obliterated, for example, the union between matter and spirit experienced in sexual acts, according to Walt Whitman.
2. *Monistic mysticism*: An experience in which the soul is isolated from all that is in time and space. Here matter is repudiated, flesh is abhorred, and sex is the enemy of eternal peace, as described by the Buddha.
3. *Theistic mysticism*: An experience of the ecstasy of eternal love, as the self is united with God.

Zaehner considered the last of these experiences to be superior to the others, for it is, in his view, the result of Divine grace. He is widely

---

[123] Otto writes about the numinous as follows: "[I]t will be useful, at least for the temporary purpose of the investigation, to invent a special term to stand for the holy minus its moral factor or moment, and, as we can now add, minus its rational aspect altogether" (p. 6). Jacqueline Mariña says that it is a view shared by Friedrich Schleiermacher in "Friedrich Schleiermacher and Rudolf Otto."

[124] Zaehner, *Concordant Discord*, chap. 3. Yandell, *Epistemology*, pp. 25–32, adds to *Monotheistic* experience and *nature* experiences; *Nirvanic* experience is associated with Buddhism, *Kevalic* experience is associated with Jainism, and *Moksha* experience is associated with Hinduism, Jainism, and Buddhism, for a total of five.

considered to have brought his Christian perspective into the assessment of experiences that come with the label "mystical," but his acquaintance with Hinduism is also in evidence. A study that attempts to be exact would seemingly differentiate experiences from one another, and so bring numerous views into play, including those offered by religions and by recognized forms of mysticism and spirituality.

NEAR-DEATH EXPERIENCES (NDES)

Raymond Moody, a medical doctor and philosopher, is widely credited with having first discovered the details of the phenomenological experience of recovering from what appeared to observers to be a state near death, primarily among people resuscitated by new life-saving equipment. His *Life after Life*, first published in 1975, has become a classic on the subject, but much more information has been gleaned since then, with *International Association for Near-Death Studies* and its *Journal for Near-Death Studies* serving as a vehicle for the dissemination of accounts and critical responses to them.

The following items are identified by Moody as having significance:[125]

1. Hearing pronouncement of "death"
2. Hearing an uncomfortable noise
3. Feeling that one is moving through a long dark tunnel
4. Finding oneself outside one's own body, but capable of seeing one's own body in the normal environment
5. Emotional upheaval over resuscitation attempts
6. Awareness of new body
7. Awareness of strange properties of the new body
8. Awareness of "spirits" of other already-dead people
9. Inability to communicate with living, although often attempted
10. Encounter with a "being of light"
11. Evaluation of one's life, and playback of major events
12. Approach of a barrier incapable of being crossed
13. Feeling required to return to normal life
14. Reluctance to return
15. Feelings of intense joy and peace
16. Reunited with one's physical body
17. Reluctance to share experience
18. Feeling the ineffability of the experience

[125] *Life*, pp. 13–16.

19. A profound impact of the experience on life
20. New views of death

Moody creates what he describes as "A Theoretical Model"[126] in which no single experience seems to have all of the above properties; no single property is found in all experiences; some near-death experiences have no features of the above kind in them at all; the order of events varies; and the completeness of an experience seems to depend on how far into the "death process" a person gets. Also, although the source is personal, some reports have corroboration in the experience of others, for example, where those undergoing resuscitation can later report on who was present in the room at the time.

SIR ALISTER HARDY

Hardy's schema was based on a study of 3,000 first-hand accounts of religious or spiritual experience obtained over eight years by Hardy and research associates. The classification scheme created with the assistance of a curator includes more than 100 separate categories, but in order to make this classification system more workable here I will keep the twelve main categories as he presents them, and then add only some of the subcategories that he identifies:[127]

1. Sensory or quasi-sensory (SQS): visual
   a. Visions
   b. Illuminations
   c. OBE, etc.
2. Auditory
   a. Voices guiding
   b. Gift of tongues, etc.
3. SQS: touch
   a. Healing
   b. Comforting, etc.
4. SQS: smell
5. Supposed ESP
   a. Telepathy
   b. Precognition
   c. Clairvoyance, etc.

---

[126] Moody, *Life*, pp. 13–16.
[127] Alister Hardy, *Spiritual Nature*, pp. 26–29.

6. Behavioral changes: enhanced, or "superhuman" power in humans
   a. Healing
   b. Exorcism, etc.
7. Cognitive and affective elements
   a. Security
   b. Joy
   c. Reverence
   d. Hope
   e. Horror
   f. (Plus seventeen more)
8. Development of experience
   a. Gradual growth in experience
   b. Identification with ideal human figure
   c. (Plus twelve more)
9. Dynamic patterns in experience
   a. Being beyond the self
   b. Self-actualization, etc.
10. Dreams
11. Antecedents or "triggers" of experience
    a. Natural beauty
    b. Prayer
    c. Music
    d. Sexual relations
    e. Childbirth
    f. (Plus sixteen more)
12. Consequences of experience
    a. Purpose in life
    b. Religious belief, etc.

The lists presented in this chapter suggest that experience and phenomena having RSM significance have only begun to be collected, and that some of the forms that are known, such as dreams, exorcism, and ESP, do not readily fall into some natural hierarchy or classification.

EMMA HEATHCOTE-JAMES

The lists presented to this point indicate that the experience and phenomena having religious or spiritual significance have been widely noted by human beings, although exact description and appropriate terminology have not been fixed, and perhaps never will be. Moreover, since such phenomena are found all over the world, numerous distinct descriptions exist in various languages, some readily translatable from one language to another, no doubt, while others are likely not. My interest here is not primarily in language, but in the phenomena that have occurred and what they indicate, suggest, or imply about orders of reality beyond those that are open to a scientific public. We cannot ignore the language differences, of course, but we cannot make too much of them either, in view of the fact that satisfactory translation is often possible. Translatability suggests that similar perceptual cues are occurring across linguistic boundaries. Since "raw" experience is always susceptible to having conceptual frameworks imposed upon it, "exact descriptions" remain an ideal about which we can only fantasize. Still, discussion must begin somewhere.

In a study of contemporary encounters with angels,[128] Emma Heathcote-James found 800 people in Britain who reported such experiences. This study is important because it focuses on one kind of experience, thereby allowing us to see the inevitable variations of RSM experiences. She earned a doctoral degree from the University of Birmingham for her work, which gives her study some credibility, for doctoral committees at public universities typically include people having varying beliefs about the possibility of such experience. She was not writing for an audience whose religious commitments discourage them from entertaining RSM experience as a serious phenomenon. Her chapter titles indicate that some angels were heard to speak, some were seen, some were touched, and so on.

DIGRESSION ON LEVITATION

Levitation is generally considered to be the act of rising into the air, seemingly because of some "spiritual" power acting upon the levitator. I have mentioned above the references made to it by Poulain, by Davis, and by Rosemary Guiley in her *Encyclopedia*. Davis adds a curious qualification to her entry in listing levitation among RSM experiences, namely, "the *sense of* rising up."[129] In this remark Davis indicates that the perspective she prefers to take on experience is the phenomenological one, as this is present to a percipient. The phenomenon of levitation as seen from an external perspective is of course that of seeing (another) rising into the air. Although I have not made an effort to research levitation, and have not stumbled upon many actual allegations, I did come across one in the course of my research into Christic visions.[130]

---

[128] Heathcote-James, *Seeing Angels*.
[129] My emphasis.
[130] *Visions of Jesus*, pp. 44–45.

Robin Wheeler indicated that he had experienced a Christic encounter that he wished to share, but he enigmatically added that his wife needed to be present when he gave his report to me. I understood later in the interview that he wished to refer to his experience of levitation, and hers. Robin reported that two beings repeatedly appeared to him in his bedroom in a series of events in which his destiny was seemingly being decided. One of these figures was (or was taken to be) the Christ, and the other was (or was taken to be) a demonic being that had the form of a human being without skin. Robin said that his struggles with these two beings lasted an entire night, and Robin's wife reported that during these events, each lasting a half-hour or so, Robin "floated in midair in a horizontal position about a foot above the bed ... his body ... perfectly rigid," and his head bent so far back that she thought his neck would break. Although she did not see the two figures that appeared to Robin, she could ask him what was happening as each event occurred, and he would describe the conflict taking place between them. Robin was not aware of his levitation, however, although during the fights he could see his wife seated near him as well as these two other beings, who seemed as real as ordinary persons. The place he seemed to be in did not fit with the physical description of their bedroom, however, and so belongs to visions in which extraneous elements are more-or-less blended in with ordinary ones. If we take the reports at face value, we see that some aspects of what Robin experienced were witnessed only by his wife, while other features were witnessed only by him. Robin had no sense of rising into the air, which Carolyn Davis identifies as central to the phenomenon of levitation, since his levitation was seen only by his wife. This case suggests that we cannot begin our description of experience simply with what is phenomenologically transparent to the experiencer, for Robin was unaware of his levitation. It also suggests that, wherever possible, we must examine what both experiencers and observers bring to events. The claim that Robin levitated is a conjecture, of course, made to interpret the reports of Robin's wife.

A remarkable instance of levitation comes to us from the life of St. Joseph of Cupertino, who also allegedly performed miracles. *The Catholic Encyclopedia* describes the life of St. Joseph as "one long succession of visions and other heavenly favours. Everything that in any way had reference to God or holy things would bring on an ecstatic state." It also states: "frequently he would be raised from his feet and remain suspended in the air." This case is particularly interesting because witnesses to his levitation include a Pope, two kings, the Duke of Brunswick, and the philosopher Gottfried Leibniz.[131] Perhaps I am impressed by the witness of a fellow philosopher, for I expect philosophers to exercise impartiality, insofar as they are able, in their reports of remarkable phenomena. With levitation we are clearly near the domain of miracle, although the matter of physical laws being contravened or violated, if this is considered essential to miracle, is not as obviously present when a human levitates compared with a wooden stick becoming an asp after being thrown upon the ground, which Moses and Egyptian priests of his time are said to have done.[132] In reflecting on the action of gravity in some ordinary event we might consider a ball that is thrown into the air, where the momentum given to the ball by its thrower overcomes the gravitational power acting on the ball. Just as gravity is not suspended or violated as the ball ascends, so levitation, if it were to occur, might not mean that gravity is not in force, but only that some force greater than gravity is also present, perhaps from a source neither visible, nor tangible, nor perceptible to any other senses. St. Joseph's levitation is generally construed as due to Divine influences in his life, probably because of the miracles of healing he is said to have performed. Once one spiritual Order is recognized as real, another comes into view begging to be recognized. Christianity deems some cases of levitation to be caused by powers that are diabolical, and the history of "miracle" in Eastern Orthodox and Roman Catholic contexts is fraught with uncertainty about the source of the unusual powers that are active in and around human beings.

Those of us with a scientific bent want to ask many questions about the circumstances in which unusual phenomena arise, but our normal ability to do so seems to be inexplicably limited. In the discussion that follows I will attempt to include as much in the matter of "description of experiences" as one can find, and not confine my attention only to the phenomenological feel of experiences. This creates complications, of course, but no harm comes, as far as I can see, from approaching an event from all perspectives on it that are available.

---

[131] Godwin, *Angels*, p. 223f. The article "St. Joseph of Cupertino" in *The Catholic Encyclopedia* does not mention these very noteworthy observers or his levitation; cf. www.newadvent.org/cathen/08520b.htm (accessed June 26, 2018). To add to the controversy, a Franciscan article observes that when Joseph was canonized in 1767, the investigation preceding the canonization looked at 70 incidents of levitation; cf. www.franciscanmedia.org/saint-joseph-of-cupertino/ (accessed June 27, 2018).

[132] *Exodus* 7:9–12.

2

The General Theory of Spirits

My discussion thus far supports the claim of Daniel Pals that I quoted in the Preface, namely, that "Religion consists of belief and behavior associated in some way with a supernatural realm of divine or spiritual beings."[1] That (alleged) spirits are featured in the belief systems of virtually all peoples hardly requires further substantiation; whether the beings deemed to be real are actually real is the central question. The Theory of Spirits that I will sketch and discuss in this chapter is really a cluster of theories, not a single theory, but for convenience, I will generally refer to it as one theory rather than many. We get a vivid portrayal of part of this theory in an article written by Richard Rorty (1931–2007) when he was Professor of Philosophy at Princeton University. In "Mind–Body Identity, Privacy, and Categories,"[2] he argued that a new way of thinking of the mind–body problem could be developed, a view that competed with the effort to show that mental states were identical with yet-to-be-discovered neurophysiological ones, as articulated by, among others, my doctoral advisor, J. J. C. (Jack) Smart (1920–2012) at the University of Adelaide, South Australia. Rorty argued that the Theory of Mind (or mental states) might eventually be eliminated, in just the way that demons had been successfully eliminated in Western thought: The disappearance form of the Identity Theory suggests that "What people used to call 'demoniacal possession' is a form of hallucinatory psychosis."[3] Rorty evidently considered the Theory of Demons to have been successfully eliminated. Another significant twentieth-century

---

[1] Pals, *Nine Theories*, p. 338.
[2] Originally published in 1965 and reprinted in Rosenthal, *Materialism*.
[3] Rorty, "Mind–Body Identity," p. 27.

philosopher Alfred North Whitehead (1861–1947) asserted in his Gifford Lectures forty years earlier (1927–28) that belief in evil spirits was both primitive and in need of elimination,[4] which suggests that he did not consider the belief in evil spirits to have been completely obliterated at that time. Whitehead famously defended a theistic form of Process Theory, but Rorty seems to have rejected support for any form of religious reality.[5]

Rorty and Whitehead treat the Theory of Spirits in just the way I propose to treat it here. This theory must either purport to explain certain unique events, or it needs to be eliminated from our descriptive–explanatory repertoire. I shall regard the Theory of Spirits as one that possibly refers to unobservable – or theoretical – objects, or possibly to ones whose effects are occasionally observable – seen or heard or touched, and so on. I shall speak here of the Theory of Spirits, but what I have in mind is some version of it, since very many are possible. This feature resembles theories that we find in atomic physics and psychology, say, where the Theory of Subatomic Structures is really a cluster of similar theories, or the Theory of Human Personality is a cluster of closely related theories rather than a single one. Theories purport to identify the features of *something*, but the difficulties that ordinarily attach to investigative efforts only allow us to say some things accurately, whereas other features remain obscure, even mistaken, so theories evolve to reflect growing information and conceptual changes. I will illustrate this point further as discussion proceeds. I am adopting an attitude of critical realism here, so I deem theoretical efforts to be to discover, as best we can, actual features of the cosmos. Limitations of one kind or another might prevent us from having as close a view as we might want, depending on the topic under discussion. In a recent book on the challenges of articulating the requisite *metaphysics*[6] for such a science, Anjan Chakravartty, Professor of Philosophy at the University of Notre Dame, advances a view of realism that is an evolution of realism itself, describing it as *semirealism*.[7] Philosophy is not static, for just as theories in the natural and social sciences change, the topics that constitute philosophy's central core, including realism and its competitors,[8] are undergoing comparable evolution.

---

[4] Whitehead, *Process and Reality*, p. 150.
[5] Postel, "High Flyer: Richard Rorty Obituary."
[6] This term has many misleading connotations, so I try to avoid it, and use "ontology" in its place. I construe Western philosophy as having ontology as its one overarching preoccupation, although in some periods, language or (mental) concepts appear to dominate.
[7] Chakravartty, *A Metaphysics for Scientific Realism*.
[8] See Miller, "Realism" for comments about noncognitivism, instrumentalism, nominalism, idealism, subjectivism, and anti-realism that compete with realism for adherents.

I have discussed this approach to the General Theory of Spirits elsewhere,[9] and in this chapter, I will augment this previous discussion. In treating the Theory of Spirits as postulating theoretical objects, possibly unobservable ones, I am following the brief suggestion about religion put forward by W. V. O. Quine in a book published half-way through the twentieth century,[10] and echoed by David Lewis, his doctoral student, in a visit to the University of Adelaide in the early 1970s when I was working with Jack Smart. Some pressing issues relating to the Theory of Spirits, or any theory concerning the cosmos, perhaps, are expressed in the following questions:

(a) Is the theory intelligible?
(b) Is the theory testable?
(c) Is the theory plausible (or true)?
(d) Is the theory indispensable to a complete view of the cosmos?

I will discuss the first of these questions in this chapter and leave the others to subsequent ones.

INTELLIGIBILITY

We can hardly consider questions about a religious theory's intelligibility without reference to the logical positivist (or logical empiricist) movement, many of whose proponents cast religion in an unfavorable light. Philosophy professor at London and Oxford, A. J. Ayer (1910–89) famously asserted that because "the religious utterances of the theist are not genuine propositions at all they cannot stand in any logical relation to the propositions of science. For the sentences which the theist uses to express such 'truths' are not literally significant."[11] The positivists were not uniform in their views, of course, but Ayer's remark not only captured anti-theistic sentiments already felt then among philosophers but also bolstered them. Various recent philosophers still disparage the intellectual status of religion as though logical empiricism had not suffered severe setbacks or had not been defeated.[12] Thus, John Searle, Professor at the University of California, on the scientific and naturalist worldview asserts:

---

[9] See especially Wiebe, *God and Other Spirits*, chap. 3.
[10] Quine, *From a Logical Point of View*, p. 50.
[11] Ayer, *Language*, pp. 117–18.
[12] See Passmore, *A Hundred Years of Philosophy*.

... [Naturalism] is not an option. It is not simply up for grabs along with a lot of competing world views. Our problem is not that somehow we have failed to come up with a convincing proof of the existence of God or that the hypothesis of afterlife remains in serious doubt, it is rather that in our deepest reflections we cannot take such opinions seriously.[13]

Near the time of his death Rorty wrote: "empirical evidence is irrelevant to talk about God," which is a viewpoint that applies equally to theism and atheism.[14] The question of intelligibility is often expressed in conjunction with one over testability, which is a position understandably deriving from the emphasis our culture generally places on "science" and the testability of its claims.

The third question of a theory's plausibility (or truth-likeness) only arises if the prior questions about intelligibility and testability have been positively answered. The fourth question concerning the dispensability of a theory has to do with a theory's significance for a comprehensive description of the cosmos and explanations for events. This is a point on which theists and atheists are clearly divided. Whether the Theory of Spirits is dispensable is perhaps the most important question of the four. I am thinking here about the capacity of a theory to survive every effort either to reduce it to other theories whose ontological commitments are incontestable or to eliminate it completely. We might consider the Theory of Mind, which attributes mental states and processes to all *persons*, not just humans, as one whose status was carefully monitored in the twentieth century as physical sciences progressed. Whereas many philosophers considered mental states to be reducible to neurophysiological phenomena, by the discovery that the denotations of the commonsense view would be identical to the denotations of neurophysiology, others thought that the Theory of Mind might be eliminated entirely. The latter possibility now seems to have been removed as a likely option, inasmuch as we are at the point of being able to identify the neurological phenomena that at least *accompany*, if not *constitute*, mental states. I will assume here that some parts of the Theory of Mind will be reduced as neurophysiology eventually takes the place of (much of) it. I will also assume that other parts of mentalism will be *eliminated* as neural discoveries make particular parts of the Theory of Mind otiose. I also expect that new discoveries about "mind" will be made that are a result of neurophysiology itself,

---

[13] Smith, "Metaphilosophy," p. 199; quoted from Searle, *The Rediscovery of the Mind*, pp. 90–91.
[14] Rorty and Vattimo, *The Future of Religion*, p. 33. Rorty reiterates the point in "Some Inconsistencies."

discoveries that have no counterpart in the current Theory of Mind. The Theory of Mind is perhaps indispensable, for it contains a conceptual framework that will long remain central to the teaching of infants and children, even though they abandon this theory as they mature. I will develop my ideas here as though a similar result could befall the Theory of Spirits. I do not think that spirits (or mental states) should be protected by some ad hoc measures.

An important discussion about the peculiar features of religious language took place in 1955 in a symposium featuring Antony Flew (1923–2010),[15] then from the University College of North Staffordshire; Oxford University professors, R. M. Hare (1919–2002), Basil Mitchell (1917–2011), and I. M. Crombie (1917–2010); as well as several other philosophers and theologians. It has been widely republished, usually under the title "Symposium on Theology and Falsification." Flew famously argued, using the parable of a garden tended by a gardener who is never seen, or heard, or smelled by bloodhounds, or detected by the electric fence surrounding the garden: "Just how does what you call an invisible, intangible, eternally elusive gardener differ from an imaginary gardener or even from no gardener at all?"[16] He was drawing attention to the resistance of the theist to allow any evidence against their theistic belief. In this discussion, Hare notably suggested that having a theological belief is to have a *blik* about theological matters, which is a feature of beliefs for which no reasons exist. He remarks: "It was Hume who taught us that our whole commerce with the world depends upon our *blik* about the world; and that differences between *bliks* about the world cannot be settled by observation of what happens in the world." This discussion occurred in the context of the enormous influence of Ludwig Wittgenstein (1889–1951) upon language and its interpretations – an influence that Richard Rorty captured in his edited book, *The Linguistic Turn: Essays in Philosophical Method*, in 1967. The central topics in this symposium were the remarkable language of religion and the place of evidence in RSM discourse, having as its background the far-reaching doubts about the possible role of evidence in religion's articulation, doubts arguably created primarily by logical empiricism (or positivism), and attention to some of the peculiarities of reasoning about religion.

During the early decades of positivism philosophers could isolate religious *statements* from the rest of the commonsense domain and comment

---

[15] Flew et al., *Theology and Falsification*.
[16] Ibid.

on them as though such claims did not belong to unique conceptual structures – *theories* – whose expression involved numerous interrelated statements. Perhaps the Harvard historian Thomas Kuhn (1922–96) can be credited with having uncovered the larger context in which a statement must be placed in order to be adequately appreciated and understood.[17] His observations about the *paradigms* within which theories and the events they explain are typically placed gives us a larger view of conceptual structures.[18] An even larger vista is provided by the conjectures of Imre Lakatos (1922–74), according to which inquiry takes place in the context of *research programs* that might permit a theory that is technically falsified to be retained for the purposes of further research.[19] We can perhaps view biological evolution as a research program, some parts of which are still in need of corroboration. Lakatos spoke about a protective belt of theories designed to allow a particular theory to be developed and tested, where the protective belt is itself rendered immune from testing for a time. These remarks here only provide a snapshot of work that continues to be done on the structure of theories and cannot be given any more space. The discussion of religion by Flew and various Oxford philosophers mentioned earlier does not capture the detail sketched here and exhibits the unfortunate practice of evaluating particular statements apart from a conceptual framework.

In considering the intelligibility of a claim or, more accurately, the intelligibility of a theory in which a claim is embedded, we can profit from some reflection on particular theories that have exercised the human imagination and have nothing to do with spirits. We might consider the theory of a luminescent ether, for instance, which exercised the critical thought of physicists from Isaac Newton onward, and perhaps even from some earlier time, depending on how we read the ancients and the medievalists on the propagation of light. The notion that light was propagated from the sun and stars by some medium known as an ether is not without plausibility, since propagating light through a literal vacuum appears contrary to conditions under which actions and their causes occur in human experience. The theory was clearly intelligible

---

[17] *Scientific Revolutions*, first published in 1962. Quine's view of epistemological holism – the interconnectedness of many theories – was perhaps also an influence.
[18] According to historian of physics and personal friend, now deceased, Thaddeus Trenn, Kuhn's views were anticipated by Ludwig Fleck (1896–1961), *Genesis and Development of a Scientific Fact*, first published in German, and translated by Trenn and Frederick Bradley.
[19] Lakatos, "History of Science."

in some important sense of this term, which came into focus with the work of Albert Michelson and Edward Morley. They found the Ether Theory to be (likely) false since it has contrary-to-fact implications and seems inconsistent with other branches of physics. We can see from this example that a claim about the ether was really about a theory that purported to explain how light from the sun and the stars reaches the earth. Although the larger context of a particular claim might not be immediately apparent, a closer scrutiny of it reveals that a *theory* is being assessed for intelligibility, testability, plausibility, and indispensability. A similar remark is pertinent to the Theory of Spirits.

The intelligibility of the Theory of Spirits cannot be examined in toto because it is much too large to be considered in that form and too varying from one culture to another. We can consider widely known kinds of specific expression of the Theory for Intelligibility, however. Here is one:

> *Case 1: Drottningholm Phantoms.* The British newspaper, *The Guardian*, carried a story on January 4, 2017, in which it reported that Queen Silvia of Sweden believed the royal palace where she resided was haunted. "There are small friends … ghosts. They're all very friendly but you sometimes feel that you're not completely alone," she said. This documentary also said that Princess Christina, the king's sister, backs Silvia's claims of the Drottningholm phantoms. This newspaper report did not say exactly what led the Queen to assert the existence of ghosts, but in 2010, the Swedish newspaper, *Aftonbladet*, also published an article about the palace's ghosts, specifically mentioning a "grey man" and a "white lady."[20] I take it from these descriptions that sights (apparitions) of one kind of another have been reported, not merely inexplicable gusts of cold air or creaking of floors, say, or some other phenomenon suggesting that "someone invisible" is walking nearby.

This is just one small snippet of a very large conceptual structure in which ghosts or phantoms are said to exist, and are also assigned properties, or are described as having some relation to other objects or beings. This conceptual structure is so much a part of the history of earth's peoples that some variations on it can be found in virtually every culture. This in itself is cause for some astonishment, inasmuch as it speaks to similar

---

[20] Reported by Lara Rebello, *International Business Times UK*, updated news report January 6, 2017.

human powers of extrapolation, or pure invention, or the capacity to formulate testable theories.

The exact sense impressions that might have contributed to such beliefs among the Swedish monarchy are not mentioned in the newspaper article, but this snippet on its own is intelligible, I submit, and would have to be intelligible for the Theory of Spirits to be effectively denied. Ayer seems to have conflated truth and intelligibility, for I can easily imagine that not just this snippet but the whole Theory of Spirits might be *false*, or *mistaken*, or *in error*. To say that, however, is to know roughly what it is that is being denied. Searle seems unwilling to consider whether opinions about ghosts can (and should) be taken seriously, and Rorty seems convinced that the matter of ghosts is devoid of evidence. These deprecating remarks about God or religion put the Theory of Spirits on the defensive, of course, but I submit that the Theory is *intelligible*, as the next case also shows.

> *Case 2: The Burnaby "Evil Spirit."* In *Visions of Jesus*, I relay some experiences described by Pauline Langlois, when she was living in Burnaby, British Columbia. Her first visionary experience consisted of an apparition of the Christ (she thought) who appeared near her bed as she lay contemplating suicide. She reached out her hand to determine whether her eyes had deceived her and found that her hand encountered something solid to the touch. The experience removed her desire to die and gave her some hope to live. She reported that she did not believe in a spiritual world to that point in her life, but subsequent events involving no visible agents convinced her that an evil spirit, as she called it, was trying to scare her. For the next six months doors would slam behind her, plants would move across the table, water taps would switch on and off, music would come from the corners of the rooms, and furniture would move across the floor of their own accord. At first, she wondered if she had "gone crazy," as she put it, but when members of her extended family witnessed these events as well, she thought that there must be some other explanation. She went to several priests for help. One gave her holy water to sprinkle on her home, especially on her daughter, about whose safety she was worried, but that did not help. Pauline finally traveled halfway across Canada to consult the family priest in Ontario, whose insight she respected and in whose parish she grew up. When he heard about the troubling events, he instructed her to take "the Good Spirit" with her

to confront them. This is what she did, she said, telling "the Good Spirit" to take care of frightening events each time they occurred, until they finally stopped.

This account is intelligible, I submit, so a subsection of the (General) Theory of Spirits is capable of being engaged. Some might think that Pauline hallucinated the events she attributed to an evil spirit. This position in effect allows the Theory of Spirits to be construed as intelligible but false. The alternative here to a spiritual being is given in naturalistic terms, by advancing mechanisms internal to an experiencing subject. I will discuss hallucinations more specifically in Chapter 5.

The Canadian philosopher Kai Nielsen has quite consistently construed Christian theism as *devoid of factual meaning*: God talk has not been given intelligible directions for its coherent use, he claims, and nothing could make propositions about God true.[21] Nielsen specifically addresses Christian theism, so it is possible that some of the difficulties he advances might not apply to all aspects of the Theory of Spirits. They are instructive, however, in considering the questions relevant to a theory's intelligibility. Nielsen asserts that to say that God is that being on which the world depends is to say nothing at all, for no sufficient conditions for dependency have been elaborated or apparently can be. Also, to speak of God as self-existent being is to utter another incoherent proposition, he says, for no rules have been discovered for identifying something as self-existent. Similarly, to speak of a being as transcendent is to speak of something obscure, for if something is experienced, it is ipso facto not transcendent. He observes that Hebrew-Christian religious traditions hold that God created the world out of nothing, but this is not intelligible either, he claims, and no advance is made here if God is thought of as the final cause, as opposed to an efficient cause. Moreover, to say that God acts without a body is also incoherent, for in our experience, the actions of persons occur by means of a body, and to speak of God as ineffable is no more coherent than to say that God acts without a body. In addition, to speak of Being or Being itself, rather than God, makes no sense, according to Nielsen who plausibly rejects the view that theological claims are only symbolic, rather than literal. He defends philosophy's role in critically discussing various forms of life, which, in his judgment, is most rational if lived atheistically. Nielsen defends the criterion of meaningfulness he is using, arguing that it is not a simplistic

---

[21] Nielsen, *Philosophy and Atheism*, chap. 5.

verificationist criterion. That is probably correct, but positivism's baleful influence over the discussion of religion many decades after Ayer is evident from Nielsen's remarks. It is not clear that Nielsen would take a similar approach to the ghosts and evil spirit in the examples I have adduced as intelligible, but even such finite spirits are often said to act without a body, to be transcendent, to be incapable of clear description, and so are ineffable in this sense. His general approach to theism is easily assimilated to portions of the Theory of Spirits that do not speak of the Christian God specifically, putting them too in an unfavorable light. Many philosophers do not discuss spirits other than God, thereby suggesting, perhaps without meaning to, that finite spirits have no relevance to religion and spirituality. My approach is different here, for reasons that will become more apparent in Chapter 3, where I discuss the testability of claims.

Another example of a portion of the Theory of Spirits that strikes me as intelligible comes from an account reported in my *God and Other Spirits*:[22]

> *Case 3: Abbotsford Visitor.* Tom Arthur (not his real name) of Abbotsford, British Columbia, said that he was a nominal theist for most of his life. He occasionally went to church but did not take "religion" seriously until he was asked to be a pallbearer at the funeral of a friend. The service made him think about God and the direction of his own life. When the funeral was over, he prayed to God, asking him to reveal himself if he was real. Tom added, "But please don't scare me." Nothing happened for a week or so, but not long afterward when he and his wife returned home from shopping, they noticed that their bedroom light was on. They were sure that they had shut it off before going out and wondered if someone had been in their house. They did not notice anything missing, however, and so gave the incident little attention at the time, thinking that maybe they had left the light on and forgotten that they had done so. A similar incident occurred a few days later when they again went out; only this time, the light and the television set in their bedroom were both on when they returned. They were sure that they had not left both the light and the TV on. They examined the doors and windows, but none of them showed any evidence of an attempted entry. They phoned their son to find out if he had paid them an unexpected call, but he had not. They even phoned the previous owners of the

---

[22] Wiebe, *God and Other Spirits*, pp. 63–64.

house just in case they had kept a key to the house and had come over for some reason. The former owners assured them that they had not been to the house. Tom's wife was so spooked by these incidents that she wanted to sell the house, but Tom wasn't ready. Then a third incident occurred a week or so later. They came home to find their bedroom light on and Tom's good suit laid out on the bed as though he was supposed to go somewhere. It was the same suit he had worn to the funeral and the kind of clothes he would wear to church if he went. Tom wondered if "someone" was trying to get him to go to church and if that someone could be God. The strange events stopped when he and his wife started going to church.

Tom evidently construed the invisible agent at work in his home to be God because of the prayer he had prayed, and because of the wholly beneficial effect on his life, as this was evaluated afterward. Christian tradition has allowed that an angel, rather than the Supreme Deity himself, might have done this, although this ambiguity concerning God and the angels said to do his bidding does not generally interfere, for Christians, with the claim that the ultimate agent was God. Tom evidently saw or heard nothing directly of the supposed agent in his Abbotsford home, and Christian tradition allows the appellation "God" to be used in contexts such as this. In Chapter 3, I will raise the issue of testability of claims concerning God, but for now I submit that Tom's description and explanatory account can stand as intelligible. Some might construe the strange events as hallucinatory, I suppose, but because his wife witnessed the same events at the same time, and in the same place, the claim of hallucination is improbable. I submit that Tom's claim is intelligible.

A curious case of encountering an angel comes from a study that Emma Heathcote-James of the University of Birmingham undertook for her doctoral degree. Among the more than 800 responses was an incident in which about half of the people present in a church in England, including its rector, reportedly saw a being they consider to have been an angel during a baptismal service.[23] A reporter from *The London Times* also made contact with the rector about the incident, who spoke on the condition that his church would remain unidentified.

Case 4: UK Angel Encounter. Times reporter Carol Midgley quotes the rector as saying:[24]

---

[23] Heathcote-James, *Seeing Angels*, pp. 46–47.
[24] "Sent from Heaven," *The London Times*, December 12, 2002.

The General Theory of Spirits 45

Suddenly there was a man in white standing in front of the [baptismal] font about 18 inches away. He was a man but he was totally, utterly different from the rest of us. He was wearing something long, like a robe, but it was so white it was almost transparent.... He was just looking at us. It was the most wonderful feeling. Not a word was spoken; various people began to touch their arms because it felt like having warm oil poured over you. The children came forward with their mouths wide open. Then all of a sudden – I suppose it was a few seconds, but time seemed to stop – the angel was gone. Everyone who was there was quite convinced that the angel came to encourage us.[25]

This case differs sharply from the earlier cases I cited and indicates something of the variation that falls under the general heading of encounters with spirits. Some critics of religion and RSM experience focus excessively on one type of case, find some flaw in it or in its kind, and disparage the whole lot. This case from the UK is intelligible, just as many stories of angelic encounters are that have been handed down through many religious and spiritual traditions. The fact that young children react to supposed angels in ways consistent with their understanding of the import of what is transpiring suggests that these descriptions are intelligible. Perhaps adults might be convinced that these accounts are ill-conceived or false, but cases involving spontaneous reactions of children seem unlikely to be contrived with their collusion. This case involves reports of sensory experience, evidently meshing well with the intersubjectively observable world of fonts, oil, children, rectors, churches, and so much more belonging to "the ordinary world." This case is also interesting for the phenomenological detail it suggests concerning "the feeling ... of having warm oil poured over you." Many experiences that are deemed to have RSM significance might consist of nothing more than such a feeling and in the absence of any visual or other sensory experience are construed as having no ontological significance, especially by those who are especially critical of religion. However, I will say something more in Chapter 5 about this juxtaposition of intersubjective sensory experiences.

Another snippet from the Theory of Spirits can be advanced as intelligible, this time coming from the curious world of "spirit painting," which fascinated Sir Arthur Conan Doyle, of Sherlock Holmes fame.

> *Case 5: Spirit Painting. The Vancouver Sun,* one of the major newspapers in our province, republished an extraordinary story on January 17, 2017, which was first published in the *Daily Mail* in Great

---

[25] *The London Times,* and *The Vancouver Sun,* December 12, 2000; cf. Heathcote-James, *Seeing Angels,* pp. 46–47.

Britain on December 16, 1919. It is a story about Kathleen Spencer, daughter of Robert Beaven (1836–1920), who was the sixth premier (1882–83) of British Columbia, the province in Canada in which I have lived for more than forty years. Kathleen married Viscount Churchill in the UK and so gave British Columbia an important connection with her cousin Winston, who is still credited with having "won World War II." Kathleen painted a piece called "The Light" in 1919, and Doyle wrote in a letter about Spencer and her work in the *Daily Mail*: "The remarkable thing about this head (in 'The Light') was that it was done upside down. Mrs. Spencer worked at it solidly for about three hours, and when it was finished, wondered what on earth she had done: it was only on turning it upside down that a perfect head of Christ appeared." Doyle thought this was proof that Kathleen's hand had been guided by "a force from beyond," writing: "When a masterpiece is produced by one who has no technical skill, and when it is exposed for all to behold, the most skeptical must admit that there is something there behind their ken." Doyle argued that a spirit could sometimes take hold of a living person and guide them, and he suspected that this was the case with this "periscope" painting of Jesus that was exhibited in London, England, in 1919. The artist's mother-in-law said that Kathleen's gift was "psychical in origin," especially since the painting was done upside down. Whether this painting still survives is unknown. Newspaper reproductions of it present a blurry figure from mid-torso to the top of the man's head, too indistinct to be of much interest. However, the figure of a bearded man with an oval face and full head of hair are clearly in evidence. He is looking up, and with his (partial) form visible in profile, resembles "the received likeness" of Jesus.[26]

Doyle's interests in "spirit painting," along with "spirit photography," belong to phenomena that would today be described as paranormal. He described Spencer's ability as either akin to or an instance of "the discerning of spirits," of which St. Paul wrote. In doing so, Doyle attached some Christian significance to paranormal phenomena, placing them on a footing with "gifts of the Spirit" as offering evidence for the larger order of Beings said to influence the natural order. This theory snippet

---

[26] I have discussed the problem of "the received likeness" of the Christ in *Visions and Appearances of Jesus*, chap. 8.

is clearly intelligible, although naturalists would be inclined to posit other psychological forces, none of which are supernatural, as alternative explanations. Doyle's claim *is not unintelligible,* however.

DEFINING "SPIRIT"

I have offered no definition of "spirit" to this point, the reason for which arises from the fact that it, and similar terms, denotes a theoretical object (being) that is perhaps not observable, and so is comparable to terms found in the natural and social science. Different kinds of spirits are featured in the comprehensive Theory of Spirits, each having a sufficient number of similar relations to one another that bringing them under one rubric is understandable. The propositions forming the Theory of Spirits consist of a vast array of claims, some of whose statements assert the existence of some particular beings, others that ascribe the properties (attributes) such beings have, and still others that ascribe the relations these beings have between one another, or to other things, *including things not in dispute.* It is the last of these relations to which I will call special significance. In the heyday of positivism, the (descriptive) terms of a theory were required either to *denote* observables (things, properties, and relations) or to be *definable* in terms of observables. These measures were designed to preserve the empirical meaningfulness of the theory. Rigid measures were initially proposed by which terms purporting to denote such theoretical entities could be construed as empirically meaningful, but in view of the success of many theories postulating theoretical entities that did not measure up to the early rigid standards, that methodology has had to be altered to reflect this change. Carl Hempel (1905–97) observes how the initial (strict) criteria of verifiability and falsifiability, and then the weaker criteria of confirmability and disconfirmability, are featured in the debates concerning scientific research during the first half of the twentieth century.[27]

Herbert Feigl's (1902–88) work reflects some of these changes in the understanding of theories postulating theoretical objects. He was a member of the Vienna Circle who interacted with early members, including Moritz Schlick, Karl Popper, and Ludwig Wittgenstein. Later Feigl became a philosopher at the University of Minnesota where he was instrumental in establishing the program known as Minnesota Studies

---

[27] Hempel, "Problems and Changes."

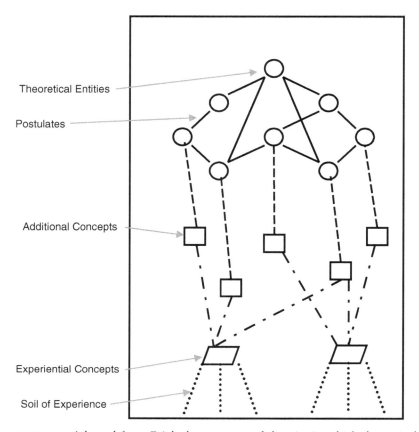

FIGURE 2.1 Adapted from Feigl, the structure of theories in which theoretical objects are postulated

in the Philosophy of Science (1953). The "tower pattern" in Figure 2.1, adapted from Feigl, pictorially portrays the structure of theories in which theoretical objects are postulated. Here it is used to depict the structure of physical atomism in which well-known theoretical entities are postulated to exist.[28] Feigl interprets the circles at the top of the pattern to stand for concepts that are basic and unique to a theory, such as the characteristics of waves–particles featured in subatomic physics. Basic concepts include those required for expressing the four fundamental forces to which entities are subject, such as gravitational force, which is applicable everywhere, as well as to the strong force, found only in

---

[28] Feigl, "The 'Orthodox' View."

the nuclei of atoms. The heavy solid lines between the circles at the top represent the postulates that are part of the theory; these are articulated using only the terms purporting to denote theoretical entities, their properties, and their relations to one another. An example can be found in laws that specify positions at which negatively and positively charged ions are featured in atoms. The squares stand for additional concepts that are defined by reference to the basic ones, such as the concept of kinetic energy, which is defined by reference to the masses of the waves–particles and their velocities. Such concepts link those belonging exclusively to the theoretical domain with those that belong to the domain of observables, such as the concept of the half-life of radioactive substances discovered by Ernest Rutherford. The parallelograms represent the concepts relevant to the theory that are formed directly by experience, such as the phases in which matter can exist, for example, as liquid, gas, or solid. The lines between squares and parallelograms stand for the conceptual linkages that give credence to a wide variety of terms in a theory, for example, those describing the properties of inert gases. The "soil of experience," signified by the dots extending below the parallelograms, is the (narrow) domain upon which positivism unsuccessfully focused its efforts to give meaning and significance to the full range of scientific statements.

Feigl conceives of the data obtained by way of human experience as "seeping upwards" toward the unobservable features of a theory as though the dotted lines at the bottom represent capillaries taking nutrients from "the soil of observation" to the elements of a theory that experience and experiment can influence only indirectly. From the theories describing the theoretical entities that are postulated to exist, predictions about expected events are inferred, and from correct or incorrect predictions, the theories about theoretical entities are either corroborated or undermined. The observations of events in cloud chambers and in the emulsions through which subatomic particles are directed have provided an empirical basis for theories about some of the subtle objects found in atomic physics.[29] Feigl's portrayal of the relationship between concepts derived from observation, and the concepts concerning unobservable or theoretical matters (objects, properties, relations), might suggest a straightforward way of defining theoretical concepts, but it is not. He discusses the work of Rudolf Carnap (1891–1970), Hempel, and other

---

[29] See, for example, P. A. M. Dirac's prediction from his equation determining the wave function of electrons, that a particle exists that is the opposite of the electron (antielectron), discussed in Nambu, *Quarks*, pp. 42–44.

theorists on operational definitions, bridge principles, correspondence rules, and other mechanisms for giving meaning to theoretical terms. By the time Feigl wrote "The 'Orthodox' View of Theories" (in 1970), criticism of positivism had taken its toll, and his account is nuanced to reflect not only objections to the demand for definition by exclusive reference to observables but also his sympathy for a complex, perhaps incomplete, interpretation of how terms purporting to denote theoretical entities acquire their meaning.

David Lewis (1941–2001), for many years a professor at Princeton University, suggests that a significant insight into the mechanisms giving meaning to theoretical terms can be acquired by looking at fiction, where neologisms (newly coined terms) are typically introduced and become widely understood. Before the fiction is told, the neologisms have no meaning, but after it is told, they do.[30] We might wonder what *precisely* gave them their meaning, but this is a question for which we might never find the complete answer. Traditional empiricists such as John Locke, George Berkeley, and David Hume evidently sought answers to questions about how complex concepts are acquired, suggesting that we somehow abstract concepts from simple experiences seemingly having a common element and compound the concepts in plausible ways to account for the impressive array that an ordinary person possesses. These theories do not explain how we obtain concepts of abstraction and compounding, however, suggesting that these empiricists conjecture about the sources of concept formation. While we might not find the sources by which common concepts are acquired, we should not assume that either the concepts or the propositions in which the concepts are featured are thereby rendered unintelligible.

Lewis here proposes a significant alteration in the views articulated by philosophers interested in theories postulating theoretical entities. He suggests that theoretical terms do not need to be *defined* in terms of observables but only need to be embedded in a narrative structure where all the *other* terms in the theory *are already intelligible*.[31] No account explaining how intelligibility is obtained is provided. The fact that intelligibility is obtained is found in the fact that many questions about the objects postulated in a narrative can be answered. This is not a blanket ontological endorsement of spirits, of course, for we also recognize some forms of the Theory of Spirits in which the postulated entities are too

---

[30] Lewis, "Psychophysical and Theoretical Identifications."
[31] *Ibid.*

remote from intelligible concepts to be defensible. When we reflect for a moment on the phenomena in which spiritual entities have been historically construed to be implicated, the list is long and curious. Theories in which spirits are embedded as causal agents have been irresponsibly employed to explain almost anything. This is a substantial difficulty and probably accounts in part for the abandonment of these theories by the scientific community in the last two centuries or so. Our religious and spiritual forebears probably did not know that they were doing a disservice to this branch of cognitivity by postulating spirits too freely. The positivistic strictures upon religion, and upon theories concerning theoretical entities in general, were dramatic, drastic, and often justifiable. Fortunately, eight decades of philosophy of science[32] have brought more moderate views of theory structure into play. Narratives that describe and explain events in terms of the activities of spirits, whether these are spontaneous events or ones apparently triggered by human actions, embed a portion of the Theory of Spirits and implicitly define their attributes, as well as identify their relations to other things. In this respect, the Theory of Spirits is comparable to theories of unobservable (or rarely observed) objects found in the physical and social sciences.

The meanings of terms purporting to denote spirits are especially provided in causal relationships to objects or events whose existence is not in doubt. An implication of this is that no succinct "definition" can be provided of "spirit" and cognate expressions, for their meaning is provided by theory. Here we have an explanation for the fact that anyone can understand (more or less) what the Queen of Sweden is talking about when she speaks about her castle being haunted. No difficulty (or benefit) arises in calling these "beings" phantoms rather than ghosts, for the primary issues here are not linguistic, but ontological. Naturally, epistemic questions that arise from such claims must also be addressed, which I will discuss in Chapter 4. One might not expect Thomas Aquinas (1225–1274) to make remarks that are consistent with my comments here on methodology, but he does. He remarks about the difficulty of offering a conventional definition of God, writing:

Although we cannot know in what consists the essence of God, nevertheless in this science we make use of *His [presumed] effects*, either of nature or of grace, in place of a definition, in regard to whatever is treated of in this science concerning

---

[32] I am using *The Journal of the Philosophy of Science* as a benchmark here, which was established in 1934.

God; even as in some philosophical sciences we demonstrate something about a cause from its effect, *by taking the effect in place of a definition* of the cause.[33]

Aquinas prefers another method of definition, namely, the one made famous by Aristotle, in which an object is found to be in some genus and then some differentium is found in which that object differs from all others in the genus. Aquinas cannot find this kind of definition, so he relies on "the cause of some effect" in explicating the notion. Here he is both extraordinarily modern and, as I shall show below, extraordinarily Socratic.

I have not spoken to the issue of the spirit of a human person to this point. One might perhaps address many features of the Theory of Spirits without taking a firm position about spirits of humans (or, perhaps, humans being spirits). One final example will finish my (incomplete) argument here that theories that have terms that denote spirits can be intelligible. This is not a blanket approval of theories purporting to denote spirits, however.

> *Case 6: Ayer's NDE.* A curious report of an NDE is associated with the last days of Sir Alfred J. Ayer, philosopher extraordinaire, widely known for his atheism and denial of an afterlife. However, after an NDE in America, he expressed significant hesitation. He was quoted in an article titled "What I Saw When I Was Dead" in *The Sunday Telegraph* on August 28, 1988 as saying:

My recent experiences have slightly weakened my conviction that my genuine death, which is due fairly soon, will be the end of me, though I continue to hope that it will be. They have not weakened my conviction that there is no god. I trust that my remaining an atheist will allay the anxieties of my fellow supporters of the British Humanist Association, the Rationalist Press Association and the South Place Ethical Society.

Ayer's account of his NDE is as follows:

I was confronted by a red light, exceedingly bright, and also very painful even when I turned away from it. I was aware that this light was responsible for the government of the universe. Among its ministers were two creatures who had been put in charge of space. These ministers periodically inspected space and had recently carried out such an inspection. They had, however, failed to do their work properly, with the result that space, like a badly fitting jigsaw puzzle, was slightly out of joint. A further consequence was that the laws of nature had ceased to function as they should. I felt that it was up to me to put things right.

---

[33] Aquinas, *Summa Theologica*, First part, q. 7; my italics.

I also had the motive of finding a way to extinguish the painful light. I assumed that it was signaling that space was awry and that it would switch itself off when order was restored. Unfortunately, I had no idea where the guardians of space had gone and feared that even if I found them I should not be able to communicate with them. It then occurred to me that whereas, until the present century, physicists accepted the Newtonian severance of space and time, it had become customary, since the vindication of Einstein's general theory of relativity, to treat space-time as a single whole. Accordingly, I thought that I could cure space by operating upon time. I was vaguely aware that the ministers who had been given charge of time were in my neighborhood and I proceeded to hail them. I was again frustrated. Either they did not hear me, or they chose to ignore me, or they did not understand me. I then hit upon the expedient of walking up and down, waving my watch, in the hope of drawing their attention not to my watch itself but to the time which it measured. This elicited no response. I became more and more desperate, until the experience suddenly came to an end.

Ayer evidently saw his NDE as having (modest) evidential relevance to the question of postmortem survival. His reference to supporters in various societies being *anxious* about the inferences he drew from his experience is of some interest. Perhaps he felt pressure from his friends about the things he said much as one in some religious organizations experiences pressure from other members in offering an interpretation of personal experience. Ayer was right, perhaps, to view his NDE as having more evidential relevance for human survival than for the theory of theism. More to the point, however, I observe that nothing about his NDE account is unintelligible, and even Ayer seems to be convinced that this is the case. In order to illuminate more of the manner in which terms for unobservables acquire meaning, I will turn again to subatomic physics.

LAMBDA-BARYON PARTICLES

The recent history of physics includes remarkable "observations" made of unobservable subatomic objects, such as neutrinos that stream from the sun and pass through the earth as though it were no obstacle at all. Their presence is detected by sophisticated detectors placed in carbon tetrachloride vats a mile or so below the earth's surface.[34] Other entities are "observed" in events that are captured in cloud chambers and emulsions through which known particles (waves–particles) pass. Figure 2.2 from the Berkeley Lab describes the circumstances behind the production of a lambda baryon. On the left-hand side is the image from the particle

---

[34] See Shapere, "The Concept of Observation."

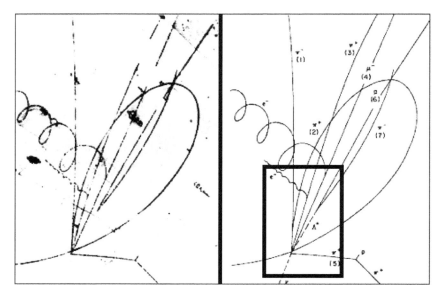

FIGURE 2.2 Lambda-Baryon particles

chamber, and on the right is the diagram that provides an interpretation of it.[35] I have placed a smaller rectangular box featuring thick lines on the right side, around the detail in which I am particularly interested.

A neutrino that is devoid of charge and consequently not imaged on the left corresponds to the dashed line at the bottom of the drawing on the right. It enters the chamber from the bottom and collides with a proton entering the chamber from the left (shown by a solid line). This collision produces three positively charged particles (labeled as 2, 3, and 5), two negative ones (1 and 4), and a neutral one – the lambda-baryon particle pictured by a dash on the right and identified by the lambda (Λ^*). This baryon particle has an extremely short life, decaying within one-billionth of a second. It produces a distinctive "V" when it decays into a proton and a pi-meson (6 and 7). The existence of this lambda-baryon particle is (causally) inferred from the set of observable events shown. A great deal of physics is presupposed in this "inference" of course, as well as some assumptions that do not belong exclusively to physics, such as the assumption that causality pervades the domain of description and explanation.

[35] From Close et al., *The Particle Explosion*, p. 183; also at www.bnl.gov/bnlweb/history/charmed.asp

The problem of how a theory postulating theoretical entities could be intelligible has been answered: Terms purporting to denote crucial entities are defined by the attributes given to the entities, and by the relations these entities are assigned to objects, some of whose existence is not in doubt. This is not a simple answer to the problem of definition, but it is one that helps us understand the role of unobserved objects, especially their causal powers, as well as their capacity to be acted upon by other objects. Other relations besides causality obviously figure in the (full) definition of a theoretical object, such as temporal order, but causality carries special weight. Terms, including those for spirits of different kinds and ranks, have meaning, just by virtue of being included in a theory in which their supposed denotations are ascribed properties and held to be in relations to things that are not in doubt – including ordinary objects accepted as real by commonsense and science.[36] When we speak of spirits of departed persons, for instance, the entities referred to are ascribed relations to things that are not in doubt, such as living persons. The crucial relations here are between a living person – the bearer of personal identity while a body is alive – and the entity deemed (by the theory) to be the postmortem bearer. The issue of ongoing identity in postmortem existence appears to be hardly different than the ongoing identity found in living things generally. We might *teach* in a logic class the (partial) character of the identity relation by reference to objects having several names or descriptions (such as "Venus" and "the Morning Star") or by examples drawn from arithmetic (such as "$7 + 5 = 12$"), but in actual life, we encounter the ongoing identity in a plant, or animal, or human person, where the strict identities just illustrated are not present.[37]

Various fields of science and exact inquiry, besides physics, have been opened up by theories that postulate the existence of theoretical entities, for example, genetic theory, whose origin goes back to the "inheritance factors" (genes, now observable) postulated to exist by Gregor Mendel to account for the similarity in traits between parents and children; evolutionary theory that postulates natural selection (Charles Darwin) and

---

[36] Philosophers who have followed such phenomenalists as George Berkeley in denying the existence of the (so-called) external world have put themselves out of the prevailing discourse and also introduced a distraction requiring attention even as more pressing issues about the reality of unobservables demand a response.

[37] See Dennett, "The Self as a Center of Narrative Gravity" that takes advantage of the obscurity in assigning continuing identity by claiming that successive space-time structures are not identities, so that one person, supposedly, is really a set of nonidentical states. This (Humean) position is thinkable, but not plausible.

other mechanisms in order to account for the flourishing of genera and species among flora and fauna; tectonic plate theory in geology that attempts to account for earthquakes, continental drift, and the similarities among land forms, flora, and fauna, among now distant parts of the earth; and psychological theories that attempt to account for normal and abnormal behaviors among people by virtue of unobserved processes or structures, such as the unconscious in the theories of Sigmund Freud and Carl Jung. Virtually all fields of physical science appear to postulate entities that are rarely or never observed. Social sciences also make extensive use of "objects" that are seemingly unobservable or difficult to observe, for example, self, nation, language group, culture, economy, capitalism, and society, so the methodological principle under discussion here occurs in virtually all exact inquiries. As long as logical positivism was ascendant among theorists in Western thought, unobservable objects were viewed with suspicion and regarded as having little significance in theorizing, but the demise (or decline) of positivism has allowed a deeper understanding of the structure of theories to develop. Of course, various entities once postulated to exist have come to be seen as nonexistent and so reduced by elimination;[38] phlogiston is one of the better-known examples from the history of chemistry, where understanding developed of the roles played by fundamental elements such as oxygen and carbon in oxidation, calcification, and other primary chemical changes. Science and other exact studies, as we presently have them, would not exist if it were not for the theories featuring the kinds of postulated entities of which I am speaking.

Theories that postulate theoretical entities have structures and logical features that are not found in other branches of empirical inquiry. These theories do not fit into the classical view of the structure of a science, according to which definitions and intuitively plausible first principles that set out the essential properties of the objects under examination (laws of nature) allow deductive inferences to be drawn that detail the content of the exact inquiry.[39] This ideal is most readily illustrated by Euclidean geometry and by the axiomatization of Newtonian physics, but hardly any other exact studies exhibit the finely structured character of the deductivist model. All theories continue to be tested by examining

[38] For a discussion of numerous kinds of reduction, see Hooker, "Towards a General Theory of Reduction," pp. 38–59, 201–36, 496–529.
[39] Anaxagoras has been credited with identifying observation and the use of logic as two vital principles of investigation, and so having been first to advance a view about the nature of science, in Gershenson and Greenberg, *Anaxagoras*, p. 5.

their deductive implications, but the deductivist model is too limited to account for the accomplishments in science and other exact inquiries. Moreover, it unreasonably hobbles science concerning an appropriate or preferred method. Inductivist models are now accepted everywhere, where probability measures become central to description and hence to explanation.

A different way of thinking about the world is required if we accept the plausibility of theories that postulate theoretical objects in order to account for otherwise inexplicable events. The American philosopher Charles Saunders Peirce adopted the term "abduction" to distinguish the third form of theory from deduction and induction. One important consequence of reasoning with theoretical objects is that the five different criteria advanced by John Stuart Mill for detecting causal links between events or objects cannot be applied. Even probabilistic claims generally require that conjectured relationships allow for the observation of the related events or objects. The tests by which theories postulating theoretical entities are examined for plausibility are much harder to execute than tests for theories dealing with observables, and the critical scrutiny to which such theories are subject is indirect. I will discuss some of the relevant factors in Chapter 3. Theories that postulate theoretical objects or processes are apt to undergo many modifications, as first attempts to identify relevant theoretical objects are replaced with simulacra in which the postulated entities are given slightly different properties. A widely known example of this is found concerning the structure of the atom as it developed in the nineteenth and twentieth centuries.

Claiming that something exists, when it does not, and failing to claim the existence of something that is real, are, comparatively speaking, reasonably significant errors. Less grievous errors occur when we ascribe the wrong attribute to a thing or fail to note a relation between two objects. Even universal claims might be granted an exception or two, providing the universal statement is generally reliable. Here we have a rough guide to the notion that one theory might be modestly flawed, whereas another theory is seriously wrong. These notions apply to the Theory of Spirits as much as to any other theory, postulating the existence of theoretical objects. So the real question for the Theory of Spirits is whether any one variation has a realization (is true) in our world. Here the modern age confronts the medieval and ancient ages, for the latter explicitly assert the reality of many things that are now dismissed as quaint, or sentimental, or irrational, or "primitive," or just mistaken. The conflict between the modern and the earlier ages can be located squarely in this feature of "the Theory." Theories that postulate theoretical entities are by their very nature susceptible to innumerable variations. The corroboration or the undermining of such theories might take many years to come to fruition, if it ever does. We can see that those who value exact results might be keenly disappointed with theories that postulate theoretical entities. Inasmuch as we accord to scientific theories the gratuity of not needing to be true exactly, I suggest that we accord a similar concession to the Theory of Spirits.

I assign more attention than usual, perhaps, to the *relations* that the supposed denotations of theoretical terms bear to things about which no (serious) disputes exist. I would want to include these in the (standard) definition of objects if we were able to say so succinctly – I am not sure that we can. Many philosophers follow Leibniz's *Law of Indiscernibles* in defining objects. This Law asserts that "a" is identical to "b" if and only if every attribute of "a" is an attribute of "b," and vice versa. The Law actually makes an assertion about the (identical) denotation of attributes but says nothing about the *relations* that "a" and "b" have to other objects.[40] Saying nothing about relations leaves one with a world of individual objects whose places within structures are ignored or considered insignificant. The world we inhabit is one in which relations are crucial, however, whatever these relations happen to be. We sometimes can only offer incomplete accounts of them, but to the extent that we can, we have more than isolated individuals that possibly "create" no structure at all.

WESTERN ORIGINS OF HUMAN SOUL (SPIRIT?)

The sources of science and philosophy in the West are usually seen as beginning with the pre-Socratics, since these were first to speculate about ultimate kinds of things, their causes, and their effects. Thales, Empedocles, Anaximander, Heraclitus, and their contemporaries are typically identified as belonging to this group. Socrates has been quite widely credited with having given to Western culture its unique understanding of soul (*psuche*), which is not far from how spirit (*pneuma*) in human life has also been understood, inasmuch as he considered soul to last beyond the death of "the body in which it lived." According to the Cambridge classicist John Burnet (1862–1928),[41] Greek literature prior

---

[40] See Findlay, *Meinong's Theory*, p. 208, for remarks by the Austrian philosopher Alexius Meinong (1853–1920), making properties and relations essential to a thing's identity.
[41] Burnet, "Socratic Doctrine."

to Socrates associated soul with events that were part of unconscious life or semiconscious experience, for example, prescient dreams, apparitions of the dead, and trance-like states in which a god was thought to speak – RSM experience, in short. However, Socrates extended the concept of soul beyond these phenomena to include mental states found in everyday life, including making choices and acquiring knowledge. Socrates did not repudiate the "spiritual" events in which soul was previously implicated, and so the concept he worked with served both religion and psychology. Other prominent twentieth-century Plato scholars, for example, A. E. Taylor (1869–1945)[42] and Francis Cornford (1874–1943),[43] agree with Burnet in construing Socrates as having left this profound deposit in Greco-Roman-Christian thought. Curiously, another prominent nineteenth-century classicist Erwin Rohde (1845–96) says nothing in his eminent study *Psyche: The Cult of Souls and Belief in Immortality among the Greeks* about the innovation that Burnet, Taylor, and Cornford ascribe to Socrates. Pre-Socratic Ionian philosophers evidently set the stage for Socrates' innovation by encouraging speculation about the nature of soul,[44] but Socrates seems to have left his own lasting imprint on the concept.

Socrates introduces the term "*psuche*" in a curious way in his discussion with Crito over the moral legitimacy of trying to avoid the sentence of death passed upon him by the Athenian court:

In the matter of just and unjust, fair and foul, good and evil, which are the subjects of our present consultation, ought we to follow the opinion of the many and to fear them; or the opinion of the one man who has understanding, and whom we ought to fear and reverence more than all the rest of the world: and whom deserting we shall destroy and injure *that principle in us which may be assumed to be improved by justice and deteriorated by injustice* – is there not such a principle?

And

And will life be worth having, if *that higher part of man* be depraved, which is improved by justice and deteriorated by injustice? Do we suppose *that principle, whatever it may be in man*, which has to do with justice and injustice, to be inferior to the body?[45]

---

[42] Taylor, *Socrates*, p. 132.
[43] Cornford, *Before and after Socrates*, p. 50.
[44] W. K. C. Guthrie in his *Introduction* to the 8th ed. of Rohde's *Psyche* defends Rohde by saying that his focus was on immortality and the cult of souls, not the origin of the concept (p. 24).
[45] Plato, *Crito* 48a; my italics.

In these remarks, Socrates introduces the concept of soul *indirectly*, by describing events in which the soul (alleged) is causally implicated. Socrates does not attempt to define soul in the Aristotelian way, using genus and *differentium*. Neither does he seek to define it by attempting to identify simple things that might constitute it – indeed, the soul has been widely deemed by those who accept its existence as being itself a simple, and so incapable of definition. Neither does he analyze soul in the way in which Plato (Socrates?) analyzes knowledge (apparently) as justified true belief, which seemingly identifies the three individually necessary and jointly sufficient conditions for something to be knowledge – a strategy that some modern philosophers, for example, Bertrand Russell,[46] have identified as the characteristic of their philosophic method. Interestingly, nothing about the "definition" introduced here by Socrates requires that soul be construed as nonmaterial, although other texts suggest that he thought it was.

Socrates uses the strategy for giving reference to an obscure object by locating it within an account of events with which it is supposedly causally implicated. Socrates and Crito agree that *people* can improve or deteriorate, and they also agree that this is not simply the improvement or the deterioration of people's bodies. So they conclude that it is something else – the soul, whatever that might happen to be – that improves or deteriorates. In other early dialogues, Socrates is portrayed as also having construed the soul to be capable of wisdom or foolishness. It is in the nexus of these complex causal chains that the soul is more fully defined, although whether Socrates was aware of the innovation he was introducing in definition is unclear. Because the nature of what is being indirectly characterized is nebulous, one can hardly say that one knows precisely what is being talked about, which is consistent with the famous Socratic position that he only knew that he did not know. Aristotle derides those that eschew his preferred method of definition and instead rely on dialectics, which he describes as "a method that is futile and indeterminate."[47] Although Plato is not mentioned, he is the most famous dialectician on record in prior Greek history and is arguably the person Aristotle has in mind; of course, Aristotle might have been thinking of various pre-Socratics.

---

[46] Russell, *The Atomism Lectures (1918)*, lect. VIII. Russell illustrates this method of definition by reference to his analysis of definite descriptions, which he considers to have undermined the then widely held position among philosophers that a distinction between existence and subsistence was plausible.

[47] Aristotle, *De Anima*, bk. 1, pt. 1.

The Socratic view that the soul was immortal[48] and would be judged in some postmortem judgments[49] firmly linked the soul with religion, of course. This feature of the soul was enthusiastically embraced by Christianity, during whose long hegemony[50] over intellectual life in Western civilization, the soul's supposedly immaterial nature and independence from matter were emphasized. St. Paul contributes in a curious way to the Theory of Spirits as we find it in Western thought. He writes: "For what *person* (Gk: *anthropon*) knows a man's thoughts except the spirit (Gk: *pneuma*) of the man which is in him?"[51] The long-standing tradition in Western culture has been that someone's thoughts, which include sense perceptions, memories, feelings, desires, attitudes, concepts, propositions, and so on, are known to the one who has them. The notion of spirit as Paul uses it here is ascribed very expansive power. It impressed St. Augustine so much that he made it a cornerstone of his theism,[52] claiming that the one responsible for creation had to have powers at least as great as the self-knowing mind we discover ourselves to be.

We still generally deny this power of self-knowledge to animals, but of course we might be shown wrong by some future developments in cognitive science. We readily concede that they have sense perceptions that resemble ours in many cases, perhaps even outstrip ours in certain circumstances, but their own awareness of their own perceptions is something that (now) eludes our efforts to establish; *mutatis mutandis* with beliefs, attitudes, desires, concepts, and all the other mental states that form the distinctive content of our mental life. Of course, we now consider human mental life to include what Paul is attaching here to spirit, for self-awareness is considered as much a mental state as any sense perception, or memory, or concept, or proposition – as we remember some event, for instance, we (generally) know that we do so. No particular harm arises, as far as I can see, in "carving out" the extraordinary feature of self-knowing found in folk psychology and placing it in a theoretical context so that it is shared with folk religion.

Since knowledge of my own thoughts is itself a thought, supposedly known by the spirit of the human in whom the thought is found, if we follow St. Paul, I also (seemingly) know that I know my own thoughts.

---

[48] Plato, *Phaedo*, 79b–e.
[49] Ibid., 63c.
[50] See Smith, "Metaphilosophy" for an interpretation of this influence for about 1000 years.
[51] *I Corinthians* 2:11.
[52] Augustine, *On the Trinity*, 14.12, p. 15.

We can see the possibility of the beginning of "an infinite regress" here. This is somewhat disquieting, for we might not knowingly experience level after level of knowledge. However, if we had no such experience at all, that would cast doubt not just on the infinite order seemingly triggered but also on the notion that if we know something, we also know that we know it. Perhaps we should be cautious here and *claim* only that while we know our own thoughts, we believe that we know them, rather than knowing that we know them.

From the objective standpoint in which science is generally pursued, self-awareness is an attribute that we assign to another, but in our own case, we say that the power of introspection allows us to observe this about ourselves; of course, we attribute an identical power to anyone who is (now) considered a person.[53] Cartesian philosophy once pretended to have a significant difficulty in knowing that anyone other than oneself was truly (or had) a mind, but the unreasonable limitations that this stance once placed on epistemology and ontology have largely disappeared. These strictures were absurd, of course, and could hardly be maintained outside philosophy classrooms, but maybe they benefitted novitiates there. Although we might not know exactly how Paul intended his general description of a human being as "body, soul, and spirit" (or maybe "body, mind, and spirit"), he might have considered the (human) spirit to have the power to know all one's (own) mental states. This is not a definition of a spirit, but it could be viewed as an expression of a central relation to the Theory of Soul–Mind–Spirit as it has been expressed in the Western tradition (and perhaps elsewhere). I am not focusing here on language but on the "objects" that language purports to denote or assumes as real in its expression. The objects that have been construed as real come with properties or attributes, including ones that contribute to being the kind of things they are, and then come with relations to other things. Relations can be asserted in a theory to hold between things that are later found to be nonexistent, of course, in which case no relation actually holds. I do not consider the ontologies that we construct to be the final word on what exists and on how things are, but we rely on them, even though we might try to convince ourselves that we are primarily thinking about words, not things. Although Paul does not explicitly say that I cannot generally know the thoughts of another, he might be

---

[53] This point is now a delicate one, since laws and practical decisions are being challenged about prenatal life and the state of those suffering from brain diseases that impair the continuity of memory.

implying that. In other words, my spirit (however awkward that sounds) knows my thoughts and only my thoughts (generally); it does not know yours, and your spirit does not know mine (generally). This is perhaps a "law" concerning spirits, but Paul does not say enough to be explicit on the point.

Descartes is celebrated for having given the sharp distinction between an immortal soul and a mortal body, thereby heightening questions about the nature of the soul, about the meaning of claims that humans have souls, and about the soul's relation to the body. The post-Cartesian developments of the concept of soul are well known: Cartesian dualism was questioned, and various other views of soul and the soul–body interaction were advanced, including materialism, idealism, parallelism, the double-aspect view, epiphenomenalism, and the preestablished harmony view. The term "soul" was eventually replaced with "mind," which does not carry the religious associations of "soul" or "spirit," and eventually "mind" was replaced with "mental states," which does not suggest a questionable substance but only properties of something. Conscious mental states and processes are now widely seen as properties of a *person*, as are physical attributes, and spiritual aspects of human experience are often ignored.

Early in the twentieth century, naturalistic theories of psychology, such as behaviorism, explored strategies for eliminating references to minds and mental states, in part because of the "spooky stuff"[54] mind was thought to be. A decisive methodological shift toward mental states took place in the last few decades of the twentieth century, as theorists who were broadly sympathetic to physicalism, such as Jack Smart,[55] Hilary Putnam,[56] and Richard Rorty,[57] began to look on mental states favorably, arguing that they could be interpreted as "theoretical entities" postulated by a theory that purported to explain human behavior. Wilfrid Sellars argued that a language allowing references to thoughts, sense impressions, choices, feelings, memories, and other mental states or processes – the language of what is now widely known as *folk psychology* – could be viewed as expanding the expressive powers of a language containing only descriptive terms that refer to "public properties of public objects located

---

[54] For a representative expression of this view, see Churchland and Sejenowski, "Neural Representation and Neural Computation," p. 227.
[55] Smart, "Sensations and Brain Processes" and "Conflicting Views about Explanation."
[56] Putnam, "Dreaming and Depth Grammar."
[57] Rorty, "Mind–Body Identity, Privacy, and Categories."

in space and enduring through time" and logical expressions, however impressive the latter language might be.[58] Sellars does not suppose either that the "inner" episodes need to be located in a separate substance,[59] which is how classical dualists about mind and body had understood mind, or that they need to be understood as physiological in character, which is how most materialists insisted on understanding them. These "inner" episodes are simply entities postulated by a theory that purports to provide a causal explanation for verbal acts and other acts typical to human life.

We can speak about anger, for example, by virtue of its causal relationships to various readily observed phenomena that are typically conjectured to cause it,[60] such as rude gestures and verbal abuse, and the phenomena it is conjectured to typically cause, such as violent acts. If verbal abuse, say, is selected as a typical cause in introducing this postulated state, then anger is partially (or contextually) defined by this causal relation. Once anger has been introduced as a postulated entity, it can be used in descriptions and explanations of other phenomena. If verbal abuse of a person is followed by bouts of self-deprecation in that person, but self-deprecation has not been used to introduce anger, we can offer the conjecture that anger, in conjunction with other causal factors, not all of which might be known, causes self-deprecation. This statement is not an empty truism but one that purports to add to our understanding of the causal role of anger. In the larger context of the theory that emerges, anger is ultimately characterized by the complex cluster of events in which it is implicated in causality and other relations. This position for understanding mental states and processes is a more fully worked-out view of the one hinted at by Socrates, which took nearly 2,300 years to blossom.

Since the Theory of Spirits is a theory about beings *with* minds, or perhaps even beings *comprised of* minds, we have to consider that the background relevant to the testing of claims is appropriate to the kind of entities that are in question. The testing of claims in physics or biology might only be marginally relevant to claims about spirits; claims about human persons are much more relevant. We learn to identify the features unique to human minds in the context of everyday life and language, where the concept of mind makes its frequent appearance. We

---

[58] Sellers, *Science, Perception and Reality*, p. 178. This is drawn from the essay, "Empiricism and the Philosophy of Mind," which was first given in lectures at the University of London in 1956.
[59] Sellers, *Science, Perception and Reality*, p. 187.
[60] Lewis, "An Argument for the Identity Theory," p. 20.

can acquire some sense of the richness of this concept by a review of the study of mind offered by Gilbert Ryle (1900–76) in 1949. He is widely seen as a key representative of ordinary language philosophy, of which his book *The Concept of Mind* is characteristic. This style of philosophy is also widely seen as reflecting the shift of philosophical interests of Ludwig Wittgenstein published as *Philosophical Investigations* (1952), which differ sharply from that exhibited in his earlier writing *Tractatus Logico-Philosophicus* (1921). Ryle describes his book as offering "what may with reservations be described as a theory of the mind."[61] He targets for criticism "The Ghost in the Machine," whose source he considers to be primarily Descartes who construed the differences between the physical and the mental "as differences inside the common framework of the categories of 'thing', 'stuff', 'attribute', 'state', 'process', 'change', 'cause' and 'effect'."[62] Ryle argues that a category mistake occurs here, for the mental is (mis)construed as something that it is not. He holds that "the phrase 'there occur mental processes' does not mean the same sort of thing as 'there occur physical processes', and, therefore, that it makes no sense to conjoin or disjoin the two."[63] Neither traditional dualists nor modern identity theorists construe the mental in quite the manner that Ryle does under whom Jack Smart had studied.[64] When Jack Smart was said to have committed "the Australian fallacy" for advancing the Identity Theory, I surmise that this was a reference to Ryle, or to a circle of his supporters, who disagreed with the approach that Jack Smart took toward mental states.[65] Ryle's study offers an instructive overview of mental states, discussing them under familiar headings such as "Knowing How and Knowing That," "The Will," "Emotion," "Dispositions," "Self-Knowledge," "Sensation and Observation," "Imagination," and "Intellect." The mental states that are canvassed include ones featured in accounts of interactions with spirits, but Ryle hardly mentions spirits. Neither does he show interest in RSM experiences. If the ontological power of religion rests in RSM experience, as I am arguing here, we can hardly be surprised at the failure to find significance in religion among analytic philosophers.

---

[61] Ryle, Introduction to "*Concept.*"
[62] Ryle, *Concept of Mind*, p. 9.
[63] *Ibid.*, p. 12.
[64] Chalmers, "Australasian philosophy family tree," http://consc.net/tree.html (accessed May 13, 2017).
[65] See the obituary of Jack Smart, "Vale J. J. C. Smart,"
www.monash.edu/news/articles/vale-j.-j.-c.-smart (accessed May 13, 2017).

Defining mental states contextually, by identifying the causal roles they are deemed to play in the theory that postulates their existence, has allowed theorists to revive folk psychology as a significant theory and to postpone questions about ultimate realities implicated in human behavior and experience until a time when the relationships between the levels of inquiry presupposed by scientific research are clearer. The various reductionist positions made popular in the philosophy of mind during the twentieth century, for example, Identity Theory, functionalism, and eliminativism, can all be articulated with respect to the contention that mental events are "theoretical entities" postulated by a theory purporting to account for human behavior and experience. Developments in neuroscience itself suggest that it will discover hitherto unknown, and consequently unexpressed, relationships between mental states.[66] Just as the Theory of Mental States has been revived, I wish to contribute here to the revival of the General Theory of Spirits, and just as the former is subject to reduction, I construe the General Theory of Spirits to be subject to possible reduction, for we cannot tell in advance of empirical inquiry how a particular theory will fare. The classical distinction between mind and matter as two different kinds of substance does not need to be advanced in explicating mental events, and I do not see it as a requirement for endorsing the Theory of Spirits. Indeed, no firm position needs to be taken on the kinds of substance found in the universe, for all positions are conjectural to one degree or another.

The difficulties with theism advanced by Nielsen over what I am describing as intelligibility are open to a response from the perspective on theories I have advanced in this chapter. We should not think of logical positivism as having had complete or fully articulated positions on difficulties with religious and spiritual language. Friedrich Waismann, a significant figure in early expressions of positivism, recorded early conversations with Wittgenstein and others associated with the Vienna Circle where the limits of language are noted, particularly as it relates to ethical and religious language.[67] Positivism recognized difficulties associated with establishing criteria for the proper use of a term and for intelligibility, and with religious language this is exacerbated. So Nielsen's call for exact or complete criteria for the use of religious terms is too demanding upon commonsense itself, let alone science. Wittgenstein's insights about language, expressed most notably in *Philosophical Investigations*, have

---

[66] Churchland, "Reductionism and Antireductionism," p. 64.
[67] Waismann, *Wittgenstein and the Vienna Circle*, pp. 68–69, 117–118.

been universally considered and widely embraced. He is well known for having affirmed that the meaning of a term is found in its use, which then requires close attention to all the contexts in which the term can be correctly used in order to articulate that meaning. An implication of this view is that *imposing* a meaning on a complex term might misrepresent the way the term is actually used. Perhaps advancing explicative definitions,[68] which contain substantial reportive elements, but possibly some stipulative ones as well,[69] is a way to advance the cause of clarity in the use of language.

Nielsen's complaint that God cannot act without a body will need to await my discussion in Chapter 3 of an allegation in which causal efficacy appears to be exercised "without a body" in any conventional sense. His complaints against those who revert to construing God as a final cause, or as Being itself, appear to me to be well served. His complaint that theists do not elaborate on sufficient conditions for dependency strikes me as one deriving from insufficient attention to the cautious, conjectural approach to description and explanation that has come with recognition of the important role that abductive reasoning has acquired as theories postulating unobservables have become known. He protests that to speak of transcendence is obscure, for if something is experienced, it is *ipso facto* not transcendent. I would offer as a rejoinder that the lambda-baryon particle transcends the world of observation, at least in a sense well known to commonsense.[70] The notion of transcendence has evidently been forged in the commonsense domain, but, like many such concepts, it has limited value in illuminating the remarkable world of unobservable or theoretical objects. Nielsen is right in saying that propositions that assert that God is self-existent being and created the world out of nothing need fuller explication than that conventionally found. I observe that the former editor of *Philo: A Journal for Philosophy*[71] Quentin Smith compares the claim that the universe was created by a timeless point with the claim that the universe was created by God.[72] He evidently considers the reference to God

---

[68] Rudolf Carnap was famous for advocating explication, as in *Logical Foundations of Probability*, chap. 1, pp. 1–18.
[69] A difference between ordinary language philosophy and (standard) analytic philosophy is embedded in this remark.
[70] Shapere in "The Concept of Observation" argues that the term "observation" is being increasingly used by physicists to refer to phenomena in which only remote effects are observed, such as collisions of neutrinos with carbon tetrachloride molecules.
[71] This journal ceased to publication in 2014 and has joined the efforts of other organizations that criticize thoughtful approaches to religious beliefs.
[72] Smith, "Time Was Created by a Timeless Point," p. 96ff.

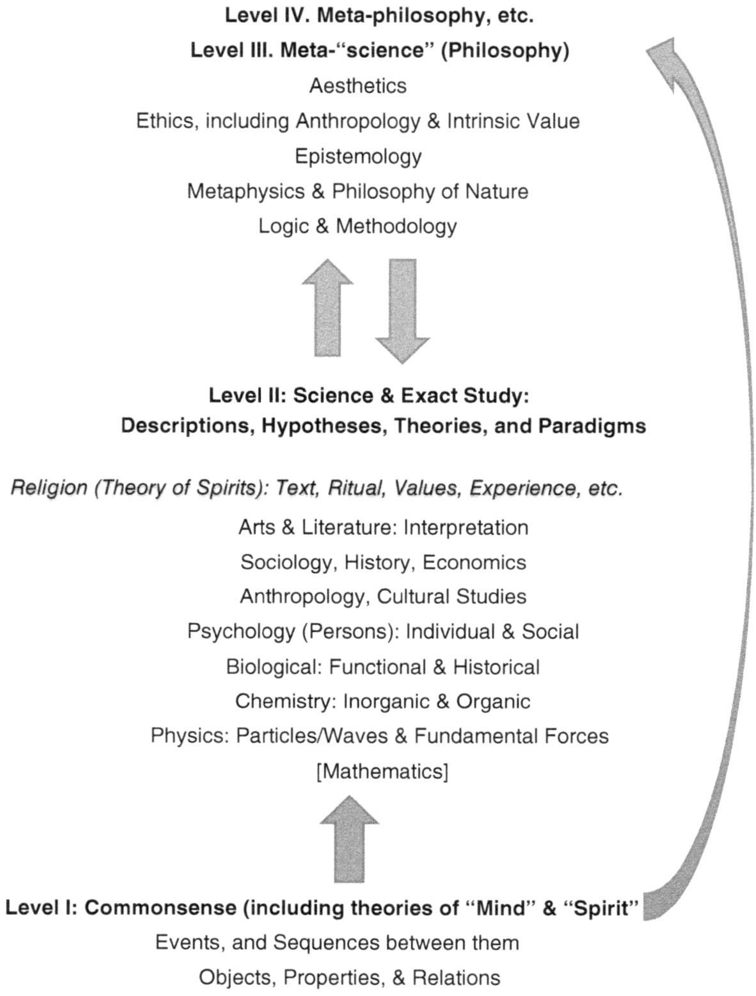

Level IV. Meta-philosophy, etc.
Level III. Meta-"science" (Philosophy)
Aesthetics
Ethics, including Anthropology & Intrinsic Value
Epistemology
Metaphysics & Philosophy of Nature
Logic & Methodology

Level II: Science & Exact Study:
Descriptions, Hypotheses, Theories, and Paradigms

Religion (Theory of Spirits): Text, Ritual, Values, Experience, etc.
Arts & Literature: Interpretation
Sociology, History, Economics
Anthropology, Cultural Studies
Psychology (Persons): Individual & Social
Biological: Functional & Historical
Chemistry: Inorganic & Organic
Physics: Particles/Waves & Fundamental Forces
[Mathematics]

Level I: Commonsense (including theories of "Mind" & "Spirit")
Events, and Sequences between them
Objects, Properties, & Relations

FIGURE 2.3 The relationship between Commonsense and Science

to be intelligible, even though this Being does not exist. I will have further remarks on God in Chapter 3.

Figure 2.3 summarizes much of the widely endorsed view of the relationship between Commonsense and Science, but I have incorporated the activity of philosophy, as I see it, and created a place for Religion as a study of spirit in general.

Comments on Figure 2.3:

The General Theory of Spirits

1. This figure should be read more-or-less from the bottom up. Commonsense, to which the Theory of Spirit clearly belongs, once provided us with the most basic insights into the nature of the world [symbolized by the broad arrow between Levels 1 and 2]. The sciences are now our best known critical achievements, whose insights are increasingly being configured in conceptual terms defined in mathematics. The commonsense framework is found in every basic language in all the world's peoples, among which rough commonalities can be found, as well as differences, no doubt.
2. Commonsense has obviously influenced philosophy (symbolized by the long narrow arrow on the right-hand side), but no significant influence occurs in the opposite direction, that is, commonsense might not be significantly affected by claims (or discoveries) by philosophy. The relationship between science and philosophy is different, for science influences philosophy, and philosophy has some impact on science (symbolized by the two broad arrows between Levels 2 and 3), perhaps best seen in methodological shifts that are proposed by philosophy and then accepted by science.
3. I have chosen to depict the scientific framework using the familiar physicalist hierarchy that places physics at the base of the pyramid of science, with chemistry dependent upon it, and biology upon chemistry, and so on. Psychology is the domain in which the Theory of Mind makes its appearance. Its concept of person is central to other widely recognized social sciences.
4. The Theory of Spirit is one part of the commonsense domain whose elimination has been anticipated by modernity, perhaps because of premature confidence that the Theory of Mind would be eliminated. If the eliminativists about mental states in the closing decades of the twentieth century had been correct, the Theory of Mind would either have disappeared or be disappearing now. Those who view mental states as defined by their function have taken the upper hand, and whether this explanatory role can be reduced to neurophysiological states and process is still an open question.
5. Physicalism has stressed the value of reduction as a goal toward which science should work. I have no quarrel with reduction: If we can find one, we should embrace it. I do not think that imposing it upon all critical inquiry promotes the growth of inquiry, however. I see the social sciences as endorsing many unreduced concepts as central to their critical studies.

6. "Naturalism" is an important term for understanding contemporary science. *The Stanford Encyclopedia of Philosophy* interprets ontological naturalism as holding that "all spatiotemporal entities must be identical to or metaphysically constituted by physical entities. Many ontological naturalists thus adopt a physicalist attitude to mental, biological, and other such "special" subject matters. They hold that there is nothing more to the mental, biological, and social realms than arrangements of physical entities."[73] Asserting this thesis of "nothing more than" in the absence of careful consideration of phenomena involving spirits seems premature.
7. I assume that all parts of science, including paradigms, are open to testing, possible refutation, and to reformulation using modified or new conceptual frameworks, within which new theories are offered. I have placed the General Theory of Spirits in special lettering, since its place in the hierarchy of scientific and exact inquiries is contested, and some would grant it no place because of its supposed lack of intelligibility.
8. Meta-philosophy pervades critical commentary, and meta-philosophy itself is subject to criticism. Figure 2.3 could be viewed as coming from meta-philosophy. This abstract and remote branch of philosophy sometimes give philosophy its "bad aroma," but many more people engage in it than we might expect.

We can offer a minimalist sketch of the Theory of Spirits, perhaps, although the actual form that it takes depends very much upon local beliefs in which spirits are thought to be implicated. We can safely say that little of the medieval understanding of the spirit-infused world now remains among the intelligentsia of modern culture, whereas more is to found among those who take directions from their own experience, and from shared public feelings and fears, perhaps. When especially heinous crimes occurred several decades ago in a city of more than 100,000 residents, only thirty miles from Toronto, Canada's largest urban area, the residents insisted on burning down the house in which the crimes were committed. This was an unusually "medieval response" to the horrific rapes and murders, hardly the expected response of people with a "thoroughly modern mindset." The ancient practice of "cleansing by fire" was arguably in view, with varying convictions, I presume, about the efficacy

---

[73] See David, "Naturalism." Well-known American philosophers John Dewey, Ernest Nagel, Sidney Hook, and Roy Wood Sellars are cited as having special significance.

The General Theory of Spirits

of this method of removing an evil presence from a community. Perhaps enduring beliefs include that a world of benevolent super-beings exists, mirrored by diabolical ones who work to undermine their influence, and that humans are caught in the maelstrom when these two engage each other. These three are the major categories on which I will reflect in the ensuing pages, with some excursions into more out-of-the-way topics.

This understanding of ourselves as persons is capable of being extended to spirits, who are also persons, evidently, but in ways discoverable only by personal interaction with them. Such interactions are often too fleeting to provide an adequate account of how they are "minded" or "mindful" beings, but other interactions are more revealing. In the *Burnaby "Evil Spirit" Case*, for instance, we detect a being who is familiar with the use of restrooms, who opens and closes doors in an "appropriate sequence," comparable to the actions of an ordinary or normal human person. Whether it is conscious of creating anxiety or fear in those witnessing the events is unclear. The *Abbotsford Visitor* exhibits comparable "mindedness," but never acts during the times Tom and his wife are home, only when they are out. It seems intent on achieving a particular end, for when Tom starts attending church, the events come to an end. This appears intentional to Tom and also to his son. Naturally, church is not the only context in which spirits are encountered, even invoked on occasion such as at funerals, but it perhaps remains the main one in Western culture. The ominous effect the "visits" to Tom's home had on his wife are curious, and we cannot say that all of the effects were unequivocally pleasant. Was this unintended? Inevitable? If we are speaking of the Deity here, we might say that some of his acts create uneasiness, even fear. The important point here is that events unfold that have some of the markings of acts involving persons in which attributes, including intentions, are revealed, the understanding of which is grasped by virtue of previous familiarity with "minded" human acts, even though speech does not accompany the acts; this is a feature of both the *Burnaby* and the *Abbotsford* cases.

3

Testability and Evidence

I surmise that my discussion of the intelligibility of the Theory of Spirits in Chapter 2 will be met with some disbeliefs. My critic might light-heartedly raise the medieval question here about the number of angels who can dance on the head of a pin, perhaps to show that the discussion of spirits has no practical value, or, more likely, to show that this kind of question has no answer because the claims about spirits, while intelligible, could have no answers since empirical methods do not exist from which an answer might be obtained. I will begin by advancing an actual allegation concerning spirits that is testable. If a theory is testable, it certainly is intelligible,[1] but the converse seemingly does not hold (and might not matter).

In order to address the problem of testability of the Theory of Spirits as perspicaciously as possible, I draw attention to a curious exorcism with a testable feature that said to have been part of the life of Jesus of Nazareth, whom Christendom considers to be the Christ. The NT describes a case in which demons are said to have been exorcised from a man and sent into swine feeding nearby. This is the description from *The Gospel of St. Luke*:[2]

The Gerasene Case: Then they arrived at the country of the Gerasenes,[3] which is opposite Galilee. And as he [Jesus] stepped out on land, there met him a man from the city who had demons; for a long time he had worn no clothes, and he lived not in a house but among the tombs. When he saw Jesus, he cried out and

---
[1] The link between these concepts is logical, it appears.
[2] *Luke* 8:26–33.
[3] Also known as Gaderenes.

Testability and Evidence 73

fell down before him, and said with a loud voice, "What have you to do with me, Jesus, Son of the Most High God? I beseech you, do not torment me." For he had commanded the unclean spirit to come out of the man. (For many a time it had seized him; he was kept under guard, and bound with chains and fetters, but he broke the bonds and was driven by the demon into the desert.) Jesus then asked him, "What is your name?" And he said, "Legion"; for many demons had entered him. And they begged him not to command them to depart into the abyss. Now a large herd of swine was feeding there on the hillside; and they begged him to let them enter these. So he gave them leave. Then the demons came out of the man and entered the swine, and the herd rushed down the steep bank into the lake and were drowned.

Most examples of resorting to spirits in description and explanation are much more implausible than this one, such as when people routinely construe mental illness as a condition brought about by demons[4] or construe every spontaneous remission of cancer as brought about by God. Such remarks are generally untestable, even though they might be intelligible. The striking account of the *Gerasene Case* clearly has features about it that allow us to understand how a central feature of it might be testable. I have chosen to use the account in St. Luke; the two other synoptic gospels that treat this incident, St. Matthew and St. Mark, say that two demoniacs were involved, not just one. These are differences that biblical scholars address, but I will not address the problem of resolving such variations here. If two men, rather than one, were involved, we would be required to conjecture about their equal involvement in the bizarre request to enter the swine, as well as the simultaneity, or otherwise, of the effect upon the swine. The case is complicated enough with just one demoniac, so I will stay with Luke's account. I will briefly discuss the question in Chapter 5 about the evidence for demonic activity, including possession, but in this chapter, I will focus on the testability of claims about spirits.

This account clearly implicates two subbranches of the Theory of Spirits; so if it is testable, then it has consequences for both diabolical and Divine orders. That feature makes this case extraordinarily efficient, inasmuch as only one order or the other is generally in focus in RSM experience. We might raise legitimate questions about how we might recognize experience implicating just one kind of order, unlike this case where each order is more clearly seen in the light of the other. The testable component of the *Gerasene Case* involves the threat of Legion to enter the swine. Although the account is sketchy on the kinds of details

---

[4] Cf. Goldberg, *Speaking with the Devil*.

we might demand today of anything empirical, the transfer of "something horrible" is evidence for the exorcism having been completed, and with that, evidence for the reality of two orders of spirits appears to be at war with each other. The transfer is the testable portion. The time frame for the exorcism and the transfer appears to be small, but not enough detail is provided to speak more adequately on this.

Compare this transfer case with one that I heard about when I lived in Adelaide where Leo Harris exorcised a spirit from one man, which then entered another (seemingly). In this case[5] "the voice" in the first (older) man said, "We [the plural form was used] don't want to go, but if we have to, we are going to enter X." X was a younger man known to Leo from the congregation of perhaps 1500 that he pastored in Adelaide, which was a city of about 700,000 people at the time. Within a half-hour or so of this exorcism, Leo received a telephone call from the mother of the younger man who had been named. She begged Leo to come to the house immediately because "something strange had come over her son." Leo did not consider her phoning him at the very time that she did to be at all a coincidence, given what had just happened in his office. When Leo arrived at the house, he was ushered into the room where the younger man was resting, and upon shutting the door behind him, Leo heard the threatening voice that he had heard in his office a short while ago saying: "We told you we would get him, didn't we?" This exorcism claim was testable because an implication of it was that something would happen to the younger man. If nothing at all had happened, the exorcism claim would have been strongly disconfirmed.

Here is a test case in which one possible outcome speaks to the falsity of the exorcism claim, inasmuch as it provides grounds for dismissing exorcism altogether and the spiritual orders said to be implicated; however, the other outcome confirms the existence of the two spiritual orders in an apparent conflict. The fact that something was said by "the voice" coming from the younger man indicates that the predicted event occurred; the behaviors (not described) that disturbed the younger man's mother are also corroborative, although on their own might not count for much. In this case, testing of the prediction was completed in less than one hour, and it provides us with a clear view of testability. The *Gerasene Exorcism Case* combines the prediction and the predicted event into such a short temporal sequence (apparently) that the two must be teased apart

---

[5] I have discussed this case in *God and Other Spirits*, chap. 1, and in "Deliverance and Exorcism in Philosophical Perspective."

(conceptually) to be seen for what they are. This is not needed in the case from Adelaide. These two exorcism cases contribute to my conjecture here that a more complete form of the General Theory of Spirits would uncover novel features. The possible activity and causal efficacy of other-than-human minds are shaped here by empirical information. The claim that the minds here are other-than-human is a conjecture, of course, but we know enough about the limitations of human minds to advance this with confidence.

Some merit exists in examining the *Gerasene Case* in the light of the account of the lambda-baryon particles discussed in Chapter 2. Nothing about the *Gerasene Case* is unintelligible, just as nothing about the lambda baryon being produced in a collision of subatomic particles is unintelligible, even if the object is unobservable. Neither is either claim ineffable, that is, too great to be described in words, for the claims about the baryon particle and about the *Gerasene exorcism* are set in spatio-temporal–causal contexts by which the postulated entities are functionally defined. In just the way that we "see" the baryon particle, we "see" the entities (beings) that are implicated in the exorcism of the Gerasene demoniac. Even "God," who usually escapes detection, is "visible" for a split second. However, nothing more than a split-second "trace" in the space–time–causal continuum presents itself to the observer in either case.

A person would not need to "be religious" to interpret the strange set of events involved in the *Gerasene exorcism*. If an empiricist were to hear the "strange" greeting addressing Jesus as the Son of the Most High God, she might be puzzled or confused, but since the man's behavior in general seems to have been bizarre, this verbal barrage might be considered nothing more than a variation on a theme that was common for the demoniac. Even the conversation about "entering" the swine nearby could be seen as one more instance of bizarre verbal behaviors exhibited by the demoniac. However, when the order is given to "Legion" to leave the man, and permission is given to enter the swine, everything changes. A causal sequence seems to have been triggered, for the man in whom the bizarre behaviors were found becomes normal, and the swine begin to behave in a peculiar way, as though something passed from the demoniac to the swine. No religious background in spirits or commitment to their reality would be needed to this point, for one might postulate "something-we-know-not-what" to account for the transfer described. If one were to have an "empirical disposition" and were to be in a physics lab where the lambda-baryon is generated, but be relatively unknowledgeable about physics, one might again postulate "something-we-know-not-what" to account for the strange "gap" seen on the photographic plate. One need not already have accepted the reality of subatomic particles, particularly those that are not observable to the basic human senses – sight, touch, hearing, taste, and smell – perhaps because one has imbibed too long and hard at some positivist source. However, anyone with a disposition to identify causes is apt to identify the cause as "something-we-know-not-what." Nothing about the lambda-baryon particle exhibits the features of minds as we have come to understand them from our interactions with humans (and also with animals), again revealing something about our understanding of minds.

The theory that postulates the reality of lambda-baryon particles gives intelligibility to the portions of the theory making mention of such a particle, by providing both attributes of such particles (perhaps), and, more importantly, offering relations to things that are not in doubt. Here the central relation of causality carries something of a presumption about it, because we might not know the extent to which causality is a feature of our universe. We generally assume that it pervades the order of experience, but some doubt, of course, about this assumption is feasible. The intelligibility of the lambda-baryon theory is supplied in part by the assumption of causality. The intelligibility of the *Gerasene Exorcism Case* is also provided by causality pervading the sequence of events described. Since the entity (or entities, perhaps) that leave(s) the man and enter(s) the swine is never "directly observed," its (their) reality is provided by the role the evil spirits are assigned in the account. The intelligibility of the two "theories" is roughly comparable and is independent of the unusual strictures that positivists placed upon theorizing in general.

A curious feature of the *Gerasene Case* is that "God" is construed as having been active – at one moment the demoniac is overwhelmed by destructive forces, and at the next moment, he is freed. Although some theorists might baulk at calling the power "God," Jesus himself is modest enough elsewhere to suggest that this power is over and above those abilities he possesses as a human being and that this power either is God or comes from God. I surmise that if one were to observe, not merely read about, the events in question, he or she might wonder if he or she had momentarily "observed" the power that is God. I will describe another event in Chapter 5 where "God" seems momentarily visible. Nielsen is right in thinking that no being is encountered in the exorcism who could be described as a creator, or as self-existent Being, or as final cause, or as one that lacks (or has) a body. The last of these descriptors takes on a whole new meaning if we make a transition from the commonsense (preatomistic) world that Nielsen seems to be thinking of to the world of physics where the solidity of bodies actually becomes a remark about the impenetrability of certain atomic structures by objects as large as human hands – physics has changed our understanding of bodiliness to impenetrability, by substituting a *relation* between objects for a *property* of them. Nielsen's worries about transcendent being are also beside the point, for we can assert that something was experienced by the demoniac; consequently, the experience satisfies Nielsen's condition for not being transcendent. His worries about God being ineffable are more to the point. Because we cannot observe the beings postulated in the exorcism, to describe either of them as ineffable is to minimize the degree to which we actually do understand. Our understanding is provided by the causal context in which the events occur, events that are linked to the everyday world by such relations as causality, and spatial or temporal proximity. Nielsen seems to be responding to forms of theism that belong to the a priori tradition of theism, rather than an empirical one.

The demons, said to be Legion – a play on a word, at one time functioning as a name, and another time as an indicator of the number of demons said to be involved – clearly suggest that they *are* minds or *have mindedness*. We are given the discourse that occurred between the diabolical agents, somehow speaking through the demoniac, and the Christ – a term that I use here to indicate that some agent is present above and beyond (apparently) the earthly Jesus of Nazareth. The speech of both parties is evidently suited to the context, and is also redolent with intentionality and purpose, since swine are mentioned and are actually feeding nearby. Recognizing objects is a striking mark of minds. The terminology here is difficult to settle upon, but everything about the account suggests that Legion can hear commands perfectly well and respond to them in intelligible ways. He can identify himself as Legion; he can sense objects in its immediate vicinity such as the swine; he can understand that what I am calling "a transfer" from men to pigs is possible; and he can appreciate something of the unique identity of the Christ and his power to send evil spirits to the abyss, which is generally taken in the NT to be the realm of the dead.

All spirits seem to be minimally minds, but with varying attributes, depending upon the class of spirit to which they belong, perhaps, and by their authority or rank. In *Visions of Jesus*, I relate the account of a visionary who returned to her home and found her property ringed by beings of about her height (average), whom she construed as angels. They made (seeming) signs of obeisance to other beings above her head who were initially invisible, but who became visible as she and her family were about to enter their home, beings that were eight or nine feet tall. The smaller beings showed deference to the taller ones, whom she took to be personal guardian angels, one for each of her husband, their son, and herself. They entered the home of the visionary and her family, but the other angels did not.

The involvement of a human mind and of swine in the story of the *Gerasene exorcism* is curious. One might be loath to accept the possibility that a demonic spirit – a mind – could be "attached" to a human being, or to swine, for that matter. However, animals have long been considered to be "familiars" in accounts of bewitching, where influences are perhaps transmitted from a "witch" (or "wizard") to "the bewitched" with the help of an animal, a cat perhaps, so the Gersasene account could be seen as corroboration of this belief. The claim is intelligible, even though the "mechanisms" by which such "transmission" occurs remain obscure. The exact attributes of theoretical objects might be obscure, along with their relations to things not in doubt, so conjectures involving theoretical objects have a significant amount of indeterminacy about them. By the causal role assigned to these (putative) objects, some of their features become intelligible.

The two orders of spirit in the *Gerasene exorcism* account stand out very sharply against the backdrop of each other. We sometimes hear people go on at length about the presence of evil in some person, or the presence of God in some religious service, and while both claims are intelligible and could possibly turn out to be plausible, the grounds for claiming them are generally so insubstantial that they do not warrant acceptance. Religious categories for describing or explaining phenomena have been so abused and overused that their value can legitimately be called into question. Moreover, in many cases, we simply compare one mundane human situation with another in which the diabolical, or divine, influence is alleged to be present, but that influence is undetectable. Those who are deeply committed to viewing the universe as marked by RSM phenomena can easily impose their viewpoints on what are really very ordinary matters. The shocking truth is that in some religious quarters such an imposition of a conceptual framework upon rather mundane matters is viewed as some sort of virtue – having "faith" perhaps, or being profoundly spiritual. The Theory of Spirits has features that make irresponsible use of it quite easy. All theories that posit unobservable entities are subject to abuse, but the psychological impact of the Theory of Spirits deserves special respect, for the fear that the theory can arouse can be manipulated to personal advantage.

One conclusion that I draw from the *Gerasene Case* is that some claims about spirits are testable. I do not extend this conclusion to most claims about diabolical and divine spirits, but only make it about some such claims. Perhaps it almost goes without saying that the conjecture that divine and diabolical spirits are real *does not follow from* the data sketched, just that the conjecture in question is testable. The phrase "*does not follow from*" is one of the most pernicious phrases found in philosophy. It seemingly derives from an era in which theorists were expected to advance truths that were beyond question, or truths that no sane person would doubt, from which, using Rules of Deduction, many other claims (Theorems) could be advanced as true. The nature of *sound* argumentation, in which valid arguments are put forward from truths, guarantees that if we begin with truths, then we argue only to additional truths. In this way, considerable bodies of related truths could be advanced, once commonly known as sciences. This legitimate method of presenting an understanding of some subject area was celebrated in the ancient world. However, it has proved too narrow to account for argumentation in the modern age. Induction was already recognized in Aristotle's time, but neither deduction nor (conventional) induction covers the innovation in modern thought described as *abduction* or as *retroduction* by Charles Saunders Pierce. Here we encounter the stratagem (also found in antiquity) of postulating theoretical objects in order to explain observed phenomena seemingly in need of explanation. Modern science, including physics would be seriously incomplete and methodologically impotent without abduction.

The discussion so far suggests that answers to questions of testability and evidence concerning the General Theory of Spirits are neither uniform nor simple. Some subfields carry implications about the existence of several kinds of spirits, and some perhaps carry implications concerning the human order. We have every reason to suppose that the Theory of Spirits will surprise and stretch our critical capacities, much as every general field of exact inquiry in unquestionably naturalistic domains already does. I surmise that we can learn much from naturalistic inquiries, especially those in which unobservable objects are postulated to exist. These unquestionably make the identification of evidence challenging. I do not assume that views on evidence are exactly uniform, but what to put in the place of this claim is unclear. Ernst Mayr, zoologist, remarkable biologist, and winner of the Darwin Medal in 1984, argues that biological life cannot be reduced to the atomic structure of its constituent physical parts. He argues that biological explanations require reference to both

DNA components of a thing and its evolutionary history. He observes that successful work in physics hobbled biological studies for a time, since biology was considered to require adherence to the methodology that is significant to physics.[6] The differences he takes note of suggest to me that every claim about spirits requires close attention to particular nuances of the theory.

GOD

I have made a number of references to God in this book, and some comment on my conception(s) of God is in order, especially as I embark on a fuller examination of testability and evidence. Of course, I stay with remarks in Chapter 2 according to which the import of a term is found in the set of narrative statements in which the term is used, but some further clarifications are in order. God is considered to be the greatest conceivable being by St. Anselm,[7] from which other descriptions have developed, among them those that ascribe infinite attributes to God. Aquinas considers God's disclosure of his name to Moses[8] at the scene where a thornbush was in flame but was not consumed – I AM THAT I AM – to give expression to the unique kind of existence of one whose essence is to exist. The biblical account is interesting for the theophantic character it ascribes to God:

Exodus 3: "Now Moses was keeping the flock of his father-in-law, Jethro, the priest of Mid'ian; and he led his flock to the west side of the wilderness, and came to Horeb, the mountain of God. And the angel of the LORD appeared to him in a flame of fire out of the midst of a bush; and he looked, and lo, the bush was burning, yet it was not consumed. And Moses said, "I will turn aside and see this great sight, why the bush is not burnt." ... Moses said to God, "If I come to the people of Israel and say to them, 'The God of your fathers has sent me to you,' and they ask me, 'What is his name?' what shall I say to them?" God said to Moses, "I AM WHO I AM." And he said, "Say this to the people of Israel, 'I AM has sent me to you.'" God also said to Moses, "Say this to the people of Israel, 'The LORD, the God of your fathers, the God of Abraham, the God of Isaac, and the God of Jacob, has sent me to you': this is my name for ever, and thus I am to be remembered throughout all generations."

Aquinas holds that no other existent thing exhibits existence as its essence, for every other thing or being that does exist, whether terrestrial or

---

[6] "The Autonomy of Biology." Andrew Brigham drew this to my attention.
[7] St. Anselm, *Proslogion*, chaps. 2–4 is the classical source.
[8] Summa Theologica (ST) 1, 3, 5.

celestial, only happens to do so; nothing else has a structure comparable to HE WHOSE ESSENCE IS TO BE.[9]

In expositing Aquinas's approach to understanding God, Eric Mascall (1905–93), Professor of Historical Theology at the University of London for many years, claims that Aquinas's being whose essence is to exist is equivalent to St. Anselm's view of God as a being greater than which cannot be conceived.[10] The infinite properties that God is understood to have, according to Anselm's understanding of maximal greatness, result in the well-known view that God can only be defined by the use of attributes that are understood as *analogies* to comparable attributes found in humans. This view is expressed in the doctrine that God is above every other form of being, since he is the ground and archetype of all else that exists. Mascall also interprets Aquinas's famous five "proofs" for the existence of God – as the first cause, as necessary being, and so on – as *implications* of the insight that God is he whose essence is to exist,[11] which means that the common philosophical practice of presenting Aquinas's five ways as deductive proofs, as though they satisfied expectations of logic, misrepresents them.

One could quibble with Mascall's claims, but I will not. I stop only to observe the conceptions of God readily found, some of which I have mentioned in the following:

1. God is the Being who essence is existence.
2. God is the Being who exists necessarily (while all other beings only exist contingently).
3. God is the Being a greater than which cannot be conceived.
4. God is the Being with maximal greatness (equivalent to 3?).
5. God is the Being with an infinite number of excellences (and no deficiencies), each present to an infinite extent (Spinoza's concept);[12] sometimes three attributes are the object of special attention, namely, infinite benevolence, infinite power, and infinite knowledge.[13]
6. God is the Being who revealed himself to Abraham, to Isaac, and to Jacob (according to *Genesis* in the Hebrew Bible).

---

[9] *Ibid.*; my italics.
[10] *He Who Is*, pp. 11–13.
[11] *Ibid.*, p. 37, my italics; cf. Harris, "Can 'Creation' be a Metaphysical Concept?" p. 150, for a similar view.
[12] Spinoza, *Ethics*, Part 1, Axiom 6.
[13] The problem of evil arises from this set of attributes.

The self-identification of senses 1 and 6 in the epiphany to Moses is significant.

The approach I take to the "definition" of God is in keeping with my discussion in Chapter 2, which happens to be consistent with remarks from Aquinas that I have quoted above.[14] I construe God (and other spirits) as defined primarily by (apparent) causal ties to other objects (or beings), some of which are observable. No obvious mechanism exists for limiting the way in which a putative referring term is given further reference in the context of a complex theory. The fact that such a theory purports to introduce God into the causal domain in which humans live does not obviously conflict with other stratagems for giving meaning to the term "God." The being who is God in the Theory of Theism, as I envision it, might in fact be identical to the one whose essence is to exist, or to the one who has maximal greatness, and so on, but the method I have advanced, being empirical in character, neither requires this nor rules out God's being the unique self-existent one. In this respect, the method I have proposed allows a postulated entity to acquire a rich description, albeit one that is subject to modification as its attributes becomes more fully known.

I would not describe the attributes that God possesses as *analogous* to the attributes found in other things. Aquinas was concerned to distinguish univocal ascription from equivocal and analogical ascription. When we address theories in which unobservable objects are postulated, we are often unable to determine how much or how little an attribute of that object (or a relation in which that object is featured) is like another. We attribute causal power to some spirit, for instance, but cannot say very much about the ways in which that causal power resembles or differs from cases in which we know much more about causation, because of our detailed knowledge of both the causes and the effects in the natural order, for example. I do not see how all the possible questions about similarities and differences can be answered, primarily because we may be dealing with an unobservable object. The fact that (most) theories are intelligible allows us to cautiously affirm that the vital terms in it are also intelligible. I see intelligibility as conferred on terms by virtue of their (intelligible) linkages with other terms that are already intelligible. Although empiricists have set tasks for themselves in showing how intelligibility originates with the most basic of terms, I am assuming that intelligent communication occurs without a complete description of its origins.

---

[14] See Chapter 2, p. 51.

The approach I am taking here to the understanding of "God" is in contrast with that central to rationalistic approaches to understanding "God," which seem to be in ascendancy now in Western culture and can hardly avoid making God even more remote than he already seems. We have no *obvious* experience with a being whose essence is to exist, although it is imaginable that we have more experience with such a being than we know about. I suppose that such a being would be "one greater than which cannot be conceived," but I am not sure why one would give assent to this proposition. More troubling are those descriptions of God that resort to infinite attributes, such as infinite knowledge, or infinite power, or infinite goodness. Spinoza gave classic expression to a rationalistic approach in the view: "God, or a substance consisting of infinite attributes, each of which expresses eternal and infinite essence, necessarily exists."[15] Here God is a being with maximal greatness, since the infinite attributes are infinite are number.

While no one could assert that the "humbler God" encountered in a burning bush is not identical with a God having maximal greatness, the two approaches to theology differ sharply from one another. Advancing Spinoza's God, compared to the empiricist labors over possible theophanies as expressions of God's reality, has all the benefits of theft over honest toil. We might wonder how we could offer grounds for thinking that an infinite being with an infinite number of attributes, each present to an infinite degree, could exhibit its presence. We could look at the *Gerasene exorcism* from this perspective, for instance, and wonder if anything about the accounts of it offers grounds for thinking that such an infinite being was encountered, by the demoniac, say, or by any bystanders. It is clear that such a God has attributes that are in no way *testable*. Whether defenders of this form of theism recognize the extent to which they play into modern atheism is unclear. I will construe God hereafter, unless I give indication to the contrary, in the humbler fashion outlined by the structure of theories, in which theoretical objects, perhaps unobservable in some readily recognized sense of this complex term, are postulated to exist as items in a causal nexus. Perhaps it goes without saying that virtually all the philosophic terms I am using in this book are also definable by their positions in the context of theories in which they are used, since the ontic properties and the epistemic grounds for asserting such properties are seemingly empirical.

---

[15] Spinoza, *Ethics: First Part*. Proposition 11.

TESTABILITY

Testability is a concept that places emphasis upon the human capacity and opportunity to conduct tests of one kind or another, in order to establish a causal link between one phenomenon and another. John Stuart Mill is famous for having articulated five principles for determining whether one thing is cause of another. Such Millian principles include determining whether a putative cause and a putative effect are present together, or are absent together, or whether more of the putative effect occurs along with more of the putative cause. All such claims depend upon being able to make independent observations of causes and effects; naturally, such observations are impossible when we are dealing with unobservable objects. We might say that all theories postulating unobservable objects share this difficulty, which means that more subtle measures must be in place in order to assert plausibly that some theoretical object is in the causal nexus of some particular phenomenon, such as the ability to paint with considerable authority without having had any lessons, as alleged in the case of Kathleen Spencer. Perhaps this claim is testable in the sense that we can predict it to be repeated, or maybe it is susceptible to having a cause plausibly cited that is naturalistic in origin, which would falsify the original claim about its source being in some spirit or mind other than Kathleen Spencer. The latter would amount to reduction by being eliminated in favor of some other theory, perhaps articulated using the typical constructs of psychology, and consequently a chapter of naturalism, or soon to be one. In all the discussion here about the testability of claims concerning spirits, we must remember that spirits are minds of one sort or another, whether embodied or not (whatever this might mean). So they are living beings and more akin to humans that to any animals that we might know well.

We could say that modernity is predisposed to look for natural causes for events, so that proposing a cause that is spiritual in character is contrary to the way in which critical inquiry is apt to be done. The principle as work here is:

Principle of naturalism: Natural explanations should first be sought for phenomena, before considering any nonnatural or supernatural one.

This principle exhibits a bias in favor of naturalism and is supported in the writing of William James from a century or so ago.[16] However, it might not reflect a plausible understanding of the cosmos. I will go along with it, but I observe that a proponent of the Theory of Spirits is given

---

[16] James, *Varieties*, p. 18.

a significant obstacle to overcome, which I acknowledge as a challenge here. We could view modernity as having chosen to ignore or minimize any theory postulating spirits, perhaps with a view to examining the explanatory power of naturalistic explanations without the distraction of unpredictable beings known as (nonhuman) spirits. This interpretation accords with:

Principle of Simplicity:[17] A hypothesis that is simpler than another is preferable.

A related principle is:

Principle of conservativism:[18] Theories that are already used in explanations are preferable to new theories advanced to explain inexplicable data.

Whether simplicity is a mark of truth is debatable.[19] Moreover, a criterion for simplicity is needed to make this principle workable, but I think that plausible criteria of simplicity can be formulated by those who work in a particular field of scientific or critical inquiry. Of course, we might end up with different criteria, including some not reducible to others. These are the challenges of theorizing.

I should perhaps observe that I am not particularly interested here in claims that would be deemed miraculous. Terminology is not consistent around this term, but by it I mean those claims, roughly, in which the natural order is somehow overridden or perhaps violated.[20] For example, I do not consider the alleged visitation of the angel Gabriel to the Virgin Mary, as described in *The Gospel of St. Luke*, to be a miracle, but Mary's conception of a male child without ordinary human intercourse I do consider miraculous. If humans share the cosmos with spirits – spirits that are somehow distinguishable from one another and also from us – this fact would make our lives more complicated, but it would not be obviously incommensurable with what we are discovering through scientific and other exact studies. We can quite easily consider the possibility that minds might exist on planets not yet discovered – otherwise projects such as SETI (search for extraterrestrial intelligence) would make no sense and be little more than a waste of public and corporate financing. Enthusiasts

---

[17] William of Ockham (ca.1285–1347) is its most famous proponent; it has been very widely discussed and embraced. The principle was known prior to William, but he referred to it so often it became his; cf. "Occam's Razor," *Encyclopedia Britannica* www.britannica.com/topic/Occams-razor (accessed September 3, 2018).
[18] Quine and Ullian, *The Web of Belief*, pp. 44–45.
[19] Cf. Edmonds, "Simplicity is not truth-indicative."
[20] See Larmer, *The Legitimacy of Miracle*, pp. 27–46.

of the alleged UFO (unidentified flying object) incident near Roswell, New Mexico, in July 1947 claim that aliens – intelligent beings of one sort or another from some galaxy other than ours, perhaps – visited the earth. So claims about the existence of minds (neither human nor animal) is not obviously a form of supernaturalism, and consequently not a specious form of it. We do well to focus on those that yield testable results.

We must be especially cognizant of the fact that we are interacting with beings who are persons (*with minds*). When we think of the testability of claims concerning spirits, we are helped by thinking about the testability of claims about human persons as these are informally viewed. Our unique form of being is important because it is clearly distinct from any animal, whose relations to existing things and whose attributes might be indeterminable. At the end of Chapter 2, I sketched some of our insights concerning human beings, insights that are far-reaching and somewhat mysterious. Perhaps we can reflect for a moment on human behavior involving some thoughts and planning, not appearing to be merely reflex behavior. We might observe, for example, that a daughter comes regularly to visit her elderly mother; perhaps two or three times a week, often bringing her mother some food. On the basis of this observation, which is neither exhaustive nor exact, we conjecture that this behavior will continue into the future. Here is a testable claim. We expect a similar pattern to endure, and if it does, our conjecture is confirmed; if it does not, then our conjecture is disconfirmed, even falsified. The Theory of Mind, without which life is hardly imaginable, is central to this (rough) generalization, and to its test implications, including its confirmation or disconfirmation. This example is from such a familiar part of the Theory of Mind, and is so fully integrated into it, that we could almost overlook our knowledge of it.

We are now in a position to comment directly on the testability of the examples in Chapter 2 of claims seemingly involving spirits. The fact that one subbranch, namely, the *Gerasene Exorcism Case*, is testable lends credence to the possibility that others are as well, but this cannot be bluntly asserted, for particular kinds of cases must be critically examined.

1. The case of the *Drottningholm phantoms* is perhaps testable, but we might not be able to identify readily the circumstances in which the phantoms can be identified again. The feeling of some preternatural presence is not enough to satisfy those who are understandably skeptical of the reality of spirits, for some ordinary psychological state might have been misinterpreted. When I discuss hallucinations in the section "Apparitions" of Chapter 4, I will also say

more about *seen* apparitions. One would need to know more about how often the Drottingholm phantoms show up and how they do so, exactly. Perhaps some patterns are detectable that allow predictions to be made, such as showing up on the anniversary of some previous resident's death, or their birth, and so on. Psychologist Carl Jung famously predicted the action of some spirit in his interactions with Sigmund Freud in the midst of a heated argument between them about the reality of the paranormal. Jung's biographer Aniela Jaffé writes: "Later in the evening, however, in the course of an argument about paranormal phenomena, a seemingly unaccountable detonation went off in Freud's bookcase. When Freud dismissed Jung's parapsychological interpretation of this event, Jung predicted that the same thing would happen again, and so, to Freud's consternation, it did."[21] I presume that many such predictions have been made in various parts of the world and have not been accurate; however, finding an accurate one in the lives of prominent academic figures is reason for pause. We should observe that this case is not one in which we can pair the putative cause with its supposed effect.

Immanuel Kant decries the absurdity and folly in thinking that a person might be "possessed of a spirit" who knows and shares insights about the future or any other matter.[22] His remark is found in lectures that were published in 1797, based upon the manual he used in a course on anthropology, which he taught for about thirty years. Kant treats the existence of God with respect, but the larger ontological question of (finite) spirits – or minds that are not obviously infinite – is dismissed with scorn. Kant treats the claim that prophesied events (what he calls "inevitable fate") might be causally dependent upon human free acts as involving a contradiction, for the concept of "an unconditioned destiny (*decretum absolutum*) involves a mechanism of freedom, and so contradicts itself."[23] Kant delights in undertaking an analysis that appears to lead to "contradiction" in some claim, as in his widely known (and flawed) articulation of the ground of moral imperatives.[24] This is a key component in the critiques that follow his form of philosophical analysis,

---

[21] Jaffe, *Memories*, p. 152.
[22] *Anthropology*, sec. 36; in sec. 53, he construes a mind as perverse that has a taste for "mystical books and revelations that transcend sound human understanding."
[23] *Anthropology*, sec. 36.
[24] *Groundwork of the Metaphysics of Morals* (originally published in 1785).

which is my field of training and professional experience. I surmise that he either experienced no locutions or insights, as Jung seemingly had, or decided to ignore both. Kant notes that the belief in witches had not been fully rooted out in his time, citing a case of a Protestant minister in Scotland who testified to the existence of witches in a witchcraft trial.[25] Although belief in spirits does not coincide with belief in witches, the two are so closely connected that repudiation of one is virtually repudiation of the other.

A different perspective is put on the accuracy of predictive "words" by at least one biblical prophet. The Hebrew prophet Jeremiah reports that the word of the LORD came to him: "Behold, Han'amel the son of Shallum your uncle will come to you and say, 'Buy my field which is at An'athoth, for the right of redemption by purchase is yours'." Assuming that we are reading Jeremiah here, not a later editor, Jeremiah reports that when his uncle did just this: "Then I knew that this was the word of the LORD." I surmise that Jeremiah might have had questions about the "words" that came to him, more specifically, whether God himself might be behind these "thoughts." Of course, no simple way of comparing modern experience with that of the ancient era exists, apart, perhaps, from determining whether the predicted events actually occur, and even then we cannot get into the phenomenological detail needed to compare one such experience with another. The demand, in effect, that I pick between Kant and Jeremiah is a curious one. I now find myself going with the prophet rather than the philosophers, but in an earlier time, Kant would have been an easy winner.

In 2003, I received "a word" that substantially changed my intellectual life. I had gone to my office at the university where I was teaching on a spectacular summer morning. I was absent-mindedly looking at an article sent to me by a philosopher in the US when a "voice" spoke to me: "Phillip, why don't you write an article on the reality of evil spirits and send it to this journal" – meaning the one in which the article I was looking at was published. The interaction had no (detectible) emotion at all, for everything was at the cognitive level. I took it to be an invitation, primarily, not a command, but the invitation was strong. This "word," if that is what it was, took no more than two to three seconds to deliver, and then everything of significance was over. My full first name was used and the tone was friendly, and I wondered whether the Divine Order was behind it. I am sure no one would have heard what I "heard" and cannot

---

[25] *Ibid.*, sec. 13. Kant observes that the Scottish judge had scoffed at this testimony.

explain further what transpired there. This "word" was not imagined, for imagined thoughts have quite a different phenomenological quality for me. The invitation seemed to have a test implication attached to it, but the actual formulation did not include this feature, for I was never told that the journal that was indicated, *Religious Studies*, would actually publish my article;[26] I was only told to send it there. While I consider God to have been its source, which is a conjecture, of course, I have mulled over the possibility that he has an interest in ontology as philosophers understand this.

2. The *Burnaby "Evil Spirit"* claim was apparently testable in some imprecise sense during the peculiar period of time that the phenomena described above took place in Pauline Langlois's home. She reported that various members of her family witnessed the movement of plants that she saw and heard the inexplicable music that she heard in her home. She attributed these phenomena to an evil spirit in view of the fact that the events were not associable with human beings. The events suggesting that someone invisible entered her apartment, used her washroom, and then left the apartment were not witnessed by any other person, to my knowledge. This sequence would understandably be psychologically impressive, especially in the absence of a human being. Testability in the form of some reasonable expectation of repetition is applicable here. Adding to the curiosity is that the unwanted phenomena abated and then disappeared after Pauline "confronted" the evil spirit by invoking the Holy Spirit. This feature evokes Mill's criteria for identifying supposed cause and effort, where the presence of one can be associated with the presence of the other.

3. The case of the *Abbotsford "Visitor"* perhaps carried no reasonable expectation of being continued, even at the time the sequence of events occurred as described in Case 3 of Chapter 2. Tom seems to have had no such expectation himself, and so did not construe the events as belonging to some predictable and testable sequence. Each strange "visit" to his apartment was surprisingly different. Some apparitions tend to be repeated a number of times before coming to an end, and during such a time the expectation of continuation is reasonable; of course, we do not know whether an apparition is a one-off case, or whether it is apt to be repeated. The

---

[26] The article is titled "Finite Spirits as Theoretical Entities."

fact that the "visitations" end when he decided to go to church was taken to be significant, and is significant.

Some apparitions seem to be connected with unsolved murders or with the absence of rites of burial of murdered people. In those cases the apparition might appear only for as long "as needed," and is testable in the sense that a general prediction of its recurrence might be true. My brother-in-law who has been a teacher for many years in and around Winnipeg, Manitoba, now retired, conveyed an incident to me in which a married fellow-teacher and his wife were involved. They reported some odd events in their home: lights were left on, doors were opened when they were out, their furnace was turned off at night, and so on. So they made inquiries of a psychologist about these matters, who put the teacher's wife into a hypnotic state. In this state, she saw a man who said that he was only trying to get their attention and indicated that he liked them and did not wish to distress them. He reported that he had been murdered on the site where their home now stood, which was once land that Native bands of Manitoba occupied. He said that his murder had never been solved and his body had never been properly buried, so he instructed her on how this should take place: they were to make a small model boat made of paper, set it alight, and let it sail on the river adjacent to their home. After this consultation with the psychologist, they researched the topic of the Native bands that lived in the exact area where their home now stood, and in an *Encyclopedia* article, she saw a sketch of a man from that band, whose clothing was identical with what she had seen under hypnosis. This article also described conventional burial customs for that band, and when they followed them, all odd events stopped. We could perhaps say that the hypnotic state suggested events that turned out to be accurate, and in this sense, the supposed spirit-experience was testable.

4. The *UK Angel Encounter* is extraordinary for the kinds of epistemic issues it raises. We certainly might predict that similar events might occur in the future, perhaps in some other place, and in this sense, the claim about a spirit (an angel) is predictable in general. More importantly, this case presents an instance of intersubjective observation, so that the report of one person can be corroborated (or not) by another, and so is testable. The notion of testability generally carries with it the idea that we might formulate conditions for testing a theory, bring about the requisite conditions for the theory's application, and then wait to observe whether or not

the test implication occurs. This approach is closely related to the notion of a test result being replicable. However, this condition is not applicable to every kind of study. Many cosmological and geological phenomena are ones that we cannot control, so bringing about the requisite test conditions is not possible. Other studies belonging to sociology or history, such as testing whether protracted unemployment predisposes a population to unprovoked acts of violence, is not easily testable, for only a cruel despot would dare to generate unemployment in order to test its effect upon violent actions. We might compare similar populations, or perhaps similar historical conditions, in an effort to determine whether these variables are related. When moral codes disallow such tests, the luxury of intersubjective observation satisfies the requirement of testability. Heathcote-James reported: "I interviewed a lot of people about that angel, and everybody told the same story. Their descriptions were totally consistent."[27]

This account is also extraordinary for the information it provides about what was sensed by the people in the church who saw what they took to be an angel, a feeling that the rector put into these words: "It felt like having warm oil poured over you." When spiritual experience that penetrates the space-time–causal world can be correlated with a felt phenomenological experience, such felt experience has more importance than it would otherwise have. These correlated instances provide hints about what might be experienced when no marks of objectivity are featured, which characterizes most spiritual experience, it appears. Although few who are educated in Western culture might be inclined to concede that others who report only this "warm oil" sensation, in an RSM experience, have actually tapped into something beyond themselves, the rare glimpses into experiences such as the one offered by Heathcote-James and Midgley provide a basis for thinking otherwise. The reported sensation of "warm oil" is probably undergirded by neurophysiological mechanisms in human beings, but accepting this possible reduction of folk psychology has no telling impact on the significance of such an experience for folk religion. Cognitive science is expected to illuminate such issues as the difference between experiences that are derived "wholly from within" and those that are not, thereby correcting some of the overconfident claims made by those who are spiritually inclined.

---

[27] Steiger and Steiger, *Encyclopedia of the Unusual*, pp. 211–13.

5. The *spirit painting* case is not readily testable, it appears, although we might predict that similar allegations might occur in the future. Viscountess Churchill was quoted as saying that her daughter-in-law's gift was discovered just before World War I, when Kathleen Spencer expressed her desire to paint, just to make the lives of others brighter. Kathleen picked up her daughter's crayons, and "drew a perfect head of Christ." She thought she could do it again, and then bought the materials needed for painting, producing the head of Christ *upside down* in the space of about three hours. I take it from this account that Mrs. Spencer is thought to have produced two spirit paintings; from the fact that at least one was produced upside down, she was thought to have been aided by an outside spiritual source, for she had no training. Perhaps we might find someone who is reputed to have done one such painting, and then we predict that another will be done some time later. As a test of this ability, and, more specifically, as a test of the activity of a spirit acting in and through a person, it lacks epistemic force, for maybe some (normal) psychological ability caused it. This allegation of a spirit's causal influence may have been feasible to many in Doyle's generation from the widespread belief (then, in British lands) that Divine inspiration could readily be found in the Hebrew-Christian Holy Scriptures.
6. Ayer's NDE experience, which included meeting with beings of another order of reality, is not testable in itself, it appears, although the millions of similar NDEs give some reason for caution here. I will discuss NDEs in Chapter 5 and identify some features that begin to give NDE solid causal connections to the world we know we inhabit – the "undisputedly real" world.

It is clear that no single interpretation of testability is really possible. The relevant epistemology here yields as many unusual results, I surmise, as any branch of inquiry considered to be scientific. To find evidence for some theory is to say more than that the theory is testable. It is to this most important aspect of explanations for RSM experiences that I now turn.

ANGELS AND ELVES

In 2014, news was circulated reporting that 62% of Icelanders (polled) affirmed the reality of elves. This fairly high percentage, I presume, was the reason this information became international news. This news item surprised me, I suppose, for I do not share the belief and did not expect to hear such a high percentage reported from anywhere, even though elves belong generally to the class of spirits, some kinds of which I do believe to exist. I appreciate that some atheists, and other possible critics of the Theory of Spirits, would be unable to follow me in my belief in the existence of angels, as I am unable to follow those who believe in elves. I will follow Jenni Bergmann in construing elves (and fairies, perhaps) in Nordic cultures as "among the most humanoid of fantastic beings, along with vampires, werewolves, mermaids and the like, though the elf is unique in many ways, the most evident being that it usually lacks animal features and does not in most of the older accounts differ in appearance from humans."[28] In keeping with the theory of reference, I sketched in Chapter 2, elves are ultimately defined by their attributes and by their relations to undisputed objects assigned in a narrative structure, and so the Theory of Elves satisfies the requirement of being intelligible. In view of my reluctance to use imaginary cases, I am pleased to present the belief in elves in Iceland as a significant feature in a Western culture. They genuinely serve in my critical reflection on them and on angels. I might be mistaken in my epistemic assessments, of course, for my privately held views on this are open to possible correction. Even to assert that another is mistaken about an ontological assessment is to presuppose the objectivity of such a claim; consequently, much is at stake in the normal give and take about evidence, about degrees of evidential weight, and so on.

Someone might be tempted to think that the claim that elves are real would be supported by the existence of angels. However, the two orders seem independent of each other, even though both are[29] deemed to be nonhuman spirits. While my belief in angels seems reasonable (to me) and my disbelief in elves also seems reasonable, in making these remarks of how I understand the relevant epistemic relationship, I do not appear to be doing anything different than when I offer comparable epistemic estimates in domains that are indubitably a part of the relatively incontestable natural order. It is in the latter, in fact, where our "epistemic teeth" are cut. Our cultivated aptitudes can then be plausibly applied in other domains, such as the Theory of Spirits. I recognize that estimates

---

[28] Bergmann, *The Significant Other*.
[29] The use of "are" here seems to be correct, as opposed to the expression "both [elves and angels] *have* spirits." With humans the appropriate locution seems to be "humans have spirits." This linguistic convention perhaps derives from a strongly felt need to convey the thought that humans *are* bodies and spirits (or bodies and souls). The nature of the bodies of angels and elves, if they have ones, is obscure.

(or convictions, perhaps) about the epistemic weight of one thing on another can vary substantially, as my remarks on elves already shows.

We might compare the epistemic impact of claims about elves and angels with the impact of knowledge about laws of pendula and of inclined planes, both of which are subcases of the general theory of gravitational attraction. Scientists widely accept the epistemic claim that evidential support for the law of the pendulum is evidential support for the law of the inclined plane. This evidently comes about because the laws of the pendulum and the inclined plane are both *logical* implications of the law of universal gravitation. One way of explaining this epistemic claim is holding that because the law of the pendulum is a logical implication of (and so is "contained in") the law of universal gravitation, evidential support for the former is evidential support for the latter. Moreover, because of the tight logical structure found in this example, evidential support for the law of universal gravitation is evidential support for each of its implications, including the law of the inclined plane.

A similar logical structure is not found, however, with respect to the Theory of Spirits, on the one hand, and the Theory of Angels and the Theory of Elves, on the other. The latter two theories each logically imply the Theory of Spirits, but a reciprocal logical relation does not hold between the Theory of Spirits and the Theories of Angels and Elves – just because spirits exist does not mean that either angels or elves exist, for some other kind of being might exist. Perhaps a modest level of epistemic support for elves might derive from the existence of angels, if angels were to be the first class of spirits successfully considered to exist, but the amount seems negligible. We can test this intuition by asking ourselves whether the probability that elves exist (E), given the existence of angels (A), is greater than or equal to the probability that elves exist, given no information at all ($P(E,A) \geq P(E,\emptyset)$). The first value is possibly slightly higher than the second.

The principles that are operative in the case of the law of universal gravitation, and the two special instances of it that I have mentioned, are:

Special consequence principle: Confirming evidence for a theory T (universal gravitation, say) is also confirming evidence for theories deducible from T (the law of the pendulum, say)

And

Converse consequence principle: Confirming evidence for a theory T (the law of the pendulum, say) is also confirming evidence for theories from which T (Universal Gravitation, say) is deducible.

These principles have been discussed by confirmation theorists such as Hempel[30] and his critics, in conjunction with a third, the *Entailment Principle*, which expresses something of a limiting case involving confirming evidence:

Entailment principle: If one statement logically implies another, the first is confirming evidence for the second.

According to this *principle*, the law of universal gravitation is confirming evidence for the law of the pendulum, since the latter is derivable from the former. We can also hold that confirming evidence for the Theory of Elves is confirming evidence for the General Theory of Spirits, but because the General Theory of Spirits does not logically imply the Theory of Elves, we cannot use the *Special Consequence Condition* to link confirming evidence for angels with the Theory of Elves.

Hempel demonstrated that the logic embedded in the three principles just mentioned prevents us from endorsing all three, no matter how intuitively obvious each might seem, for from the three of them, we must infer that every evidence claim supports every hypothesis.[31] Here we see that some epistemic features of scientific views illuminate epistemic features of the Theory of Spirits, but we must be cautious in advancing unreservedly any of these principles, no matter how "obvious" they appear.[32] Hempel is also famous for giving expression to the following principle, which seems to have been endorsed during much of the time that induction has been recognized, which is more than two millennia:

Principle of positive instances:[33] A hypothesis receives evidential support from its positive instances, for example, "All ravens are black" is supported by the observation of a black raven.

This principle is so central to the assessment of general (law-like) statements that one can hardly imagine that it has ever been extensively denied. The "paradox" of confirmation that Hempel uncovered turns on this principle. He observed that *deductive logic* holds that "All ravens are black" is logically equivalent to "All non-black things are non-ravens"; also *inductive logic* asserts that generalizations are supported by their

---

[30] Hempel, "Studies in the Logic of Confirmation," pp. 102–03.
[31] This was shown by Hempel, "Studies in the Logic of Confirmation."
[32] Care needs to be taken in calling this principle of theorizing itself into question. If we think that science can proceed on its basis, but philosophy cannot, we call science into question for it rests on the various principles that are the study of philosophy itself.
[33] Hempel, "Studies in the Logic of Confirmation," p. 108.

positive instances, which allows us to say that white shoes (which are nonblack nonravens) support "All ravens are black," since white shoes are instances of "All non-black things are non-ravens," and the latter is logically equivalent to the former. Hempel embraced the counterintuitive result, and I partly concur. I would agree with him that the places that we might look for evidence are those in which we might find black ravens, nonblack nonravens, any nonblack things themselves, and so on.[34] Although this principle applies to spirits as well as to objects unequivocally naturalistic, the underlying difficulty is that theories about theoretical objects, which are possibly unobservable, must generally have their evidence found via some other principles.

PRINCIPLES OF EVIDENCE

The discussion of the last few pages indicates that various intuitively plausible principles concerning evidence are (tentatively) invoked in assessing theories and the evidence alleged in their favor. The challenge of theories that postulate unobservable objects is that their confirmation is often not a direct or straightforward matter. This is clear from theories in the sciences where unobservables are postulated. We might wonder how the Phlogiston Theory[35] was confirmed when it was still in ascendancy in explaining chemical changes. This invisible and intangible substance known then as phlogiston was considered so ubiquitous that it comprised the major part of every object. Since phlogiston was considered to be driven out by heat, the Phlogiston Theory might have been construed as confirmed every time a chemical change involving heat occurred. This easy confirmation seems far too easy and lends support to the approach to evidence for which Sir Karl Popper (1902–94) was famous, namely, construe as confirmatory only those reports of evidence that expose the theory under scrutiny to possible falsification as this

---

[34] The difficulty, said to be a paradox, arises from conflating the (epistemic) concept of *confirming evidence* with the (logical) concept of *being an instance of a universal generalization*. Confirming evidence unfolds in time, but the logical concept does not express a temporal notion. For example, the moment we find a white (leucistic) raven, the claim that all ravens are black is rendered incredible; finding a clutch of black ravens the next day does nothing for the falsified generalization. But each member of the clutch of black ravens is still an instance of the generalization. See my "Hempel and Instantial Confirmation," pp. 59–70.

[35] J. J. Becher (1635–82) is credited with first advancing it, when chemistry was in its infancy, we might say.

evidence is evaluated.[36] So the fact that some block of wood is consumed to ashes by fire, supposedly because heat drove out the phlogiston in the block, does not confirm the Phlogiston Theory, according to Popper, since the demonstrated fact does not expose the Phlogiston Theory to falsification. Exactly what motivated Popper to develop his curious (and controversial) approach to supporting evidence is unclear, but he was right to insist on falsifiability as *one possible mark* of science. However, Popperians can hardly insist that it is the only mark.

Principle of refutability (Popper): Only theories that are refutable are scientific.[37]

This famous principle more or less defines the unique Popperian approach to science and critical inquiry and has its adherents in discussions of religion. However, it is too sweeping to be salvageable and is falsified on these grounds.

In the final days of the Phlogiston Theory, a falsifier came into view when a body that had been oxidized by heating, and presumably had all its phlogiston driven out, turned out to weigh more than it did before heating. The suggestion that phlogiston had "negative weight," so that an object weighs more after the phlogiston is driven out, was a completely ad hoc effort to save the theory.[38] This suggests the following principle:

Principle of Ad-hocness (Karl Popper[39]): A theory that is modified simply to avoid some falsifier is not credible.

The appeal to falsifiability as a criterion for a scientific claim remains remarkably strong, even though the principle itself seems flawed. Sometimes religious claims are said to be suspect since conditions for their falsifiability are not spelled out. This is a feature of the Popperian legacy and might be feasible if it were established in the sciences themselves. However, a recent example from physics shows this criterion for scientific status to be implausible. The claim about the existence of the Higgs boson particle, predicted in the 1960s by Peter Higgs,[40] was not confirmed (weakly) until 2013 as a result of experiments conducted with the Large Hadron Collider at CERN (European Organization for

---

[36] Popper did not speak of "confirmation," since it had the whiff of inductivism, but he preferred the term "corroboration"; cf. his *Logic*, chap. 1.
[37] Ibid., pp. 40–42.
[38] Discussed by Hempel, *Philosophy of Science*, pp. 219–20.
[39] Popper, *Logic*, pp. 80–82. See Stephen, "Karl Popper," https://plato.stanford.edu/archives/sum2017/entries/popper/ (accessed May 12, 2018).
[40] "Peter Higgs," www.britannica.com/biography/Peter-Higgs (accessed June 23, 2018).

Nuclear Research), in Europe. Higgs' conjecture had an implication that was finally borne out by observation. However, the claim was intelligible and testable, even though a method for falsifying conjectures about Higgs boson particles had not been articulated. I am making reference here to an unobservable (or rarely observed) object in physics. Such claims are closer than many others to those that postulate spirits, and so offer the promise of some methodological principles for consideration in examining RSM experience.

Popper attempted to separate his critical inquiries of both Rudolf Carnap (1891–1970), at the University of Chicago, and Hempel at Princeton, arguing that his efforts did not belong to the field of *induction* according to a well-known interpretation of this method of science. He used the term "corroboration," rather than "confirmation," in order to highlight his different interests. The story of these interactions played out over decades, and still show up in discussions of the falsification of theories as opposed to their "verification." Many theories and hypotheses are universal in their form, and verifying such universal claims is extraordinarily difficult. In place of the term "verify," defenders of induction in its traditional understanding speak of "confirmation." This is where the notion of "making firmer" (confirmation) rather than "making firm" (verification) shows up. Even as I write this chapter, news sources speak of the detection of gravitational waves, predicted to exist by Albert Einstein and now evidently "observed" by LIGO (Laser Interferometry Gravitational-wave Observatory). Clearly, this is put forward as a confirming observation in the sense that it makes the existence of gravitation waves firmer, or more credible, or more probable, or more likely – however we wish to put it (informally) – than does the weight of evidence prior to its accumulation, whatever this might be. Since laws of nature are formulated as generalizations, we discover that they are harder to verify than to falsify, so finding exceptions (falsifiers) is much more probable than finding data that establish a hypothesis or theory beyond reasonable doubt. This is where Popper's methodology triumphs.

However, when we seek to defend the existence of gravitational waves, we are apt to be content with evidence that merely makes claims about their existence more credible than we previously thought. The concepts of confirmation, credibility, probability, likelihood, and corroboration all find their home in the commonsense conceptual framework, and each has been taken from that framework in order to be redefined using exact concepts. These evidently serve exact inquiries in various ways, but I prefer to use the concept of "evidence E making some hypothesis H firmer than H is on background information B alone'." The fundamental question posed in this book is whether some evidence for the existence of spirits exists. It is not a question so much about laws of nature (universal generalizations) but about the existence of spirits; consequently, confirmation, not falsification, is the essential concept shaping my inquiry. Some evidence might be obtained in an effort to falsify some theory, so I do not reject Popper's claims outright, but I do not think it is complete.

In a useful classification of evidence, philosopher Stephen Braude writes of three kinds, which I describe under the rubric of "Division of Evidence:"[41]

Division of Evidence

(a) Experimental: evidence that is capable of being obtained, subject only to effort, opportunity, financing, and similar constraints;
(b) Semi-experimental: evidence that occurs frequently enough to be recognized as an important classification, although it is neither subject to significant human control nor obtained at will;
(c) Anecdotal: evidence that occurs too infrequently to warrant notice or that occurs as peculiar one-off cases.

Experimental evidence is familiar from scientific viewpoints, in which variables are controlled so that expected effects, perhaps, are obtained. Many sciences have their evidence bases obtained in this way, including both natural and social sciences. We are all familiar, however, with particular hypotheses in geology, cosmology, or anthropology that do not allow us sufficient control to obtain test results – semi-experimental evidence. We need to be in the fortunate position to observe the implications of particular hypotheses and cannot control what are taken to be the relevant variables, so various sciences might not be amenable to having their evidence base declared to be experimental. Anecdotal evidence is generally too insubstantial for advancing the plausibility of some claim, but semi-experimental evidence can do so. The most interesting class of evidence for the Theory of Spirits is arguably that which occurs frequently enough to warrant close examination, even though it is not subject to our control. We could say that reports of ghosts are of this kind. The phenomenon occurs often enough to warrant notice, but it is not sufficiently subject to control that an undisputed body of evidence is readily obtainable. So the appearances of ghosts are testable, perhaps by predicting that they will be reported in well-known places, such as

---
[41] Braude, *The Limits of Influence*, chap. 1.

the White House in which President Abraham Lincoln lived at the time of his assassination.[42] Another famous site is The Treasurer's House in York, UK, where Roman Soldiers are said to walk still,[43] seemingly upon a Roman road beneath the cellar floor that runs from the Treasury to Roman barracks. The evidence around ghosts is semi-experimental.

Another principle that is unquestionably at work in critical evaluations of claims that spirits exist is the following:

Extreme Illuminates Obscure:[44] Examining a phenomenon in its extreme form can illuminate cases in which that phenomenon also occurs, but in a more obscure form.

This Principle seems crucial for the study of theories in which unobservable objects are postulated to exist and might have no special significance for the General Theory of Spirits. We can see, however, that this principle is implicit in the view that an extraordinary event, such as that alleged in the *Gerasene Exorcism Case*, brings credibility to some other cases possibly involving both benign and diabolical powers that do not have the clarity that the *Gerasene Case* exhibits. This principle suggests that if we have an impressive item of evidence supporting a theory – what I shall call "a decisive case" – such as the *Gerasene Exorcism*, then other claims in which weaker spiritual powers are thought to be implicated are enhanced because of the background provided by the decisive case.

I have alluded briefly to the study that Quine and Ullian undertook of what they describe as *The Web of Belief*, in a book having that title. They review the state of science at the time of publication (1978), identifying various Principles shaping exact inquiry. I have drawn a number of Principles from their writing, as well as from other sources. Their work is especially significant for they are cognizant of the importance to science of theories that postulating theoretical objects, possibly unobservable ones.

Principle of modest hypotheses (Quine – Ullian[45]): When attempting to explain a phenomenon, it is more plausible to form a hypothesis with respect to a smaller reference class than a larger one. For example, when we discover that a thing of a certain shape, size, build, etc. has a certain color, it is more plausible to

---

[42] See http://channel.nationalgeographic.com/killing-lincoln/articles/the-story-of-lincolns-ghost/ (accessed May 12, 2018).
[43] See www.britannia.com/history/legend/yorkghosts/yorkgto5.html (accessed May 12, 2018).
[44] See Wm. James, Carol Zaleski, and Steven Braude.
[45] Quine and Ulian, *The Web of Belief*.

conjecture that all things of that shape, size, build, etc. have that color than that all things have that color.

This principle is followed without much difficulty in any scrutiny of what is deemed to be the activity of one kind of spirit, such as angels. Any immodest hypothesis is quickly ruled out or at least sidelined when the principle of modesty is considered.

The following principle is applicable to all critical inquiries and does not have particular significance to the Theory of Spirits, especially to its most specific elements.

Principle of clarity precision (Quine – Ullian):[46] Theories that are precise are preferable to theories that are not.

Perhaps the caveat that applies to this principle is that whereas clarity (or precision or exactness) is an obvious desideratum in theorizing, the degree of it in a theory depends upon the amount of information needing explanation, or upon the form the data are in, or upon the history of a given theory. At the outset of some exact inquiry, we might not have enough data to warrant proposing an exact explanation. Some critical inquiry could be in a form that we might describe as proto-scientific, that is, apt to become scientific if inquiry continues in the manner exhibited to date. Data relevant to the Theory of Spirits strike me as proto-scientific.

I mentioned earlier that Thomas Kuhn is widely credited with having drawn attention to the place of paradigms or conceptual frameworks within which theories are advanced and tested. I offer this principle in two forms:

Principle of theory-laden data (Norwood Russell Hanson[47] and Thomas Kuhn[48]):

a. *Weak*: All data items are set within a framework in which certain theories about the nature of the world are already presupposed.
b. *Strong*:[49] Some data reports are so inextricably bound up with theories that the two cannot be separated, that is, reporting data requires assuming the theory the data are considered to support.

This principle is relevant when discussing the curious claims in the *Gerasene Exorcism Case*. The account is such that the events described in need of explanation, such as bizarre speech and tormenting influences,

---
[46] *Ibid.*
[47] Hanson, *Patterns of Discovery*, esp. p. 53f.
[48] Kuhn, *Structure of Scientific Revolutions*.
[49] I have discussed this version of the *principle* in "Finite Spirits as Theoretical Entities."

all are presented in such a way that both the events described and the explanations advanced for them are in a conceptual framework in which spirits are assumed to exist. Perhaps all description is theory-laden, but the theory-laden character of the *Gerasene Exorcism Case* is exceptional. In this account, the demonic powers, not the man, are said to speak to Jesus, for the strange greeting and the request to enter the swine can hardly be ascribed to the man, since asking to leave oneself in order to enter swine makes no sense. So the demonic powers, normally offered as an *explanation* for some event, are given a role in the *description* of the very events needing to be explained. Compare this case with the account of haunting identified in the *Testability* section as *The Burnaby "Evil Spirit."* Pauline came to think that an evil spirit was troubling her because "doors would slam behind her, plants would move across the table, water taps would switch on and off, music would come from the corners of the rooms, and furniture would move across the floor of its own accord." All of these actions can be described without presupposing the existence of an evil spirit. The latter is *conjectured* to exist in order to explain the strange events, but nothing in their description presupposes the very existence of spirits. The *Gerasene Case* is quite different.

We can perhaps say that the weak principle applies to virtually all descriptions of phenomena and efforts to explain them. This is a twentieth-century discovery, it appears, and has led to some endorsements of conceptual relativism and even ontological relativism. This topic is large and worthy of more comment than I will make here. I consider the fact that much successful translation from one language to another counts in favor of the view that the conceptualizations are roughly equivalent. Quine was notoriously unable to address the issue of translation in a way that satisfied him,[50] making translation a less-than-innocent issue for philosophers. I think that just as not enough confidence might be felt about our ability to translate, so too it is possible that we make too much of our inability to translate. This puts a practical spin on the issue of translation, but a deeper significance might also be present. I consider most relativistic views to be premature and insufficiently supported. A more complex statement of the role of background information is found in a principle that Imre Lakatos advanced on the basis of his review of science:

Principle of research programs (Imre Lakatos[51]): Research is generally undertaken in the context of theories whose basic form (hard core) is not questioned,

---

[50] Quine, *Word and Object*, pp. 73–79.
[51] Lakatos, "History of Science," pp. 116–17.

while portions of the theory outside the hard core are under scrutiny, and subject to change, for example, biological research in an evolutionary context, where evolution in some form is considered to be the correct background.

This principle could be found in connection with speculations over the causal role of spirits in RSM matters, but I adduce it here primarily because Lakatos noticed its actual application in science. We can always reject a principle, as Popper did, which has the effect overall of making our epistemology more tentative than it would otherwise be.

Caroline Davis's study of the evidential force of religious experience advances several principles that are relevant to the study that I am undertaking here:

Principle of cumulative effect (Caroline Franks Davis[52]): The cumulative effect of separate items of evidence for a hypothesis, each of which provides a small probability, is greater than the mere sum of these individual probabilities.

Davis advances this principle in her discussion of the epistemic power of various kinds of religious experience, but I do not think that RSM experience is any different than experience in other domains of science or critical inquiry. Assessing the probability values of particular kinds of evidence for some portion of the General Theory of Spirits represents enough of a challenge, so that determining whether the combined effect is greater than the sum of each part seems impossible. The idea is provocative but does not appear to be capable of being applied. I have observed elsewhere that we might have a report of some kind of experience, such as a Christic vision perhaps, where we consider the probability of its having occurred (as reported) as very low, say 1/1000. If we were to consider another report of the same kind as also very improbable, again 1/1000, the report of *one or the other* being accurate would arise to 2/1000. This is a feature of probability theory itself when independent reports are under consideration. I am unsure that the *Principle of Cumulative Effect* can effectively challenge standard probability theory, so as to allow us to question my example here of how probability values are ascribed to independent events. Two other thought, provoking principles from Davis are as follows:

Principle of credulity:[53] If something seems to be present, then it probably is.

And

---

[52] Davis, *Evidential Force*; see chaps. 4 and 9.
[53] Ibid., pp. 96–97.

Principle of testimony:[54] We have the right to believe the reports of others about their experiences, unless we have good reasons not to do so.

Both of these strike me as generous to a fault, but skepticism in some form might be an epistemic default for me. A further challenge with the Principle of Testimony is that some guidance around the qualification of "good reasons" is needed. I assume that these are largely drawn from our observations of previous theorizing.

I have mentioned nearly twenty principles in this chapter, each guiding (directly or implicitly) epistemic choices between competing views, and many of these principles could be found without much effort. I doubt that a complete epistemology can be offered, since I surmise that slightly different sets of principles might be appropriate for different fields of inquiry. This topic is really quite abstract and removed from scientific inquiry for various reasons, some having to do with the enormous amount of effort (and expense) involved in encouraging critical (but engaged) inquiry into epistemology. If we identify the onset of Philosophy in Western thought with the Greeks who gave both philosophy and science to the ancient Greco-Roman age, we might marvel at philosophy's modest, almost negligible, achievements. We could perhaps point to the deductive vision for science, or to the rise of inductivism as a central methodological strategy in place of the deductive vision, or to the logical positivism of the nineteenth and twentieth centuries as philosophic positions that became widely considered and embraced by considerable numbers among the critical thinkers in the Western tradition. The achievements of philosophy seem to require great efforts, whose values are hardly discernible at the time such efforts are expended and concerning which only modest agreement can be found. So I cannot say exactly which among the principles I have advanced above, and others that I have not made an effort to articulate might offer us an adequate epistemic stance from which to evaluate theories that postulate unobservables in general and the Theory of Spirits in particular. If a principle is seriously articulated and advanced that suggests that some theorists are considering it among their foundational views.

I have chosen to use the concept of confirming evidence here, even though difficulties arise in using it. In recent years Alvin Plantinga has articulated his broad interest in epistemic justification of theistic claims using the notion of *warrant*. Substantial discussion has been evoked by

---

[54] Ibid., p. 115.

his extensive use of its value in considering Christian beliefs and Christian theism in general. In keeping with the traditional view that knowledge differs from belief in that knowledge is (true) justified belief, Plantinga uses his notion of warrant to flesh out the nature of justification: "[A] belief has warrant only if it is produced by cognitive faculties that are functioning properly, subject to no disorder or dysfunction –construed as including absence of impedance as well as pathology. The notion of proper function is fundamental to our central ways of thinking about knowledge."[55] I will comment in Chapter 4 on the difficulties attending the notion of cognitive disorder in connection with experiences deemed by those who undergo them to be RSM visionary experiences. The question of whether cognitive disorder is present is not capable of being answered in a straightforward way, and to *rule out* the contemporary experiences on the ground that they are disordered for our time is to allow arbitrary assessments to be triumphant. The notion if cognitive disorder is as much a theoretical concept[56] as any other already mentioned in this chapter. The challenge of being unobservable applies as much to epistemology as it does to science itself.

Some significant difficulties also arise for claims that we somehow know directly that God is speaking. In speaking about such knowledge Plantinga writes:

The *sensus divinitatiis* is a belief-producing faculty (or power, or mechanism) that under the right conditions produces belief that isn't evidentially based on other beliefs. On this model, our cognitive faculties have been designed and created by God; the design plan, therefore, is a design plan in the literal and paradigmatic sense. It is a blueprint or plan for our ways of functioning, and it has been developed and instituted by a conscious, intelligent agent. The purpose of the *sensus divinitatis* is to enable us to have true beliefs about God; when it functions properly, it ordinarily does produce true beliefs about God. These beliefs therefore meet the conditions for warrant; if the beliefs produced are strong enough, then they constitute knowledge.[57]

Plantinga has consistently voiced his objections to having Christian claims and beliefs subjected to the evidence (expressed in probabilities) that inevitably accompany scientific claims. Although simple measures cannot be offered by which appeals to confirming evidence in RSM phenomena are rendered plausible, using evidence in assessing such phenomena is

---

[55] Plantinga, *Warranted Christian Belief*, pp. 130–31.
[56] Cf. Figure 2.3 in Chapter 2.
[57] Ibid., p. 149.

more plausible than reverting to properly functioning cognitive powers, as I will argue in Chapter 5.

We might wonder whether we can speak meaningfully of probability interpreted as evidential weight when it comes to theories that postulate unobservable objects, which the Theory of Spirits generally does.[58] The short answer is "Yes." Baryon-II particles (subatomic) were postulated to exist because of what experimenters observed on photographic plates that recorded events in a cloud chamber. The interesting question that this experiment raises is whether the probability that a lambda-baryon particle exists is greater given this experimental result than given no information at all. The answer is an obvious "Yes," which means that an interpretation of "probability" is involved that measures the evidential value of the experimental result compared with no information at all. Exactly how we would go about attempting to measure these relative values is now unclear, for no straightforward strategy can be applied – but one might come to light in time. A comparable positive answer can be given to the question whether the *Gerasene exorcism* lends evidential weight to the reality of spirits.

---

[58] Even when spirits are seen (seemingly), as in some exorcisms, the debate shifts from spirits postulated for the exorcism to the report of allegedly visible events, and perhaps to the capacity of the reporter.

4

Phenomenological Evidence

Chapter 3 on evidence leaves something out concerning the critical reflection on RSM experience as evidence, namely, the phenomenological features of experiences obtainable only (now) from those who undergo them, and the possible causal clues to obscure orders of reality they provide. The external perspective on RSM experience offered earlier already suggests the existence of beings – spirits – who interact with humans, although details of their attributes and even definitive grounds for thinking them real might still be illusive. This is the point at which phenomenological experience enters the picture. This fact should not surprise us about the forms of reality seemingly encountered.

If spirits – beings with minds who are not humans – do exist, we could hardly expect our knowledge of them to exclude our phenomenological experience. Our ordinary human existence involves significant interactions with other minds – animal and human minds – and many of the details concerning their attributes and their relations to other things come from the thoughts that are shared (or not), attitudes that are exuded (or not), intentional results of volitions that are registered (or not), or actions that are taken (or not), and so on. We perhaps understand as much about the "minds" of animals from what they do not exhibit as from what they do. Even children are not devoid of knowledge concerning other minds, but adults typically carry significant levels of knowledge of these matters, much of which is simply and quietly registered, and never spoken of in great detail. Our knowledge of the characteristics of other minds is integrated with our larger knowledge of the world. Hume's baleful influence over modernity and over philosophy needs to be identified at this point. The far-reaching skepticism he is famous for having promoted concerning other minds, the external world, and past events is insightful for its capacity to teach us about the world of sense-data, and about Quine's suggestion that ordinary objects might be seen as theoretical postulations to account for sense-data. Hume's reductive effort is by-and-large frivolous, however, which any debate over RSM experience and spirits demonstrates. When serious differences over the relevant ontological claims come into view, ordinary objects and persons, not sense-data simply, are taken to be real (in the fullest sense). Moreover, to discuss hallucinations we need some distinction, however provisional, between merely having sense-data and actually seeing (or otherwise experiencing) physical objects.

Epistemic inquiries relating to RSM experiences begin in the conscious thought of a person who has some motivation to undertake that inquiry, perhaps because of some personal experience, or the reported experience of trusted friends, or the discovery of a large database on a particular phenomenon, and so on. These inquiries are apt to be confined to the privacy of one's own thoughts, or maybe a small circle of confidants, because of the general reluctance of people to share their own RSM experiences. In part this is because of modernity's insistence that the only evidence worth reflecting upon is that which is intersubjective, but it also stems from the uncertainty that people who undergo RSM experiences harbor over how their experiences will be viewed by others. The general mental stability of those with RSM experience is apt to be questioned by others in Western culture. Some religious subcultures might encourage the disclosure of RSM experiences, but, in general, the modern age discourages disclosure. This means, generally, that the critical appraisal of the epistemic significance of RSM experiences is poorly developed, compared to many other fields of inquiry. However, even a cursory review of these experiences suggests that they might be appropriate objects of scrutiny. These experiences clearly belong to causal chains, the originators of which might be other orders of reality (or not).

A useful comparison with the kind of mindset needed for the study of RSM experience can be found in judicial systems where juries of competent adults are charged with deciding the fate of some person accused of a serious crime. The nature of criminal activity is such that those who witness it are often strongly motivated to avoid giving public expression to their opinions. The risks of being too outspoken are great enough that observers of crime privately harbor their views or only share them cautiously with others whom they can trust. Even displaying too much interest in a crime or a criminal could be interpreted as a signal that the interested person is more than an observer. When persons are required to sit on a jury, however, their epistemic judgments and opinions concerning some event are deliberately sought, with the hope that consensus will be found among all the jury members. Their critical inquiries demonstrate that people can set themselves this task of reflecting on how the evidence available affects their epistemic powers, and when we reflect on the consensus that is typically expected of juries, we might be tempted to think that some benefit might accrue in sequestering people who are RSM experiencers of one kind or another, and are dispassionate enough to stand back from their personal biases to reflect on the epistemic significance of RSM experience. Critical reflection of this kind can be plausibly construed as also being subject to possible consensus, were the effort to be expended on the matter. Again, some risk might be felt about being too outspoken on some RSM experience, particularly its significance for underwriting the claim that spirits of one sort or another are implicated. The risk of reprisal for being outspoken on criminal matters, such as being a whistle-blower in a corporation, is not the same as the risk of speaking out about one's own RSM experiences, but each phenomenon sheds some light on the other.

Religious organizations often assume that the answers to questions about spirits are already answered. They do not encourage explicit scrutiny of RSM experience, in my experience, and universities exhibit many of the same traits. My experience with analytic philosophers in Canada and Australia, generally, is that most have already answered such questions negatively – as atheism or perhaps agnosticism – although a few are theists. I have read that Christian theism is quite strongly present among American analytic philosophers,[1] but I have only had minimal contact with them and cannot comment on this with much personal authority. My modest interaction with philosophers from the UK suggests more openness there to theism than I have found in Canada. My (partial) isolation here in Canada from theistic philosophers, where I have taught for the last 45 years, as well as my background in philosophy of science, and some unexpected RSM experiences, have brought about the development of most of my own views. Although my remarks here will reflect claims central to Hebrew-Christian faith, since this is the belief-system in which I was reared, Christianity shares some common outlooks with other religious faiths and spiritual outlooks, so some of my remarks will have general applicability beyond Christianity itself. The only worldviews on

[1] Smith, "The Metaphilosophy of Naturalism," p. 196.

serious offer when I began university in 1963 were Christian theism and naturalism. I quite willingly exposed myself to the prevailing naturalism in public universities and embraced it, and I assume that everyone's adult epistemic assessments of claims concerning spirits are set within a context that is shaped by one's past. In that respect great diversity would be exhibited if everyone's history were to be collected. This history would take a unique form with each person, of course, since people change their convictions, or perhaps have their convictions changed for them.

In one other way the study of RSM experience resembles a close study of judicial systems. The latter could be examined using only the outward, observable features of it. We would document the levels of judiciaries found in a province or state, the standards of evidence required of prosecuting attorneys, the handling of evidence by police forces, the number of arrests and convictions, and innumerable other data items collectible by skilled social scientists. Now imagine, for a moment, the absence of phenomenological data, capable of being revealed only by those in whom those phenomena occur. We would know nothing about an accused's state of mind while planning or committing a crime, nothing about a jury member's misgivings or doubts about some item that was said in court, nothing about a judge's predilection in a decision to be undertaken by a tribunal she sits on, nothing about the objectives intended by those who wrote the constitutional articles on which legal structures and decisions are based, etc. The scenario I am describing here approximates to that advocated by the famous psychologist, B. F. Skinner (1904–90), who suggested that observations could be carried out in Psychology without use of "mentalist" terms,[2] since every term needed to be capable of intersubjective observation. In a similar way, the study of RSM experience would be devoid of the rich and personal description uniquely found in the phenomenological component of experience in general.

APPARITIONS

The claims that gods and devils might appear in particular forms to us, or that humans might "survive" the death of their bodies and appear to the living, generally involve "sightings" – apparitions – from which an obscure form of being as a causal source is suggested. The term "apparition" is widely used to identify a curious group of experiences that are often visual in character – hence the term "apparition," deriving from

---

[2] See his defense of this principle in Skinner, "Behaviorism at Fifty," p. 106.

the Latin term *"apparere"* meaning "to appear." Our visual sense is not the only one involved in these preternatural encounters, of course, but it remains the most important one. The sense perceptions involved in ordinary judgments about common reality are generally visual, and this is transferred, it appears, in assessments of extraordinary encounters. An important summative study of the broad range of phenomena that have been alleged as apparitions was undertaken by Celia Green and Charles McCreery in 1975,[3] based on some 1800 first-hand cases they personally researched, as well as a review of earlier published accounts, including the study in 1894 published as *Census on Hallucinations*.[4] This census reviewed the experience of 17,000 British people, in an effort to determine how frequently exceptional perceptions occurred, possibly describable as hallucinatory. Some 9.9% of people randomly selected reported some such experience.

The study of Green and McCreery considers apparitions of the living, of the dead, of the sense of tactile touch and pressure, of experiences in which knowledge beyond visual sight occurs, of auditory experience, and much more. These variations have been mooted for some time, but the recent corroboration they offer helps to bring the phenomena into clearer view. We might justifiably wonder which of these categories offer grounds for thinking that post-mortem survival is possible, which might be a form of life seemingly not dependent on the natural order of the cosmos. We might reflect for a moment on the evidential force of an apparition of the living compared with that of the dead. Apparitions of the dead, which must be the best known kind of apparition and are often described as encounters with ghosts, obviously motivate some to think that post-mortem existence is a reality, but apparitions of the living are also reported. What sense we are to make of the latter? Such phenomena might understandably be seen as shedding light on human life, giving some psychological support to old-fashioned body-soul dualism, perhaps, at least for the person who experiences an apparition of the living. Whether it would have any more significance is unclear.

When I returned to Canada in 1972 after my doctoral work, a close relative of mine told me that he had seen me (while awake) in his home in Winnipeg at a time that I was certainly in Australia, then a very long distance away. The fares for international travel were substantial in those days, and my wife and I lived on a student's budget, so the suggestion

---

[3] Green and McCreery, *Apparitions*, passim.
[4] Sidgewick et al., "Report on the Census."

that I returned home surreptitiously without even visiting the rest of my family is preposterous. The experience frightened him he said. I do not know what to make of this. Perhaps such experiences can only be plausibly evaluated in the light of apparitions of the dead. One might think that experience with apparitions would be easy to dismiss, but a closer scrutiny of the phenomenon shows that this is not the case. Perception that forms the basis of beliefs in the conventional space–time–causal world is inveigled so unexpectedly with aberrant perception that the latter makes spirit possible. They provide an obvious source of the mystery of much RSM experience.

Aberrant perception is so complex that discussion can easily fail to capture this complexity. My understanding of aberrant perceptions was enhanced by undertaking a study of Christic vision, published as *Visions of Jesus: Direct Encounters from the New Testament to Today*. The books and articles that I read in preparation for my study did not prepare me for what I encountered in one-on-one interviews. I observed that various authors had conjectured that hallucinations – a term that others use – might occur in degrees; the fact that I had one kind of experience in view, and so had something of an independent variable, allowed me to compare one kind of aberrant perception with another.[5] Here are some of the cases I studied.

Helen Bezanson Case

Helen's first Christic experience occurred when she was about twenty-one, living in Southern Ontario. She went to the Anglican Church as a child, but by the time she married and began a family she was not interested in religion. Her husband's parents took her to summer camp meetings sponsored by a Pentecostal Church, but she did not really understand what was being preached. It seemed to be coming out of the Bible, so she thought it was acceptable. Each service ended with an invitation to pray at the front, and when her mother-in-law suggested that she go, Helen did so to please her. Helen attended the meetings four times, going forward each time for prayer because doing so made her feel better about herself. As she prayed that fourth night she felt a warm presence around her, and thought that someone had touched her. She opened her eyes to see if anyone was nearby, but no one was close enough to be touching her, so she decided to continue praying. She felt a touch again, this time on one of her hands that was raised in prayer. She opened her eyes again to see if anyone was touching her, and again she saw no one, but then she felt that she ought to look up. Her words to me were: "I looked up, my eyes wide open, and I saw Jesus standing just as clear as I can see you

---

[5] Wiebe, "Degrees of Hallucinatoriness."

sitting there now, and he had both hands out like this [stretched toward her] and he was smiling as though he was accepting me finally." He made a gathering motion with his hands, as though to show her that he was accepting her, and looked so real and alive Helen thought that others must be looking at him too. She looked around to see if others were paying attention to him, but no one else seemed to notice him. She thought to herself, "What's wrong with them? They're not looking at him." She looked back to see if he was still at the front where he first appeared, and he was.

Jesus stood there some eight to ten feet away, smiling and moving. He looked much as tradition portrays him, although what caught her attention was his eyes and the motion of his hands. Helen also had the sense that she was looking at God, which gave the visual impression a characteristic that she was not able to describe more completely. Another unusual feature of the experience was that Jesus seemed to be standing on a pedestal or pillar, for he was not standing on the floor and he did not appear to be floating. Moreover, it seemed as though he stood in an oval doorway on the pedestal, surrounded in radiance in that shape. As she gazed on him she began speaking in another language, about which she knew nothing at the time. He gradually faded from view and was gone. This experience created a desire in her to please Jesus as much as she could, and to study the Bible. It also convinced her that Jesus was real. Her words were: "He's not just something that you learn about in a Bible, in a Sunday school class. Or it isn't just a story. He showed me that he was real, that he's a real person. He's not just an apparition, he's not a figment of our imagination. Nobody has even been able to tell me since that Jesus isn't real and that he can't make himself known to people, because I saw it myself, and that's all the proof I needed." Helen had a second Christic encounter some thirty years later in her home-church on Vancouver Island, and lived as a homemaker in the small community of Black Creek, British Columbia, when I interviewed her.

Helen's experience described here rules out the viability of a significant set of explanations proposed by both professional and casual theorists who endeavor to explain religious visions. Some suggest that religious visions are brought about by being deprived of sleep, of sense experience, of food, or of sexual pleasure,[6] perhaps pointing to the lives of some in monastic life who deny themselves these natural features of life, and then they experience religious or mystical visions. Much more needs to be shown in order to argue that any of these deprivations *cause* religious visions, however. The fact that Helen's first anomalous experience began with a tactile sensation, and then was followed by visual ones, can hardly be explained by any of the deprivations mentioned. Deprivations are a matter of degree, but these cannot be plausibly related to the kind of anomalous sensations mentioned. Was sleep deprivation, to take one

---

[6] Carroll, *The Cult of the Virgin Mary*, suggests that visions of the Virgin Mary occur as a result of repressed sexual impulses, p. 141f.

instance, the causal source first of a tactile sensation, and next of a visual one? How could sleep deprivation cause different perceptual anomalies so close to each other in time? Did the causal effect of different instances of sleep deprivation (over several different nights, say) vary just enough in a few seconds so that the tactile anomaly was followed by a visual one? The suggestion embedded in the sleep-deprivation theory beggars belief, giving it a probability very close to zero.

A similar question can be plausibly posed in response to the conjecture that stress was the central element explaining the perceptual anomalies, which has been proposed by psychologist Julian Jaynes in an attempt to account for the experiences of the prophets whose lives have been described in the Hebrew Bible.[7] We cannot plausibly maintain that Helen felt stress in several degrees, so that tactile sensations with their distinctive strength were first felt, then, moments later, visual ones with their characteristic strength when she faced the front. According to this theory, stress seemingly was reduced when she faced the back, since no anomalous figure was seen, and then stress was supposedly felt *to the identical amount* each time she faced the front, since the same figure was seen each time in the same place. Such a claim is not empirically impossible, but appears highly improbable. In the hands of Jaynes the theory articulated in terms of stress is just *asserted*, without the empirical corroboration it requires, since the levels of adrenalin, which is Jaynes's suggestion to measure stress, are generally not provided, and can hardly be given since RSM experience seldom occurs in a psychology laboratory.

The *Perceptual Release Theory*, which I will discuss further (in the following text), appears to be comparably problematic, for it supposes that an aberrant complex of sensations[8] was dropped into the conscious life of Helen each time she faced the front of the building, and then disappeared each time she faced the back. This is not empirically impossible, of course, just highly improbable, knowing (implicitly) what we do about the causal structure of the world. The inability of psychological constructs to account for the important differences in religious visions means that the psychological explanations have run their course, and whether they have any future significance is unclear. These explanations derive from the commonsense domain, whose content is being substantially replaced

---

[7] Jaynes, *The Origins of Consciousness*, pp. 91ff.
[8] Referred to as engrams in *Dictionary of Hallucinations* "perceptual release theory of hallucinations," http://hallucinations.enacademic.com/1415/perceptual_release_theory_of_hallucinations (accessed July 2, 2018).

by knowledge found at the scientific (neural) level. The remaining options are supposedly "supernaturalistic" explanations and neurological ones, and both domains offer promissory notes, in effect. We might also ask ourselves, "Were Helen's perceptual and cognitive abilities obviously impaired at the time of her experience?" The answer is not an obvious "Yes," which shows that cognitive impairment is a very difficult topic, not to be settled by mere assertions about who is cognitively impaired and who is not.

Barry Dyck Case

Barry Dyck was eighteen years old when his vision (his term) of Jesus took place. He was attending a Bible college in British Columbia at the time, and had gone to nearby Mt. Baker in Washington State to ski. As he skied that day, his goggles fogged up, and before he knew what was happening he went over a cliff – a drop-off of about fifty feet. When he reached bottom the tail-end of his skis struck his neck, breaking three vertebrae and herniating one disc. The pain was excruciating as he was taken off the mountain by the ski patrol, which also dropped him as they were loading him onto the ski-trail groomer. He was taken by ambulance to St. Mary's Hospital in Bellingham, where he was placed in a neck brace and traction, and was kept as immobile as possible. During the next week his ability to see became impaired as the swelling in his head created pressure on his brain, and surgery was planned to relieve the pressure.

In the middle of the night eight days after the accident he woke up to find a being standing at the end of his bed, whom he immediately identified as Jesus, the Christ. Jesus[9] stretched out his arms toward Barry, who, despite all the equipment that was attached to him and the orders not to move, sat up, grasped the hands of Jesus and begged, "Take me with you." Barry explained that he made this request to die because he was drawn by an indescribable feeling of love. Jesus somehow indicated in wordless communication that satisfying this request was not possible, and that everything would be fine. Barry went back to a fitful sleep, and during the night he took off the neck brace that was limiting his movement. When he woke up the next morning he was disappointed to discover that he was still alive! But he found that he could see perfectly, and that the swelling and pain were gone. He convinced the attending doctor the next day that he was well enough to go home, and the doctor reluctantly agreed.

Barry had been expected to be in hospital for three months, and to need a neck brace for an additional eight months. Within three or four days of returning home he resumed his regimen of running, without any ill effects. Barry said that X-rays taken by his family doctor in Seattle several weeks later showed no

---

[9] Here I will assume the identity given by the visionaries to the object or being considered to have been present with them. I have examined competing explanations in *Visions of Jesus*, chaps. 5–7, some of which obviously question the experience itself described by visionaries and consequently the identity claims.

evidence of fracture in his neck vertebrae, but that the many X-rays taken during the week in the hospital had shown obvious signs of fracture. Barry believes that he was healed during that encounter that lasted no more than sixty seconds. Barry's family and the people in the church they attended were as shocked by Barry's healing as he was. Although the church he attended did not deny the possibility of miraculous interventions, it did not encourage people to expect them. When I met Barry he was working for a trucking firm in Abbotsford, British Columbia, and has since become a stock market trader.

When we consider Barry's claim in relation to the conjecture that the Christ, or some representative of him, appeared to Barry and allowed Barry to examine him using tactile, proprioceptive, and visual (natural) powers, then initiated a sequence of events (presumably) that resulted in Barry's shocking recovery within hours of this encounter, we can appreciate that Barry's RSM experience has greater weight than Helen's. Perhaps both have some weight in favor of the post-mortem existence of the Christ, but Barry's seemingly has more epistemic weight, since it claims that the spatiotemporal–causal domain has been penetrated. The alleged healing appears to go contrary to natural laws about the rates at which people (and living things in general) recover from serious injuries, and so has the aroma of miracle, a topic on which I am not putting particular focus. Perhaps we are saying too much in asserting that Barry's recovery contravened natural *laws*, for such recovery – a part of the natural world – is not that of Newtonian physics, where some particular regularities, such as those that concern falling bodies, and revolving planets, are well established. I do not offer it here as an incontestable claim about two probability values, for the claim that Barry's case has more weight than Helen's is a conjecture, and seems as open to assessment as many claims discussed by empaneled juries in conventional penal cases. Everyone who is schooled enough on evidence and in weights of evidence appears to be in a position to comment on the comparison I have offered. I cannot see how religious beliefs or commitments would significantly alter these assessments. These assessments seem to be a shared part of intellectual life.

Even if we gloss over the alleged healing in Barry's experience, we can see that it has a significant difference from Helen's. Barry touched what he saw – I asked him very specifically on this point – indicating that his visual and tactile senses were functioning in close harmony with one another. His proprioceptive sense was also functioning "normally," although this is a point that we can easily fail to observe: He knew how his body was positioned as he lifted his torso up over the mattress, and knew where his arms and hands were as he grasped the arms of the figure that appeared to him. A skeptic might not like this way of describing Barry's actions, perhaps preferring some such description as "Barry "knew" where his arms and hands were positioned as he "grasped" the "arms" of the figure that "appeared" to him. This is the point where his healing enters the theoretical assumptions in the description: If the events that Barry described were mere apparitions, how do we account for the healing? I do not know if we can hallucinate in three perceptual systems all at once, so that sight, touch, and proprioception all occur in perfect harmony, *and are genuinely and simultaneously hallucinatory*. However, what would be the connection of this complex and life-resembling hallucination to the healing that he claims, supported by his family, and friends who knew Barry at the time, some of whom I met? No physical test exists for hallucination in several senses simultaneously, so asserting that this was what happened to Barry is a conjecture. Its future as an adequate explanation is uncertain, so those who think that the Christ, or some emissary, visited Barry hold a view that is not devoid of empirical support. The being that paid this visit is not a strict unobservable, although those who believe that the resurrected Christ exists think that he effects his impact primarily in unperceived "encounters."

Although modern physics has convinced everyone, I surmise, that reality is not quite what it appears to be, scientific thought certainly considers that *something substantial* is present when sight, touch, hearing, proprioception, perhaps even taste and smell, are all causally implicated. We are now long past the skeptical scenarios advanced by Descartes and Hume, although more modest forms of skepticism, such as the Pyrrhonic skepticism of Sextus Empiricus, still have something to commend them. We need to recognize the uncertainty that sometimes attends perception, as in religious vision, although to focus unduly on this uncertainty is to re-enter the impossible worlds of Hume and (especially) Descartes. Barry's healing corroborates the claim that "he saw and felt *something*," whatever that might have been, and thereby reinforces the thought that corporeal senses might be involved in human encounters with the Divine.

The two experiences I have related here point the direction for construing this kind of apparition as varying in degrees of hallucinatoriness (and correlatively of lifelikeness). I do not offer a measure of such degrees, since the database with which I worked was small, but some rough sense can be made of the claim that apparitions might vary in degrees of hallucinatoriness. Why this would be so is unclear. If we consider Christic visions as a category within apparitions, we might cautiously say that accounts of these can be found across the last two millennia.[10] Legitimate questions might be raised for thinking that all of the cases included in this category are genuinely *Christic*, to which we must reply that any claim that an experience is Christic is a matter of probability. I cannot see any other response to the conundrum. This will not satisfy those who think that certainties are prevalent concerning RSM experience. I would say that such a sense of certainty could be subjective, but objective certainty is another matter. The Christic apparition is of significance because it might be the most numerous kind known. Visions of Mary strike me as much better researched than visions of the Christ, but I doubt that (alleged) Marians apparitions are more numerous than (alleged) Christic ones.

HALLUCINATIONS

The one persisting objection to apparitions as a basis for advancing the existence of spirits in general is that apparitions are hallucinatory, that is, mere ephemera in a world where neural oddities emerge in unlikely places. The term "hallucination" and its cognates broadly refer to perceptions having no *direct* relation to an experienced reality. K. W. M. Fulford has offered the following list of the uses of "hallucination" in psychiatric contexts, most of which turn on the notion of sensing something that either is not real, or is not present to the perceiver:[11]

(a) normal illusions, such as the bent appearance of a stick in water,
(b) disruptions of perceptions caused by some physical cause, e.g., "seeing stars" from a blow to the head,
(c) physical symptoms, such as double vision,
(d) distortion of perceptions caused by psychological factors, e.g., the depressive who perceives an innocent remark as critical,
(e) type-I pseudo-hallucinations, i.e., perceptions without a stimulus that are experienced as real, yet are located as originating inside one's head rather that in outside space, e.g., a voice located as coming from inside one's left inner ear,
(f) type-II pseudo-hallucinations, i.e., perceptions located as originating in outside space, yet not experienced as real, for example, the alcoholic with *delirium tremens* who sees snakes, yet knows they are not there,

---
[10] See my popular book, *Visions and Appearances of Jesus*, chaps. 1–3.
[11] Fulford, *Moral Theory*, pp. 230–31.

(g) normal hallucinations, i.e., brief hallucinatory perceptions in the absence of a stimulus, experienced as outside oneself and as real at the time, as when a tired doctor, nearly asleep, hears a telephone ring, only to be assured by the hospital switchboard that she "must have imagined it,"
(h) normal imagery, i.e., images so vivid so as to be experienced in outside space, and differing from other hallucinations inasmuch as one can change them by effort of will,
(i) hysterical hallucinations, and
(j) visions (having "supernatural external stimuli?")

Fulford expresses some puzzlement about the last kind of experience mentioned, using a question mark, but does not elaborate on the qualifier that he includes in (j). He does not include the absence of perception in the presence of an object that generates perceptions (negative hallucination),[12] but this can be added to Fulford's list. Anthony David and Geraldo Busatto[13] assert that if hallucinations were to be rigidly defined as a percept in the absence of an external stimulus, where that percept is unbidden, outside of conscious control, and registered as though in external space, most of the experiences of psychiatric patients normally deemed hallucinatory would be excluded. Each of Fulford's categories could be elaborated on at length, but space prevents me. I will follow David and Busatto in generally construing hallucinations as "a percept in the absence of an external stimulus, where that percept is unbidden, outside of conscious control, and registered as though in external space." Exceptions to this interpretation will be noted. I will also use "aberrant perception" to refer to perceptions whose nature is difficult to determine, and whose classification is consequently impossible.

John Occhipinti Case

John Occhipinti was brought up in Connecticut and New Jersey, in a very devout home. His mother went to the Catholic Church every day to pray, and also attended the services of the (Pentecostal) Assemblies of God. John was a special child because of an incident that took place when he was two years of age. He fell into the river just behind their home, and was not recovered for more than half an hour. John was rushed to hospital, where doctors worked for hours to save his life. His mother was convinced John survived for a special reason, and he grew up with the background knowledge of his mother's convictions. John became

[12] Spanos et al., "Suggested negative visual hallucinations in hypnotic subjects," pp. 63–67.
[13] David and Busatto, "The Hallucination," p. 336.

serious about his faith when he was about eighteen years old. The next year he went to a Bible college in Texas to prepare for pastoral work, and this was where, in 1958, his experience took place.

John shared a room with Nathan, but could not understand what Nathan was doing in Bible college, for he already seemed to know most of what they had come there to learn. During November of that year Nathan came down with the flu, and stayed in bed to recover. Nathan was not particularly perturbed about his being sick, but said that he was in bed for a reason. Although Nathan did not have a serious illness, John felt sympathy for him, and brought him food from the cafeteria when he could, and prayed with him before retiring for the night. As he was praying for Nathan one night he opened his eyes to look at his friend lying about eight feet away. John was shocked to see someone standing over Nathan's bed, but facing and looking at John. He immediately identified the person as Jesus, in part because of the sense of awe that the appearance of the person evoked. John was about to tell his sick friend what he was seeing when Jesus reached over and placed his hand on Nathan's forehead and disappeared. At that instant Nathan leaped out of bed and ran down the halls of the dormitory shouting, "I've been healed, I've been healed." Nathan later said that although he did not see anyone, he felt something touch his head. John himself intended to go over to touch Jesus in order to establish his reality for himself, but did not get a chance to do so. He muses now on his boldness, but he was only nineteen at the time, and rather new in his (self-owned) faith.

Jesus appeared much as tradition portrays him, with a long white robe, shoulder length hair, beard, and so on. He seemed to be just under six feet tall. He exhibited no radiance, and he seemed as solid (to sight) as any ordinary person would. His skin was neither very dark nor very light, much as tradition has imagined him, but his eyes seemed to be on fire. John preferred the term *encounter* rather than *vision* to describe the experience. It was as real to him as seeing an ordinary person, and he does not think that Nathan would have felt the touch on his head if it had been "a vision" (his term). Moreover, John does not consider experiences that occur while a percipient's eyes are open to be visions. He was not aware at the time of anyone else in recent times having had such an experience, and considers it to have had two purposes: to bring healing to his friend, and to reaffirm John's desire to do evangelistic work. I assume that it also brought encouragement to students at the college, but John did not dwell on that. He lived in Scranton, Pennsylvania, when I interviewed him, and was active as an evangelist, a counsellor, and a musician.

Like Pauline Langlois,[14] John evidently tried to conduct a reality check by touching the figure he identified as the Christ, but did not get there in time – the event must have been of very short duration, but evidently long enough for Nathan to experience the touch on his forehead, and with it the healing from a condition that does not sound serious. This case carries the notion of a sign or wonder, and satisfies some of the conditions for

[14] Described in *Case* 2 in Chapter 2.

miracle as Larmer outlines them.[15] The fact that John saw (and only saw) what Nathan felt (and only felt) suggests that some transcendent Order was corporeally perceived. The claim that the two men *hallucinated* in two different sensory modalities in close proximity (spatial and temporal) to each other, *about the same object*, and in the very short temporal succession described, does not seem plausible, although the suggestion seems empirically possible. We are dealing with probabilities here, which are the warp and woof of the epistemic world we inhabit. Moreover, we have to contend with actual experiences reported, not imaginary ones that we could create, which seem to be little more than exercises in logic that seldom help us to understand the curious world we actually inhabit. Those who insist that neural sciences will show how John and Nathan might have had these closely ordered hallucinations are offering a promissory note, and whether this kind of note will ever be paid is in question. John's claim that he encountered a transcendent Order, and that his corporeal sense of sight was involved, is plausible, for the requirements for intersubjective observation are virtually met. One could be forgiven for thinking that this Order knows exactly what the conditions for intersubjective observation are, but deliberately varies them, counting on our capacity to view each set of conditions in relation to any others, so that no settled insight would be possible based on only a few cases.

This point about mass hallucination can be seen more clearly by considering the *Perceptual Release Theory*, which has a distinguished history and continues to influence views about the source of "aberrant perceptions." This *Theory*, also known as the *Theory of Dream Intrusion*,[16] claims that sensory percepts and other items of experience, such as emotions, are stored as memories, and are later assembled in peculiar ways to be experienced either as dreams, if these assembled memories occur while we are asleep, or as hallucinations, if we are awake. According to Louis West, an American psychiatric researcher well known for his advocacy of this theory, the proposed mechanism was advanced as the basis for both dreams and hallucinations more than a century ago by such prominent figures as Jean Esquirol,[17] a French psychiatrist active in early nineteenth century who distinguished insanity from mental retardation, by Hughlings Jackson,[18] a British psychiatrist who was active

---

[15] Larmer, *The Legitimacy of Miracle*. Miracles are described as (1) events that evoke wonder and (2) signs that reveal God's nature and purpose (p. 27); and as (3) events that are beyond physical nature, and (4) are caused by a transcendent being (p. 46).
[16] Blom, *A Dictionary of Hallucinations*.
[17] West, "A Clinical and Theoretical Overview," p. 287.
[18] West, "A General Theory," p. 277.

at the end of the nineteenth century and contributed significantly to an understanding of epilepsy as well as to disorders arising from injuries to the brain, and by Sigmund Freud.[19] This theory has found its way into more complex theories proposed to account for aberrant perceptions,[20] and it might be thought adequate to handle some "visions" having RSM significance. While imaginable, mass hallucination now becomes a wildly *improbable* event, for the memories of shared percepts, shared feelings, and everything else that creates our mental life would need to be dropped into conscious experience of one person at precisely the same time as it occurs in the others comprising the "mass" of people.

We cannot say that aberrant perception has no relation at all to external objects, for the constituent elements of such perceptions are (seemingly) causally produced by objects that existed externally (originally) to those who have such perceptions. We cannot plausibly issue a judgment on what is real by simply *labelling* an experience as hallucinatory, just as we cannot plausibly issue a judgment that an experience is what Augustine called a "corporeal vision" (a vision involving the outer senses) without going into the complex of epistemic and ontological issues that underlie claims about a spiritual Order. In short, the labels "hallucination" and "apparition" carry theoretical baggage with them, and the events to which they refer require scrutiny. Modernity's success in supplanting much of the commonsense domain perhaps gives it confidence that it can also successfully reconfigure ancient and medieval beliefs about the experiences of such an Order, so it is acting on a rational (inductive) extension of previous successes. Experiences involving sole perceivers are relatively easy for critics of RSM experience to dismiss as hallucinatory, and some strategies for dismissing RSM experience focus on the experience of sole perceivers, construing them as typical of the whole field. They are not, however.

Some recent discussions of epistemic issues, notably those belonging broadly to Reformed Epistemology, speak about the proper function of cognitive (and sensory) powers. An assumption about *proper cognitive function* is reasonable to make on occasion, for we have clear instances in which cognitive powers are successful, and we seemingly have clear instances in which they are not. For example, an octogenarian who complains of confused vision, as a friend of mine recently did, and then

---

[19] See his *The Interpretation of Dreams*, lect. VII, Part B.
[20] See Brasic, "Hallucinations," for a brief review of theories. For example, Horowitz, "Hallucinations," develops an approach that uses four determinants in perceptual release.

discovers that he is suffering from quadruple images, correctable by special glasses, has perceptual powers that are functioning improperly. Of course, murky cases exist in which we cannot readily determine whether a person's cognitive powers are functioning properly; apparition experiences typically raise far-reaching questions about proper function. This use of the concept of proper function is actually part of a theory in which an unobservable entity – proper function – is postulated to exist, this time at the level of epistemology itself, rather than in some more familiar setting, such as those that we find in the empirical sciences. In Chapter 2 (Figure 2.3),[21] I place epistemology at a level "above" commonsense and empirical sciences, in order to indicate that epistemology typically takes as the items for critical reflection the descriptive and explanatory statements in a science (or in commonsense) and then creates a theory about such claims. This is where we encounter the wide-ranging assertions about the varied statements, e.g., that these are the believable claims and those the unbelievable one; that these are claims for which evidence is appropriate and those are the ones for which evidence is inappropriate; that these are claims whose probability on total evidence is ½ and those for which the probability is less than ½; and so on. Further (epistemic) remarks about dubitability, indubitability, certainty, uncertainty, and many such predicates offer something of an extensive, but less than comprehensive, epistemology relevant to some particular theory. Here I am following up on an earlier remark about using Wittgenstein's insights about meaning to apply to philosophy itself. I find that my epistemic instincts are evidentialist, and I would approach the notion of proper cognitive structure as a neuropsychological construct, partially explicable by virtue of assent among theorists of various bents who attempt to (see Fraser Watts here) provide more understanding of cognitive structures than we have from a pre-psychological context in which several decisive cases are agreed upon, e.g., clearly delusional states (in which cognitive structures function ineptly) and ones that are clearly without psychopathology. Reformed epistemology, so-called, has little to offer in place of evidential claims expressed using probability values (or without such values, for that matter).[22]

Whereas I am assuming here that all of percipients whose experiences I researched gave accounts to me that are reasonably accurate, some

---

[21] *Ibid.*, p. 124.
[22] I personally favor attempting to integrate probability values into epistemic ones, recognizing that to construe these values in accord with the probability calculus imposes a conceptual constraint.

probability estimate is involved in offering this assessment. Some theorists quite readily embrace[23] what has been called *The Principle of Credulity*, which asserts that if something seems present to some person, then it probably is, barring certain circumstances, such as being high on drugs, or having a poor memory, etc. Of course, someone might want to insist that having a religious vision counts among the exceptions. However, this needs to be argued. *The Principle of Testimony*, which asserts that the reports given of experience are reliable, unless reasons exist for questioning them, is another epistemic principle on which we generally rely in evaluating epistemic claims. Richard Swinburne suggests that people who report religious experiences might be even more trustworthy when their moral values change for the better as a result of those experiences.[24] I find these two *Principles* to be exceptionally generous, but I recognize that I might be more skeptical than others about human testimony. One cannot easily show that another's claim is fictitious or fraudulent, but of course fictions and frauds exist. My concern is not primarily over these difficulties, although they cannot be overlooked; my worries are over perceptual flaws, and the possibility that experience has been misinterpreted.

An unspoken difficulty with all these experiences, deemed by those who underwent them as (visual) encounters with *Jesus*, is the exact criterion by which this assessment was made. The only "account" of his post-Resurrection appearance is found in *The Revelation of St. John*, but this book, which offers its readers a series of "visions" is not deemed to be authoritative concerning the way in which Jesus appeared in earthly form. St. John says that he had hair as white as wool, eyes blazing with fire, feet like fine brass, and other features that are evidently meant to be symbolic.[25] The NT Gospels do not give us an account of his appearance, which is an extraordinary omission, since identification of persons is made primarily by their personal appearance. A curious comment is made by St. Mark, or one of his editors, in his description of post-Resurrection appearances. This Gospel, which comes with various endings that still beguile its interpreters, includes the remark in a long ending, "He appeared *in another form* to two of them as they walked in the country."[26] This seems to be a reference to a post-Resurrection

---

[23] Such as Swinburne, *The Existence of God*, p. 303f; cf. p. 310f where its limitations are discussed; and Davis, *The Evidential Force of Religious Experience*, chap. 4.
[24] *Ibid.*, p. 323.
[25] *Revelation*, 1:12–16.
[26] *Mark*, 16:12; my italics.

encounter described by St. Luke, an encounter between the Risen Christ and Cleopas and another disciple, perhaps Peter. In Luke's account the eyes of the two disciples are said to have been prevented from recognizing Jesus. The exact nature of the event is perhaps unimportant, but what catches my attention is that Mark, or some editor, avowed that Jesus appeared in a different form. This claim is anathema to Catholic and Protestant theologians that I have met. Perhaps we are given a clue here to understanding these encounters – the normal eyesight we employ in making identifications is superseded by something else. In another place I have discussed the problem of continuing identity over a time span that includes his Crucifixion and the Resurrection.[27] The NT itself contains curious omissions concerning the identity of the Being encountered, who is identified as the Christ, so events occurring in our day could hardly offer anything but incomplete results.

Marian Hathaway Case

Marian was brought up in Swansea, Wales, as an atheist, by parents who were atheists. She said she was really a third-generation atheist, for her paternal grandfather had also been one. She wanted to believe in God when she was young, but could not find any reason to do so. When she was seventeen she had a dream in which a man with dark bushy hair came toward her with his arms open, asking her to love him. She said she knew it was Jesus, even though she did not know much about him. She had heard a story about Jesus born in a manger, who grew up to be a good man, but that was the extent of her knowledge of Christianity. Her education in a state school included prayers and religious instruction, but these meant nothing to her, she said.

Marian's visionary experience some thirteen years later occurred as she was seated in the balcony of a church, looking at the large pipe organ mounted against the front wall. The pipes began shimmering in blue and gold colors, images that reminded her of the jumpy pictures of the earliest silent movies. They gradually became clearer, and Marian found herself looking at a big face with beautiful golden hair and a golden beard. The face was so large it filled the front of the church – some twenty feet high. She thought it must be Jesus, but she was puzzled by the fact that he neither looked Jewish nor resembled the image of the person that appeared in her dream when she was seventeen. She saw him looking at the congregation with a smile and an expression of love for the people. Then she saw his arms, draped in white, move in an embrace of everyone present at the service. They were large enough to take in several rows at once. To describe his action Marian used a Welsh word meaning to cuddle, to comfort, or to love by touching someone. He loved everyone there, including her. She kissed his cheek in response, and felt his warmth, although not the feel of his skin. Because Marian

---

[27] Wiebe, *Visions of Jesus*, pp. 135–40.

did not know if this experience was real or imaginary, she closed her eyes, but she could still see him with her eyes closed. When she opened them a moment later he was still there. This went on for some time, and the experience filled her with such awe that she could hardly believe that it was taking place. When she went home that day she prayed, asking God whether it was really Jesus that had appeared to her, and if it was, why he appeared with only his face and arms. She reached for her Bible, which was still quite new to her, and opened it at random to a passage in Ephesians 1 that speaks of Jesus being the head of the church, and the church being his body. Everything fell into place for her at that moment, and Christian beliefs about him and his death became clear. This experience took place in Swansea in 1969 when Marian was thirty years of age. She worked as a library assistant when I interviewed her in 1993. I was able to interview her then in the church building where the experience occurred.

Whether Marian's corporeal senses were involved is difficult to say. The experiences of Helen do seem to have involved her outer senses, for the reality check of looking around and then back, and finding that the same figure was in the same visual space, is more impressive than the reality check that Marian attempted to use. In Helen's reality check, she was able to compare the view of the building at the front where Jesus appeared, with the view of the congregation behind her, in which nothing anomalous appeared. In Marian's reality check the contrast that normally holds between seeing a normal visual expanse with one's eyes open and the "visual expanse" that often accompanies having one's eyes shut is missing, for having her eyes open or shut made no difference. Her experience is curious, and warrants inclusion in the indeterminate category of apparitions.

The cases I have discussed in this chapter so far indicate that the following factors are evidently in mind, or are actually used, in thinking about the question of veridical visions:

1. Does looking around, and then looking back, make an apparition "objective"?
2. Does the fact that no one else present seemingly sees what I am seeing, make what I am seeing hallucinatory?
3. Is closing one's eyes and then seeing what I now see with my open eyes mean that what appears to me is hallucinatory?
4. Does seeing, and only seeing, what another touches, and only touches, mean that the apparition is hallucinatory (to both of us)?
5. If I see and touch an object, in such a way that the features of each sensation mesh well with each other, does that mean that the apparition is "objective"?
6. If a person sees, tactilely feels, and locates an apparition with the proprioceptive sense in such a way that the three sensory powers

mesh well with each other, does that mean that the apparition is "objective"? If that person is also healed in that encounter, does that mean that the apparition is "objective"?

We evidently have some idea of hallucination, but it is incompletely developed, and perhaps will not be developed until cognitive science can study the phenomenon.

Jim Link

Jim Link was watching a movie on television one evening in his home in Newmarket, Ontario, when the screen suddenly became invisible. The first thought that occurred to him, which he knew to be absurd, was that maybe he had watched so much television that he had become blind! He next realized that he was unable to hear the television set, and he thought, "Have I been watching so much TV that it is affecting my vision and my hearing?" He stood up to look out of the window next to him just to make sure his eyesight was still intact, but he couldn't see the walls. It seemed as though he was enclosed in a curtain, but he couldn't really see a curtain. A human figure then came into view at the end of the room, starting with an outline that became clearer and clearer, until he could see someone wearing long robes and sandals. He wondered, "What's going on here? Who is this? What is this?" The figure turned to face Jim, extended an arm, and beckoned Jim three times to come to him. Jim immediately thought to himself, "That is Jesus!" and the lines came to him from the New Testament, "Come to me all you who are weak and heavy laden, and I will give you rest." He thought to himself, "It's real, then, it's real. I have to ask for forgiveness and repent and receive him." At that instant everything in the room returned to normal, and he decided to become a Christian.

The figure that Jim saw was of average height, and seemed to be situated about fifteen to eighteen feet away. The robe that the figure wore was a dark blue or a purplish blue, Jim was not sure. What impressed Jim most was the royalty of the appearance and the way the figure welcomed him. The figure wore a hood that prevented its face from being seen, so Jim could not report anything about facial features. Jim had been wondering about the meaning of life, what his purpose in life was, and whether he was just on earth to work and maintain a home and watch television! He had been attending church with his wife, just to please her, but having this experience, at twenty-seven years of age, changed his outlook on life.

Jim had another experience in 1977, some fifteen years later, one evening after a Bible study in the home of his brother-in-law. He was sitting at the kitchen table, just having had coffee and something to eat. He discovered that as he tried to get up he was unable to move. He turned to tell his brother–in–law sitting several feet away about this sudden inability to move, but Jim could not see him. As he put it to me, all he could see was the face of one he took to be Jesus "from sort of three–quarters of the way down his forehead to just below his chin, just as clear as you're sitting there right now." The radiant or glowing figure seen as

Jesus had a beard and brown shoulder-length hair, like the popular images of Jesus in pictures. Just to convince himself that he was seeing something genuine, Jim looked away and then looked back again to see if the figure still was there, and he was able to do this several times. Jim was the only one in the room who could see him, however. As he got up a few minutes later to go home, he was flattened by a force that pinned him to the floor. For about three hours he was interrogated by this being about what he valued most – his job, his family, his wife, his possessions, and so on. The others in the group watched in awe but said nothing. They heard Jim's responses, but not the questions that were put to him. His brother-in-law wanted to come over to him to pray with him, Jim reported, but could not do so – it was as if an invisible line had been drawn across the floor that he could not cross. Jim describes the second experience as having confirmed his decision earlier in life to be a Christian. Jim does some oil painting as a hobby, and in the front entrance of his home hangs a painting of a biblical scene in which he tried to capture the likeness as he had seen it. When I interviewed Jim in 1988 he worked in Toronto as a supply manager for an electrical company, and also did some lay preaching. Since that time he has gone into pastoral work.

In the first of Jim's accounts his phenomenological experience involved accurate proprioceptive sensations concerning the place in which he was located, but his visual sensations did not coincide with this information. No obvious explanation for this incongruity is available; the conjecture that some powerful "mindful" agent was controlling Jim's sensory powers does not itself offer an explanation, but it suggests a direction. His second experience includes the curious aspect of being pinned to the floor with a protective region that no one could enter. This matter is intersubjective, but of course Jim's "interrogation" was private. This combination places the visionary experience in the space-time-causal domain.

I submit that the phenomenological evidence coming from those evidently experiencing apparitions adds substantially to that which can be gleaned from an external perspective. The classical emphasis upon God as Creator, or Designer, or Maintainer of the Created Order, minimizes the interactions found in RSM experience and keeps God at a distance, as the Object mostly of intersubjective intuitions. It fails to do justice to the Hebrew-Christian tradition where encounters with a Being is central, without ignoring other features of theism. Of course our skeptical age will wonder if any phenomenological accounts are reliable, as though we could do serious theorizing by accepting only those RSM accounts already accord with our cynical or skeptical outlooks about the reality of Transcendent Orders.

In order to give my interest in phenomenological evidence further credence I will turn my attention very briefly to some of the fascinating features of personal RSM experience provided by Teresa of Avila.

ST. TERESA OF AVILA (1515–82)

Teresa lived and wrote at a dangerous time in the history of the Church, for "heretics" were actively sought out, and often executed for their claims or beliefs. In the latter years of the fifteenth-century Pope Innocent VIII commissioned Heinrich Kramer (also known as Heinrich Institoris) and James Sprenger by to be inquisitors in Northern Germany. They were commissioned to determine whether "many persons of both sexes, unmindful of their own salvation and straying from the Catholic Faith, have abandoned themselves to devils, incubi and succubi."[28] The result of their study, *Malleus Maleficarum (The Witch Hammer)*, probably first published in 1486, became the ultimate authority on witchcraft for more than two centuries, continually appealed to in trials of witches in Germany, France, Italy and England. It is a fascinating medieval compendium of phenomena said to be produced by demonic powers.

Teresa exhibits her share of fear of being accused of acting under demonic influences, which means that we must read her work with that caution in mind. She speaks of both enigmatic experiences and of ones that obviously were of profound significance to her. She writes of one in which she was aware of a being near her without the use of senses:

"I saw Christ at my side – or, to put it better, I was conscious of Him, for I saw nothing with the eyes of the body or the eyes of the soul. He seemed quite close to me, and I saw that it was He. ... Being completely ignorant that such visions were possible, I was very much afraid at first. ... All the time Jesus Christ seemed to be by my side, but as this was not an imaginary vision I could not see in what form. But I most clearly felt that He was all the time on my right, and was a witness of everything that I was doing."[29]

One challenge in understanding Teresa is her effort to put her experiences in the tripartite scheme for "visions" first articulated by St. Augustine,[30] and subsequently a standard for Western (Christian) interpretation of visionary experience. The three categories that Augustine offers – corporeal vision, imaginary vision, and intellectual vision – follow the Platonic understanding of the central epistemic powers that human exhibit, namely, perception, imagination, and intellection, but the criteria for falling into one category or another are unclear. Augustine thought that only corporeal (or bodily) vision used the usual powers of

---

[28] "The Bull of Innocent VIII," *Malleus Maleficarum*, p. xliii.
[29] *The Life of Saint Teresa*, chap. 27.
[30] Discussed in Chapter 1 of this book.

sight. In a study of Julian of Norwich, Paul Molinari says that corporeal vision, as Augustine understood it, implied the causal efficacy of an external agent.[31] Not all would agree with Molinari and Augustine, however. Evelyn Underhill, whose study of mysticism went into twelve editions, suggests that corporeal vision might not involve external agents.[32] She contends that corporeal vision "is little more than a more or less uncontrolled externalization of inward memories, thoughts or intuitions – even of some pious picture which has become imprinted on the mind – which may, in some subjects, attain the dimensions of true sensorial hallucination."[33] Underhill suggests in these remarks – the only ones occurring in her extensive study of what she calls "mysticism" – that corporeal vision does not involve an external agent, but Molinari's view more accurately reflects the position advanced by Augustine.

Teresa insists that she never experienced corporeal vision, arguing that all of her experiences were imaginary or intellectual visions. In one place, however, she writes:

"[B]y the mere beauty and whiteness of a single one of the hands which we are shown the imagination is completely transcended. In any case, there is no other way in which it would be possible for us to see in a moment things of which we have no recollection, when we have never thought of, and which, even in a long period of time, we could not invent with our imagination, because, as I have already said, they far transcend what we can comprehend on earth."[34]

Her reference here to the things seen "in a moment" suggests that at least some of her experiences were of very short duration. In *The Interior Castle* she remarks that imaginative visions often last only one moment, like a streak of lightning.[35] Teresa is evidently seeking to draw a distinction between what we might call the ordinary activity of the human imagination in imagining something previously experienced, and an activity involving the awareness of something new. The phenomenological characteristics of some of her experiences evidently differed sufficiently much from those that occur in ordinary imagining that she could distinguish those experiences from the latter, but she applies the term "imaginative vision" to it, rather than "corporeal vision." Corporeal vision was thought by the Church at the time to be the most susceptible

---

[31] Molinari, *Julian of Norwich*, p. 62.
[32] Underhill, *Mysticism*, p. 281.
[33] Ibid., p. 281.
[34] *Life*, chap. 28.
[35] *The Interior Castle* (1577), Section 6.9.3.

to diabolical influence, so strong motivations existed for not admitting to having experienced corporeal vision. This account, however, suggests that her corporeal senses might have been involved. In another place she writes about some of her Christic visions that makes them sound corporeal: "At times it certainly seemed to me as if I were looking at a painting, but on many other occasions it appeared to be no painting but Christ Himself, such was the clarity with which He was pleased to appear to me. Yet there were times when the vision was so indistinct that I did think it was a painting, although it bore no resemblance even to the most perfect of earthly pictures."[36] The range of experiences to which Teresa was giving witness is indeterminate.

Teresa speaks to the question how she knows that it is Jesus the Christ who is appearing to her – a challenge from her confessors – and in doing so gives a fine illustration of the supposedly non-deceptive vision, intellectual vision. She notes that if one removes both corporeal and imaginative vision as possibilities, a third form of vision is possible: "He appears to the soul by a knowledge brighter than the sun. I do not mean that any sun is seen, or any brightness, but there is a light which, though unseen, illumines the understandings so that the soul may enjoy this great blessing which brings very great blessing with it."[37] A little later she writes: "He imprints so clear a knowledge on the soul that there seems to be no possibility of doubt. The Lord is pleased to engrave it so deeply on the understanding that one can no more doubt it than one can doubt the evidence of one's eyes. In fact it is easier to doubt one's eyes."[38] The belief in the power of the intellect to apprehend indubitable spiritual insights is remarkable, and speaks to an era in which such certainties were thought possible. The emergence here of *sensus divinitatis*, found in John Calvin, is readily understandable. Augustine considers the intellect to be beyond deception in grasping spiritual matters, remarking that "either a person does not understand, and this is the case of one who judges something to be other than it is, or he does understand, and then his vision is necessarily true."[39] Augustine's own description of his embracing Christian faith indicates that he considered his insights to be devoid of deception. Such a position has virtually disappeared in the modern age, where probabilities have replaced certainties in all areas apart from mathematics and logic.

---

[36] *Life*, chap. 28.
[37] *Ibid.*, chap. 27.
[38] *Ibid.*
[39] *Lit. Gen.* 12.14.29. He reiterates the point at 12.25.52 in the words: "But in the intuitions of the intellect it is not deceived."

This rejection of certainty is fairly recent. Dom Illtyd Trethowan offers a defense of certainty in both philosophy and theology in 1948;[40] the probabilities that mark "the age of evidence" had not fully encompassed these ancient subject areas.

Teresa offers troubling accounts of interactions with demonic powers, including an instance in which she was in an oratory, perhaps a private chapel. The devil appeared on her left hand – evidently in miniature form – and spoke to her, his mouth appearing particularly terrifying to Teresa. She reports that a great flame issued from his body, a flame that cast no shadow. He then spoke to her saying in a dreadful voice that she indeed had escaped his clutches, but he would capture her still. Finding that making the sign of the cross did not dispel him completely, Teresa threw holy water in his direction, and he did not return.[41] In describing the locutions that are from God, she says that "the words are perfectly formed, but are not heard with the physical ear. Yet they are received much more clearly than if they were so heard."[42] Clear phenomenological differences evidently attended the diabolical and the Divine locutions in her RSM experiences, allowing her to mark a distinction between them. Her accounts of her "raptures," or "elevations," or "levitations" are important, and indicate that phenomenological data are not the only ones relevant when assessing RSM experience. She writes:

"In these raptures, the soul no longer seems to animate the body; its natural heat therefore is felt to diminish and it gradually gets cold, though with a feeling of very great joy and sweetness. Here there is no possibility of resisting ... [R]apture is, as a rule, irresistible. Before you can be warned by a thought or help yourself in any way, it comes as a quick and violent shock; you see and feel this cloud, or this powerful eagle rising and bearing you up on its wings. You realize, I repeat, and indeed see that you are being carried away you know not where. For although this is delightful, the weakness of our nature makes us afraid at first, and we need a much more determined and courageous spirit than for the previous stages of prayer ... We have to go willingly wherever we are carried, for in fact, we are being born off whether we like it or not. ... Sometimes with a great struggle I have been able to do something against it. But it has been like fighting a great giant, and has left me utterly exhausted. At other times resistance has been impossible; my soul has been carried away, and usually my head as well, without my being able to prevent it; and sometimes it has affected my whole body, which has been lifted from the ground. This has only happened rarely."[43]

---

[40] Trethowan, *Certainty*.
[41] *Life*, chap. 31.
[42] *Life*, chap. 25.
[43] *Life*, chap. 28.

Levitation places an event in the space–time–causal order, and should probably be classified as a miracle since some laws of nature appear to be overridden, although the complex of forces upon a body that produce – or impair – levitation are curious. Teresa indicates that the nuns in her convent would sometimes hold her down on the ground, at her request, so that she would not be seen to levitate. We might ascribe a significant causal source to some spirit producing this levitation, but its causal power is seemingly overcome by the nuns holding Teresa down – we might wonder how human efforts to prevent levitation can be strong enough to do so. Levitation is the sort of event for which assigning a spirit as a causal source seems reasonable given some other events in a levitator's life, either simultaneous or closely connected, that are clear marks of some other form of sentience and consciousness. Of course some might rule out the causal efficacy of a spirit simply because such a source is not necessary, but then we are no longer conducting our thought along scientific lines, where causes are not necessary but only probable. In Teresa's account of levitation here we can match phenomenological features that only Teresa can offer with events in the spatiotemporal–causal world, such as when the nuns observed her levitation while they felt the levitating force rest upon Teresa's body that almost produced levitation, but did not because of their intervention.

Teresa's account is significant, and warrants inclusion as evidence for the existence of spirits, even though the species and the more specific kind of being that acted upon her might not be readily identifiable. This is typical in thought that allows unobservable objects to be postulated. We can see how the inclusion of this "grounding event" gives credibility to the larger Theory of Spirits in which the event is found. Of course we can expect any theory of this kind to be "incompletely described," but this is a problem of theories in general where theoretical objects are postulated, not a feature of only the Theory of Spirits. Many years of painstaking observation are often needed in piecing together the claims having sufficient credibility to be worthy of consideration in some theory. Mendel's work with "inheritance factors" and Semmelweiss's observations about "germs" are stark reminders of the demands for data in order to convince skeptics about unobservables. Some personal cost might also be involved, as in Semmelweiss's death in a mental hospital. He seemingly insisted on the reality of germs to such a degree that his irritated colleagues in a Viennese hospital had him committed.[44] His theory was a core notion in the development of modern medicine.

---

[44] Cf. my "Degrees of Hallucinations."

Unlike Teresa of Avila, the visionaries whose experiences I was privileged to examine were not troubled by the Platonic distinction that marked her approach to visionary experience. The Platonic-Catholic perspective that is still in evidence in its analyses has been sufficiently ameliorated in Western culture, due in part to the Protestant Reformation, that visionaries can use their own mental constructs to give sense as best they can to extraordinary experiences. The visionaries that I interviewed generally believed in spiritual realities already when I interviewed them. Their backgrounds at the time of their reported experiences varied considerably across the Christian spectrum, and some were Agnostic or Jewish. While prior beliefs shaped the accounts they gave, no doubt, they were not constrained by a prior epistemic stance in an obvious way. Some reader of their accounts a thousand years from now, if books survive that long, might say that these accounts clearly reflect the epistemic outlook of our present age, an outlook that is so close to us now that we can hardly detect it.

CATHOLIC CONSTRAINTS

The topic of Christic vision is a matter of controversy in the Church, in large measure because of the influence of theological views that discriminate against perceptual over cognitive experience. *The Catholic Encyclopedia* (1912) explains how corporeal apparitions – or visions involving the perceptual senses, including those of the Christ – might be caused. It says that in a vision

"Either a figure really present externally strikes the retina and there determines the physical phenomenon of the vision; or an agent superior to man directly modifies the visual organ and produces in the composite a sensation equivalent to that which an external object would produce…. Sometimes the very substance of the being or the person will be presented; sometimes it will be merely an appearance consisting in an arrangement of luminous rays. The first may be true of living persons, and even, it would seem, of the now glorious bodies of Christ and the Blessed Virgin, which by the eminently probable supernatural phenomenon of multilocation may become present to men without leaving the abode of glory."[45]

Perhaps we might describe this view of visions in general, expressed a century ago now, as representing historic Catholic doctrine on the matter of visions or apparitions. It curiously restricts its remarks to visual phenomena, rather than including phenomena that might involve other

---

[45] Herbermann, *The Catholic Encyclopedia*, "Apparition," www.catholic.org/encyclopedia/view.php?id=963 (accessed June 28, 2018).

senses. This effort to explain apparitions makes something of an exception of visions of the Christ, or the Blessed Mother, since these beings are deemed to have been given "glorified bodies" and to be "in heaven." The NT says this explicitly of Jesus, and Catholic doctrine has advanced the same view of Mary: Pope Pius XII in *Munificentissimus Deus* (1950) declared that she was "taken up body and soul to the glory of heaven."[46] The phenomenon of multilocation is here considered eminently probable (rather than certain), and while the grounds for this probability are not adduced, we might cite the widely mooted claim that various notables have been "seen" at different locations at the same time – this has been alleged in the twentieth century concerning Padre Pio of Pietrelcina. Such a claim requires some careful empirical reasoning about who saw someone at a given time, and who also saw (or "saw") that person at the same time in a different location. These claims are much more difficult to establish in the absence of reliable clocks.

In an *Encyclopedia* written some seventy years later and edited by Karl Rahner, a well-known Catholic priest and theologian, the article on visions focuses on "the light of infused contemplation" as marking the central feature of such experience, construing any perceptible vision as "the picture that is shown to the soul" in a "momentary form of grace." The vague language and interpretation offered in the article at this point derive from a *Spiritual Journal* written by Lucie Christine – a pseudonym for a nineteenth century French mystic, Mathilde Boutle – in 1887, which exhibits reluctance to think that outer senses might be involved in experiences seemingly involving visual perception – the picture is "shown to the soul." Many of the writers in the Roman Catholic tradition show their desire to advance views that are at least consistent with their Tradition of interpretation, if not expressed using the same or equivalent language. The constraints they sometimes exhibit are perhaps not ones often felt by Christians who are Protestant, or are deemed Protestant, such as myself. We might function without a substantial Tradition instructing us, or guarding us from serious error, for that matter. However, one cannot "just submit to" or "just embrace" some Tradition, for that is tantamount to saying "just believe." Neither the power of Tradition nor the authority of the Bible can easily dissuade those for whom the Naturalism of the modern age is – and once was for me – a voice "humming in one's ears that prevents one from hearing any other."[47]

---

[46] Para 40 and passim.
[47] Adapted from Plato, *Crito*, p. 54. Socrates says this of the Athenian laws.

The NT itself is ambiguous on whether the body of the glorified Christ was seen after his Ascension. I have discussed elsewhere[48] the problem arising from the fact that several accounts of the Ascension are given, one of which, *St. Matthew's Gospel*, locates it in Galilee, whereas *St. Luke* puts it in Bethany, near Jerusalem. The Resurrection claim itself depends substantially on appearances, so any tradition that minimizes their significance does not understand the modern era's demands upon epistemologists. In addition, at least some of the Christic appearances that occurred after the first forty days, such as the appearance to Saul (St. Paul) at his conversion, or to St. Stephen at his death, do not fit well with the view that the body of Jesus has never been seen since the Ascension. I think we can assert that the NT itself is closer to the modern age's epistemic expectations than the venerable Tradition that not only (inadvertently) makes the Resurrection relatively inaccessible, but also relegates sensory perception to an inferior place as a source of knowledge, or minimizes its epistemic value. The Tradition that construes the glorified body of The Christ as inaccessible to sensory perception is doubtful, and can be moved to the periphery when assessing the question whether the corporeal senses might be implicated in such visionary experience.

The constraints imposed upon Teresa by the Catholic Tradition are considerable, not only involving central dogmas such as the Resurrection of Christ and the Assumption of Mary, but also the three forms of "vision" articulated by Augustine. These "dogmas" effectively control her interpretation of events, so that we are hardly able to discern what might have happened phenomenologically. As in many areas of dogmatic interest, the Protestant Church has little guidance, for interpretation of the Hebrew-Christian Bible has become permeable to a fault. With a claim as momentous as the Resurrection actually is, this development is beneficial. The claim needs to be open to critical but open examination, and in this respect the loosening of religious constraints is an advantage. Many of us can still remember the constraints placed upon Western universities by Marxism-Leninism, so we know how religious or political constraints can stifle the pursuit of truth. The pursuit of truth, conducted in the most unprejudiced and thoughtful way humanly possible, remains the fundamental objective of philosophy.

---

[48] Wiebe, *Visions of Jesus*, chap. 4.

5

Evidence for the World of Spirits

The medieval Christian world is famous for its generous and fantastic metaphysical commitments, which included as many as nine orders of angels – Divine and demonic, described in *Celestial Hierarchies* by pseudo-Dionysius.[1] This metaphysical world naturally included humans, who were considered to be a second kind of rational being, with souls thought to be immaterial and immortal, possibly created at the same time as angels, but well before the creation of the first man (Adam, in Hebrew-Christian tradition). Perhaps the whole world has pretty much believed in some such metaphysical scheme, with science proving to be "the sifting humour"[2] by which cultures lose much of their RSM sensibilities. The Greco-Roman-Hebrew view of the world is still coming to grips with the scientific impetus now coursing through it. C. S. Lewis (1898–1963), British medievalist at Oxford and Cambridge, says that a third order of rational being was also considered in the West to exist, beings variously known as elves, fairies,[3] pixies, pygmies, centaurs, dwarfs, nymphs, gnomes, trolls, pans, satyrs, faunes, and by other terms. These creatures were beings having long lives – longaevi – but were variously viewed among Western medieval theorists, perhaps as daimons (or daemons)

---

[1] Lewis, *Discarded Image*, p. 70f. Some historians place Dionysius's *Celestial Hierarchies* in the sixth century, but Lewis evidently thinks it is earlier. Disputes about authorship have led to "pseudo" being attached to his name. Modern commentators, unlike medieval authors, do not think that he is the Dionysius from Athens mentioned in the NT (*Acts* 17:39).
[2] An apropos phrase from Hume, *Human Understanding*, sec. 4, Para 14.
[3] Lewis, *Discarded Image*, chap. VI. See Bord, *Fairies*, for a recent attempt to document their existence.

of Greek antiquity, or as spirits of the dead, or in other ways.[4] Interest in longaevi has clearly declined in the modern era, and the expression of definite opinions on their existence now is rare, although the recent report from Iceland about elves is an apparent exception.

The longaevi are not devoid of interest here, but my focus remains on beings that are still more widely considered to be real. Modernity's quarrels with its medieval past make positive claims about current attitudes difficult to identify and defend. This past is more-or-less Christian, depending on how we interpret this imprecise term, whose core beings are

- A supreme being, God, and holy angels who do God's bidding,
- satan and demonic powers, and
- spirits of departed human beings, and possibly also of the living.

The longaevi are evidently less resilient than these and offer substantial difficulties to those of us who are naturalistic by disposition. The mere listing of the kinds of longaevi suggests that the relevant experiences from which their reality is (causally) inferred might *not* be especially religious, spiritual, or mystical. Rather, they are apt to be seen as a part of the (natural) order of things. The principle of simplicity suggests that we posit only as many entities as needed, and inasmuch as I find myself unable to conscientiously resist this application of Ockham's Razor, I am indisputably modern. I am also open, I trust, to evidence being adduced for the reality of some of these "exotic" beings, such as fairies or elves.

The focus on ontology that I am advocating here brings philosophy back to its historic pursuits.[5] This includes a sympathetic, yet critical, review of experience that purports to be, or is at least interpreted to be, indicative of orders of reality that are not easily assimilated to a naturalistic view of the cosmos. Of course, I do not intend to extend the explanatory role of a General Theory of Spirits to events already adequately handled by physics, chemistry, biology, geology, psychology, sociology, and innumerable other fields now being served by science and exact studies. I merely seek to extend "the scientific attitude" and the philosophical one, if it is different, to areas touched by religion, spirituality, and mysticism. Although my background and experience might predispose me to view Western-Christian phenomena too favorably, I construe possible insights coming from Hebrew-Christian faith as having implications for

---

[4] Lewis, *Discarded Image*, p. 155.
[5] Cf. Mounce, *Metaphysics*, p. ix.

RSM experience worldwide. One venerable interpretation of this faith presents its Creator-Redeemer-God as knowable everywhere, independently of any historical events in which he might be implicated, whether Hebrew or Christian. I will develop this in Chapter 6. One purpose of extending human life beyond death may be so that every person might experience both the astonishing impartiality and the gratuitous goodness seemingly found in God.

Although I would be disingenuous to disguise my religious roots in Christendom, a practical difficulty facing any scholar wishing to engage RSM experience is that *everyone has some perspective or other* by which they are shaped, and possibly biased. This is true for anyone shaped by either Eastern or Western faiths; by those shaped by Islam and Judaism, perhaps because of conversion to one or the other; by those shaped by Christianity, whether it is Catholic, Orthodox, or Protestant; by those influenced by Atheism, which also has "a set of cognitive and behavioral commitments"; and by those shaped by Agnosticism and Skepticism, however disinterested and objective these perspectives might seem; and so on. Each person only has a limited opportunity in one lifetime to explore RSM traditions, with the result that our insights concerning various competing perspectives are inevitably limited. If everyone is somehow compromised, we must find ways to minimize this.

Any claim to spiritual "revelation" carries the problem that its source can seldom be identified without qualification, especially if several conflicting orders exist. The risk that a deceptive one might be involved cannot be considered negligible. A second problem is that any claim that the Most High God is implicated in an event carries the challenge of providing evidence that it is the *Most High* God, in fact. This claim has an empirical character to it, and the issue it raises is difficult, if not impossible, to resolve. Related to this issue is that if theism is interpreted to make reference to a being that is infinite in some way, since no criterion for possessing an infinite attribute is identifiable in an empirical context, the claim is always uncertain. A third difficulty arises in cases where *repeated* events occur, for showing that the same being (or Being) is encountered is extremely difficult to establish. *Evidence* for such continuity does exist, but it is not so overwhelming, seemingly, that every doubt can be silenced. We see this criticism brought up by the confessors for Teresa of Avila, who challenged her to show that it was *the Christ* that she encountered. She does not appear to have confronted them in any definitive way, although she is aware of the difficulty.

Every person who thinks that the Deity, or perhaps an emissary, has disclosed himself in some event must make up one's mind about the importance of this event. This matter is not primarily theoretical, I surmise, but profoundly practical. Several curious cost–benefit calculations now come into view, reminiscent of the calculation generally known as "Pascal's Wager": (a) Given that the probability that God has been encountered is greater than zero but less than one, and given the cost of ignoring or despising an overture made by the Deity (possibly), the (weighted) risk involved is substantial, perhaps incalculably great and (b) given the possibility that Evil is attempting to overwhelm a person, the possible disvalue here may be substantial if one fails to act in an appropriate way and thereby falls into Evil's grip. I cannot imagine greater existential questions. Some form of it is in play when a person reflects upon one's (possible) "encounters" with the otherworldly dimension. The idea that the wager is typically limited to the religious tradition(s) in which one is reared is plausible, for some RSM traditions are so far from one's own that the seemingly endless possibilities do not represent plausible ones.[6] I have chosen to act on possible overtures made to me by the Christ, seemingly, but I cannot offer a guarantee to anyone else – let alone myself – about the choices I have made. They have come to define a sizeable portion of my life, and I have no regrets. Perhaps I *know*, not just (happen to) *believe*, that the Most High God has been talking to me, but I would not say that I know that I know this, only that I believe that I know it. I also think that I am not *particularly* fortunate, for I consider all of humanity to be in the curious position of being given amounts of "Divine insight" varying from a little to much, and a corresponding amount of responsibility. This principle of fairness arises from an ethic in which justness in every sense – distributive, reparative, compensatory, and retributive – is endorsed, which is an ultimate value widely traced to Stoic or Hebrew-Christian influences in Western civilization. If we live by probabilities in every other area of life, why would we not live by them in our efforts to interpret and understand RSM experience? This would be little more than to accept our place in the cosmos as *human*.

---

[6] James, "The Will to Believe," speaks insightfully into the experience of finding ourselves "forced" to deal with options regarding religion, identifying them as (1) living or dead, (2) forced or avoidable, and as (3) momentous or trivial. So in the circumstances in which I was raised, Buddhism was a dead option, easy to avoid, and seemingly of trivial significance. However, neither Christianity nor naturalism had these features. For someone born in another part of the world, the options might be quite different.

Evidence for the World of Spirits

When we reflect for even a moment about the human minds that we know from little more than acquaintance with what we read and those with whom we dialogue, we realize that the world of human minds is vast and beyond adequate description. Each mind is individual, yet we know that various categories can be created that are appropriate as a partial description for one mind but not for another. A review of the literature and art of earth's peoples would demonstrate that much more would need to be added to any account that we might adduce as having authority. The causal evidence of minds would provide some of the suitable descriptions, but we would also need to reflect on phenomenological details provided only through personal interaction. The task suggested here by my remarks would be prodigious beyond belief, for the evidence of human minds at work is so extensive. We need to be prepared (mentally) for the possibility that any effort to provide a comparable description of spirits that were never human, as well as those that once were, would also be colossal. We could find that the individuality of spirits might play as large a place in explanation as the general categories to which spirits plausibly belong. Angels who are said to interact with human beings on occasion, for instance, might be appropriately seen as *angels*, but they might also have attributes whose combination is unique. The angel Gabriel in the Abrahamic faiths, for example, mentioned in Daniel, Ezekiel, St Luke, and the Qur'an, is given enough description to have (relative) uniqueness among beings of that form. Any descriptions of Gabriel would be tentative, of course, but that is the nature of exact inquiry and science.

"DECISIVE" CASES

The two values[7] involved in adducing evidence from RSM experience are (a) providing grounds for considering an allegation of evidence to be *likely*, that is, having occurred pretty much as described, and then (b) assessing the *evidential weight* of an item of evidence concerning some theory, here specifically, some portion of the Theory of Spirits. This can be readily illustrated. Rod, an older cousin who has been a Protestant minister for many years, and also worked for book publishers for about twelve years, reported an apparition to me of his mother. When Rod received word that his mother was dying in a hospital in Omaha, Nebraska, he

---

[7] These two measures are often given technical senses, but I am not interpreting them as such here.

went to be with her. He stayed in a hotel near the hospital where she was being cared for so he could visit her several times each day. He was awakened from sleep one morning to see his mother, my Aunt Anne, standing near his bed. She was wearing a dress that was appropriate for one who would be out in public and was looking at him. Rod asked her how she was feeling – they conversed in the Dutch-German dialect used by my ancestors – and she replied that she felt perfectly fine. She said that she could even see well, which intrigued him, for Rod knew that his mother's eyesight had failed badly. She then disappeared from view, as apparitions are wont to do, and the hospital telephoned a few minutes later to tell him that his mother had just died.

The questions that arise here are mainly two: First, how *likely* is it that Rod saw what he reported? Second, what *weight* for some feature of the Theory of Spirits, specifically postmortem survival, would such an (accurate) report have? The answer to the first question, on the likelihood that Rod accurately reported an incident, might not be viewed in a positive light by those who do not know him. *For me*, the report is as likely as any that I entertain about very ordinary events occurring around me every day. I think that such a high value is apt to be assigned only by those who know Rod well. In assigning a value here that has significance for human thought on spiritual realities, we need to be guided by a more objective outlook on the matter. Here skeptics shaped by modernity's sinister influence will wonder about his truthfulness, his cognitive powers, his attachment to RSM belief systems whose aficionados embrace postmortem survival, and so on. These issues do not arise for me, but I cannot discount the difficulties that might rise for others. Here we see the *Principle of Credulity* discussed in Chapter 3 rising to the surface, and demanding assessment. I mentioned there that those of a skeptical disposition are not disposed to give credence to reports that are supportive of RSM beliefs. A more objective assessment of reliability will be demanded, and it is one that I also recognize and respect. The issue of reliability is the prominent one here because the matter of evidential weight is so straightforward, and so powerful – if we concede that Rod saw and heard (not merely "saw" and "heard") what he reported – then the case for postmortem survival (in some inchoate form) is in place. Claims about postmortem survival (human) are complex, since they carry a variety of possibilities. One of the most important is an incomplete claim that we do survive death and continue to exist in some form, but what this form is exactly cannot be spelled out. The sciences spurn such incomplete predictions, of course, but this is still virgin territory, seemingly, where few are able to comment with authority.

THE LINCOLN COLLEGE CASE

The following is a case of an experience described by a British clergyman, possibly known to Sir Alister Hardy:

Perry:[8] "I was brought up a Unitarian and while at Lincoln College, [attended] the services at MC[9] until I realized that I had lost my faith and was an agnostic.... We were living in the country, and one evening while we were out for our usual walk between tea and supper, we saw a figure in a white robe approaching us. We recognized her as she drew near as an acquaintance. She appeared unaware of our presence. We whispered her name as she passed us and then, when we turned our heads, she had vanished. We knew that she had been bed-ridden for a year or two, and soon after our return made enquiries and found that she had died some hours before she appeared to us. I took this as proof of an after-life, but remained agnostic about a Supreme Being and the orthodox view of heaven. Two of our party are still living and may write to you. One is my brother ____ and the other is a cousin, the Rev. ____. At the time the latter was training at [the same] college for the Unitarian ministry, but this experience made him believe that the Unitarian teaching about the Resurrection was inadequate, and he transferred to the Church of England, and is now a retired vicar."

This experience is of interest here for several reasons, among which are the estimates of its ontological significance by at least one member of the group who saw (or "saw") the deceased woman. Changing religious denominations and abandoning agnosticism on the basis of this experience are reasonably dramatic and speak to its importance in assessing the possibility and nature of postmortem existence. These were students of an elite university, moreover, for Lincoln College, established in 1427 by the then-bishop of Lincoln, is a college of the University of Oxford, so we can plausibly assign a significant level of intelligence and sophistication to its students about epistemic and ontological issues. The assessment of the experience concerning postmortem existence does not construe the experience as *necessarily* implying (logically) postmortem existence, but rather postulates postmortem existence as a *cause* of the (shared) experience. The relationship here is causal, not logical, and critics of the belief in postmortem existence should not be allowed to move the debate from

---

[8] This account is housed in the research center that Hardy founded, at the Department of Religious Studies, University of Wales, Lampeter, Ceredigion, I have made only very small editorial changes in order to give consistency to spelling, grammar, punctuation, and emphasis. These accounts will be identified by "RERC" followed by the number the center has assigned to them (RERC 000445 in this case). I am using a pseudonym here; I assume that the author is a man.

[9] He uses the initials "MC," probably to denote Manchester College, where Hardy founded the research centre.

causal considerations to logical ones. A great deal of mischief has been done in philosophy by allowing these two categories of thought to be confused, and in encouraging the notion that postmortem existence must *follow* (logically) some empirical report in order to be credible. The possibility that causes might belong to the domain of the unobservable – or the rarely observable – is a matter of conjecture, but the causal claims are not thereby deprived of rationality, as I explained in Chapter 2. I will discuss this experience under some specific headings and then summarize this discussion before considering another case.

Perry's experience is not hallucinatory if he and his college friends saw – I do not say "saw" – the deceased woman. Such an experience would meet the conditions generally set for genuine perception, for it is by shared perception that we uncover the most basic features of our cosmos. The problem of "mass hallucination" is often raised at this point, as though we need to recognize the reality of *identical and simultaneous* percepts shared by several people at once, "in the absence of an external stimulus, where those percept are unbidden, outside of conscious control, and registered as though in external space." We glean from the conversation provided by Perry that he was not the only one to see – I do not say "see" – the deceased woman, who was evidently walking along the road just as any normal creature would walk. The nature of causality is such that we need to offer an explanation for the shared but peculiar perceptions, and the one that is given by Perry is that "the spirit of the deceased woman," as we are wont to say, was seen by the group. I reference the spirit of the deceased woman here, without speculating about exactly what it was that generated the similar (even identical) and simultaneous percepts in Perry and his friends. It is "a something we know not what," capable of contributing to the percepts reported by Perry. I have no objection to speaking of this as her spirit provided that we do not insist that nothing about it is *physical* – here I break with tradition. We do not *fully* know the scope of that which is physical, and so we cannot speak with authority on that which spirit must be. The probability that mass hallucination occurred is so low that it is negligible.

Apparitions of the dead are so widely known that those who report them are generally conceded to have "seen" something. The very weak description, "*appeared to* by a dead friend," is not proper grammar, but nevertheless gives the concession enough meaning so that we need not think that Perry actually saw something, rather, he only "saw" something. Philosophy has been familiar with the contrast between actual seeing and "being appeared to" since philosophy's inception in ancient

Greece. This contrast is the basis for the (Humean) empiricist conjecture that we might "construct" all experience out of "appearings." To do serious philosophy, however, we need both "appearings" and actual seeings, however incomplete actual seeings might be, given the human disposition to eccentricities and sensory imperfections. Empiricism certainly has given substantial attention to, maybe even favored, the visual sense over the other senses, and I do not dispute its importance, but only observe that the tactile sense seemingly gives us a more reliable take than the visual one on the nature of the world.

We can say that the likelihood that Perry saw (not merely "saw") a recently deceased woman is certainly neither zero nor one, that is, is neither without credibility at all nor enjoying full credibility. The nature of the event was such that no one in Perry's party was close enough to the specter, it seems, to engage with it by any sense than the visual one. I observed in Chapter 4 that the tactile sense is also involved on occasion, but we are not in a position to say whether anything might have been (tactilely) felt, had touch been attempted. The question of how much of a value between these two extremes of zero and one can be defended is the real question concerning the value of Perry's experience for defending the reality of (this case of) postmortem existence. His normal powers of perception seem to have been engaged, and this possibility becomes strong if intersubjective perception occurred. A curious factor that now enters our thought is the cogency of his claim that his companions at least *saw* the same woman. Here the "saw" must reflect some successful sense perception in which a common object was seen or observed in the same place (in much the same manner). Intersubjective perception provides such a strong presumption in favor of *successful* perception[10] that we can hardly question this condition as sufficient for actual perception. This kind of perception is such a familiar and pervasive part of our experience that we hardly stop to reflect on it. A correlative idea is that collective hallucination is such an extraordinarily difficult condition to meet, that we can hardly ever construe it as probable. If we concede that probabilities pervade all of life, including RSM experience, then we will be inclined to accord collective *hallucination* a probability barely above zero, certainly not very far above. If Perry and the friends he mentions actually did see the deceased woman, they very probably had similar visual perceptions of one-and-the-same reality, whatever form that might be. I would assign

---

[10] The "success sense" of perceive is that in which perception occurs and evidently is of a reality external to the perceiver.

a very high probability to the claim that postmortem life is real, based on the accuracy of Perry's claim. The product of the likelihood and the probability is reasonably high (below 1 but above 1/2), which illuminates the intuitive sense that collective experience of apparitions has considerable ontological weight.

This case has the capacity to be a decisive one on the matter of postmortem survival (of humans), for it might involve intersubjective observation, which is a feature of sciences and exact studies. This condition is so important that we are apt to question allegations that could be intersubjectively observed but are not. We might not be able to speak at length about *what it is that appeared* to these students, but we can justifiably assert that something real was encountered, for a sufficient (causal) condition for being real is intersubjective observation. It falls to further studies to speak with more intelligence on the curious nature of the specter, but we would be needlessly hasty to dismiss it as the object of mere opinion, not evidence. Here we touch on an important issue in the history of Western thought, perhaps even the history of thought. The cosmos has often been sharply divided into spiritual and physical categories, as though all that which exists can be conveniently placed into one category or another. My cautious pluralism, as opposed to conventional dualism, inclines me to view existing things as belonging to an indeterminate number of ultimate categories; consequently, the place for spirits is unclear. They are minds, to be sure, or perhaps we could say that these beings have minds, and this determination allows us to say a great deal, since our life as a "minded" creature generates an unlimited (collective) interest. The approach to definition I have taken in this book allows terms for objects with (some) indeterminate attributes to be construed as innocent of charges of incomprehensibility or of meaninglessness if these objects have relations to objects not in doubt.

The first question that I am asking about alleged RSM experience – the likelihood of Perry's sighting (or "sighting") – appears to conceal a cluster of questions, which include

- Did Perry hallucinate or did he actually see someone?
- Does he have full grasp of his perceptual and cognitive faculties, or does he suffer from some neurological injury or disease?
- Is Perry an honest person, opposed to misleading others, or does Perry take religious claims casually?
- Did he represent the experience of himself and his friends competently?

- Did the passage of time produce a false memory?
- Is this reported event similar to other reported events, at least in essential elements?
- Did the Alister Hardy Research Centre (if not Hardy himself) examine the allegation with care? And so on.

Each of these questions has some importance, and several have more than others, perhaps, but in our inability to answer each of these with full satisfaction, because of the wide range of epistemic issues that are ultimately involved, we are apt to come back with a "ballpark" estimate of the likelihood that Perry saw something. This position on "ballpark" estimates is strengthened if some of the assessments are based on estimates of approximate values rooted in well-known probability values that are objective in character.[11] For example, if we know that about 10 percent of the British people[12] report having aberrant perceptions associated by them with specters, then we have a guide to evaluate this particular case. Another set of questions can generate quite a different attitude toward the report that Perry submitted: Were not these students of Lincoln College, which is part of the University of Oxford, and therefore among the brightest and best informed in the United Kingdom, if not the world? Would they not appreciate the issues implicated by the report that Perry submitted? Would Sir Alister Hardy not carefully examine any such allegation before submitting it to public attention? The two extreme responses I have sketched here are excessive skepticism and excessive credulity. Perhaps broad exposure to reports of apparitions changes one's outlook on the assessment of the likelihood of the phenomenon occurring.

The issue of faults in reporting events, due to deliberate attempts to deceive, cannot be ignored, not having a probability of zero, but we must be careful here in offering a reasonable estimate that this has occurred. Although I never knew Hardy himself, I have met three subsequent Research Directors of the Hardy Trust. I have absolutely no doubt that he conducted his research in such a thorough manner that he weeded out any report that was suspicious. How such an estimate becomes embedded in our thought is obscure, and it might have to do with interactions

---

[11] See the discussion in Salmon et al., *Introduction to the Philosophy of Science*, chap. 2 (or Swinburne, *Epistemic Justification*, chap. 3), on the compliance of the relative frequency and equipossible case senses of probability with the probability calculus – a topic beyond the scope of this book.

[12] Ibid., p. 194.

with researchers in our own lifetimes and our estimates of their ethical standards. Studies of ethical misconduct in the sciences, based on papers withdrawn from various scientific fields, suggest that fraud is on the increase, but did not exceed 0.01 percent of published papers in 2007.[13] We might extrapolate, I suppose, from misconduct in the natural sciences to misconduct in the social sciences, and advance a very modest value to the claim that the *Lincoln College Case* involved misconduct.

One of the issues we cannot assess is whether the deceased woman that Perry and his friends saw considered herself to be identical to (or continuous with) the person they knew prior to her demise. We might compare this with the case reported to me by my cousin Rod, reported earlier. Several features in Rod's account contextually imply a sense of ongoing identity: the verbal remarks between the two make little sense if the being that appeared (or "appeared") to Rod was not his mother; also the apparition was appropriately dressed for going out in public, as Aunt Anne understood this, so some link with her while alive is present; and the apparition then interacted with Rod about her ability to see again, and even used the dialect that was common to their ancestry and common to them – I surmise that although she also knew English, she preferred her "native language" to speak about an existential issue, maybe even a holy matter as she saw it. The continuity of personhood revealed in the exchange is consistent with Rod's knowledge of his own mother, and the apparition (of Aunt Anne) evidently saw herself as identical to (or continuous with) the pre-mortem being known as my Aunt Anne. The continuing identity of persons, and even of animals, is something we ascribe to them on the basis, among other things, of bodily form, of continuity in space-time, and other features perhaps, such as similarity in personality, which helps to establish identity. Of course we are also aware that human beings have an awareness of themselves as persons, which contributes its own weight to the claim of continuing personhood under normal circumstances. What happens at death, phenomenologically speaking, has hardly been in (reliable) view until the closing decades of the twentieth century when NDEs became widely known. We can now say that something was perhaps known in previous centuries, from "visions" or other curious events,[14] and now we can assign a more complete and authoritative significance to what was happening before the era of NDEs. I qualify the claim to identity here by suggesting that

---

[13] Fang et al., "Misconduct accounts."
[14] Cf. Zaleski, *Otherworld Journeys*.

it is *continuing* identity that we are concerned with. The *strict* identity relation is known in mathematics and logic, but the continuing identities we ascribe to plants, animals, and human beings is a more complex relation. *Similar* space-time "slices" of these beings are evidently considered in ascribing continuing identity to two stages; we allow rather dissimilar stages to belong to one thing if we can find similarities between closer and intermediate space-time "slices."

The issue of time elapsing between an event and the report of it is important, for it speaks to such issues as the sensory and cognitive competence of the person(s) providing the initial report, and hence to powers of memory. The transmission of the report to other interested persons, and the possibility – even likelihood – that errors are made in this step must be considered. The features of this phase of dissemination of information are well known, and we have to factor in inadvertent mistakes, or memory lapses, or other flaws in the chain of evidence. The probability that the chain of evidence successfully conveys the *gist* of what occurred will not be 1, but might well be well above ½, which provides support for the reported event. In the *Lincoln College Case*, no transmission of data involving a third party has occurred, so this factor in assessing reliability can be ignored.

We can sum up the discrete items I have discussed under the general rubric of reliability and assign probability values to reflect (objective) challenges. The values I am offering here are preliminary suggestions about how the reliability variable might be calculated in *The Lincoln College Case*:

1. *Hallucinatory experience*: This is a small probability, since only about 10 percent (relative frequency) of people are reported to have some aberrant perception at some point in their lives; this does not mean that 10 percent hallucinate pretty much all the time, of course. The (subjective) probability that this case involves non-hallucinatory experience, since multiple attestation seems present, is, we might perhaps say, *very high*.
2. *Scientific misconduct*: The probability of this occurring in various scientific journals, based on a recent study, is only about .01 percent (relative frequency). I do not know if a comparable estimate of misconduct in social science and humanities is available. Alister Hardy was *first* a biologist, and knighted by Queen Elizabeth II for his work in it in 1957. I deem the probability of proper scientific conduct to be *very high*.

3. *Custody of evidence*: The competence in reporting and conveying evidence has a *very high* probability (subjective) value, since Hardy was involved, and the report came directly from a participant to the event, probably known to Hardy.
4. *Semi-experimental experience*: The experience is of a recognizable kind, for postmortem apparitions have been reported across both time and culture among the world's peoples. The probability (subjective) is *high* that the kind of item in question is not a one-off kind in human experience, but belongs to a grouping, suggesting that laws might govern its occurrence.
5. *Continuing Personhood*: The probability that the woman seen walking was identical to the person known to the theology students is *moderate to high*, since sameness of identity is generally established by nothing more than similar appearance.

These values appear dependent on one another, so their combined value might actually be a multiplication of values, the estimate of which is partially a subjective one, but not wholly so, for relative frequencies and propensities in nature are arguably embedded. I would assess the reliability as *high*.

A second main probability value needs to be considered, one that attempts to assign an epistemic weight to postmortem survival given the correctness of Perry's account of events. Since an event with multiple attestation is in view, the event provides significant grounds for asserting that (some of) the dead survive to live a postmortem life. I assign the logical probability value here as *very high*. Since the combined values seem greater than not, I regard the RSM experience of Perry and his friends as a *decisive case*. I am not offering a firm statement about the form of that existence, for example, that it is endless or immortal. I am just saying that intersubjective experience in this case warrants sufficient respect to construe it as having implications for what is real.

With this kind of RSM firmly in place, we can extend some probability to postmortem encounters that are not intersubjective. Some general arguments designed to cast doubt on the possibility of postmortem survival might begin with questionable cases, and so put the whole prospect in doubt. However, if we begin with a decisive case, the items seemingly having little evidential value, from a skeptical perspective, are given evidential significance. Other cases of a comparable character to this case can perform a similar evidential purpose. The probability values that are in play are not exact, of course, but that is how probability functions in all those cases that depart from the rare and highly idealized models in which specific values can be calculated. We need the abstract exact reasoning found in probability theory, to be sure, but its exhibition in real-life cases is exceptional. We are not dealing with cards dealt in a game, obviously, or with statistical studies of the incidence of cancer in a specific population, where readily defensible probability values are involved.

THE HERTFORDSHIRE ANGEL CASE

We can use the criteria identified earlier in order to begin the assessment of the reliability of the claim that I discussed earlier under the title "UK Angel Encounter," which took place in a small village church in Hertfordshire, near London. The occasion was a baptismal service in which the angel was seen by about thirty people, which is only half of those in attendance because the baptismal font was at the back of the church, and some did not turn around. Carol Midgley's account was quoted in Chapter 2.[15] In an interview about the incident, Emma Heathcote James reported that a young couple had moved to the area, and the wife asked to be baptized.[16] The woman was at the font near the back of the church, waiting for the rite to be performed. The rector noticed the congregation was looking intently at the woman and when he turned, there was an angel standing next to her with his hand on her shoulder. One witness fainted – she was Catholic and asked to become Anglican because of the "miracle" she had witnessed. All the people near the font of the church saw the angel. The rector gathered these people together the next day and found that they had all had the same (sensory) experience. Heathcote-James later reported "I interviewed a lot of people about that angel, and everybody told the same story. Their descriptions were totally consistent."[17] Of the 800 encounters Heathcote-James researched, 26 percent featured traditional-style angels with wings, and 21 percent featured a human form that disappeared.[18]

---

[15] Chapter 2, p. 45.
[16] This interview appears in the magazine, *Share International* (July/August 1999 issue). Heathcote-James there speaks of the rite as confirmation, but it was evidently baptism, not confirmation, since baptism, but not confirmation, involves the use of a font containing water. In her account of the incident in Heathcote-James, *Seeing Angels*, she correctly identifies the rite as baptism (p. 46). Her mistake about the correct term for the ritual conducted suggests that she is not simply speaking out of her background and has not imposed a conceptual framework on the event.
[17] Steiger and Steiger, *Encyclopedia of the Unusual*.
[18] In Heathcote-James, *Seeing Angels*, she offers percentages on the basis of a smaller database of 350 cases, and the percentages are different (p. 33).

We can evaluate this angel experience using the criteria developed in the previous section on the Lincoln College apparition:

1. *Hallucinatory experience*: This possibility seems very remote, for so many people are said to have seen the angel at once, and to have had a similar reaction to its presence. The (subjective) probability that this case involves non-hallucinatory experience, since multiple attestation seems present, is, we might perhaps say, *very high*.
2. *Scientific misconduct*: The probability of deception being involved in the report of the incident is low just in view of the fact that a reporter from one of the world's most significant newspapers was involved in obtaining an independent report. Moreover, the fact that Heathcote-James went back to the church to speak to the rector, the church warden, and to the woman who fainted, who all gave the same report each time they were questioned, indicates that the report was not marred by fraud or deception. Heathcote-James also needed to satisfy her doctoral committee at the University of Birmingham, which probably included some of a skeptical bent, I surmise, based on my own involvement with University life over five decades. I deem the probability of scientific misconduct to be *very low*.
3. *Custody of evidence*: The data that was collected did not only attract the attention of a *London Times* reporter, but because the research was reviewed by a doctoral committee at the University of Birmingham, it was given further scrutiny by a team of experts whose attitude to evidence was, I expect, demanding but fair. I consider the competence in reporting and conveying evidence to be *very high* in probability (subjective) terms. This value could be supplemented with an assessment of the (objective) relative frequency with which various groups collect and collate evidence. This topic overlaps with the previous one on scientific misconduct.
4. *Semi-experimental experience*: Experience of a recognizable kind again occurred, for reports of angels are known from around the world and across time, although we might be uncertain about the value of some of the reports from before modern times in which precautions to exclude flawed cases might not have been taken. We could say that the attitudes of modernity have put RSM claims having implications for what is real on the defensive, so that more than the usual amount of effort is required. The probability (subjective) is *high* that the kind of item in question is not an anomaly in human experience, but belongs to a recognizable kind.

5. *Integration of Phenomenological Features*: A striking feature of the encounter was the reports of "warm oil being poured out" upon those who saw the angel. Heathcote-James elsewhere describes the impact of seeing the angel as giving those who saw him – the being appeared as male – "tremendous electrifying energy."[19] The causal implication is difficult to miss, evidently advanced on the basis of Mill's methods for assessing causal connections between intersubjective objects and phenomenological features of experience. In this respect, the experience does not exhibit a causal anomaly, but conforms to the circumstances in which causation is deemed to be present in ordinary circumstances. The information is not as complete as we might find in circumstances where objects are subject to the control of a scientific experiment, but semi-experimental evidence often offers data as "just outside our reach." The probability of the claim that some anomalous object is causing a curious phenomenological effect is *high*.

6. *Personhood:* The being that appeared to the congregation evidently gave the sense of being a person, which, following John Locke, is a being with thought; intelligence; reason; reflection; the capacity to consider oneself as oneself, especially in different times and places as the same thinking being; self-consciousness; self-concern; and the capacity to be influenced by moral laws that can bring misery or happiness.[20] These nine factors are seldom applied in their entirety, since interaction with persons is often limited, but even to see an alien being interact with humans can provide a sense that the alien is a person. The sharp contrast in our experience comes from our interactions with animals, where personhood is seemingly absent.

The fact that this angel encounter was intersubjectively experienced takes it into the domain that has implications for the cosmic order. The weight of evidence here for an ontological category whose specific features are not known is still very high. Moreover, the intersubjective observation that is correlated with nonspecific sensory-like phenomenological experience gives us a probability that is high.

Encounters with angels are a subset of apparition experiences, which constitute a core experience for traditional branches of Judaism,

---

[19] Heathcote-James, *Seeing Angels*, p. 46.
[20] See Strawson, "Locke on Personal Identity" (pp. 63–67) where these nine factors are isolated.

Christianity, and Islam. The Hebrew Bible (in Genesis) describes a dozen or so apparition or dream experiences in the lives of Judaism's patriarchs, in which God is said to have made covenantal promises to Abraham, Isaac, Jacob, and their descendants. Other apparition accounts occur throughout the rest of the Hebrew Bible. Christianity describes or makes reference to a comparable number of appearances or visions of the resurrected Christ, without which the claim that he was brought back to life in some immortal form would probably never have been advanced. Islam also has its roots in an encounter with an angel, as Gabriel is said to have given the Qur'an to Muhammad. Modern apparitions or encounters with beings somehow linked to a transcendent world continue to give credibility to claims from folk religion, however incomplete these attempts appear to those who are imbued with the sophistication of the modern age. We have to factor in the possibility that accounts that have come down to us from ancient, medieval, and early modern times are flawed in various ways, and that some might be fictitious. However, I think that angel encounters are widely enough reported to warrant respect.

The angel encounter in Hertfordshire is a *decisive case* because the high combined values reflecting the likelihood that the encounter occurred much as reported, and the probability (evidential weight) that this case affords for the general claim that angels exist. Weakness in either of the two domains I have identified would render the final existential claim questionable. Other decisive cases could function in a similar capacity, further reinforcing the central claim about angels. Once a decisive claim is in place in a belief system, other claims about angels either having less likelihood or less probability become defensible from an epistemic perspective. The logical probability of H is no longer the probability of H on E, but the probability of H on E given D, where "D" is a decisive case. I will illustrate this corroborative effect of a decisive case in discussing the next case.

THE RHINELAND CASE

A case said to involve both Divine and diabolical powers was lodged with the Alister Hardy Research Centre by an Anglican priest. I speak of it as the *Rhineland Case*, and offer pseudonyms for the three men involved, in keeping with the Center's policies for the use of their collection. The events occurred in 1947 in the Rhineland, Germany. The Anglican priest who was principal in the account of the exorcism will be identified here as William, the person who underwent exorcism will be identified as Nathan, and the witness to the event will be identified as Thomas.[21]

"On the last evening of the Rhineland Keswick Convention three of us set out, at about 10:15 p.m. for a walk through a small wood which led to a village on the other side. Nathan, one of the party, started to tell the story of his life, and when we came to a clearing in the wood Thomas suggested that we should sit down for awhile. Nathan continued to relate his story. On joining the Royal Air Force he had missed the influence of home, and fell into bad company, unable to resist temptation. As Nathan finished his story there was silence. I sat with my eyes closed, wondering how I, as one of the convention leaders, could help the young fellow. What happened next was over in a very short space of time. Breaking through the silence, and crashing through the darkness with tremendous power came my voice, "In the name of the Lord Jesus Christ depart." Immediately Nathan let out a half shout, and fell toward me. He said afterwards, "At those words I saw a black form appear from somewhere at my feet and vanish into the wood, and, at the same time, something indescribable left me." I felt an urgency for prayer, and if Nathan did not pray, something would happen to him. It was at this point an event occurred so dreadful that since I have prayed that it should never happen again. It seemed as if horrifying pandemonium had been let loose; as if all the powers of hell were concentrated in that spot in the wood. I saw numbers of black shapes, blacker than the night, moving about and seeking to come between myself and Nathan, whom I was gripping hard. I saw three demon spirits, perhaps more, between Nathan and myself. These shapes were intelligences. They were different from one another. Each had a personality of its own. They began to buffet me, not striking me physically, but thrusting me backwards in spirit away from Nathan so as to make me recoil, perhaps from fear, and so loose my hold. Two other demon spirits, [were] on my left. These two were moving about with a swaying, menacing up-and-down motion, such as boxers use when seeking an opening for attack. Again I felt an intense urgency for prayer, particularly for Nathan. "Pray Nathan," I called to him, but the poor fellow could do nothing but sob. With my hands on my shoulders I cried, "The blood of Jesus Christ cleanseth[22] from all sin." Again and again I repeated the phrase. I did not notice that Thomas was silent until he said, "What a horrible atmosphere." "Pray Thomas," I commanded. "Pray for us." Together we cried with a loud voice, "The blood of Jesus Christ cleanseth from all sin." Then, after a pause, in a colossal voice such as I have never heard before or since came a verse from Scripture through my lips in terrifying power. The words were forced out of my mouth, "I give to my sheep eternal life; they shall never perish, neither shall any pluck them out of my hand." I was left absolutely gasping after this. My mouth had been stretched open wider and wider, as if the words were too big for my lips to utter. I then led with the Lord's Prayer. For Thomas this was a real climax. He saw nothing, but again felt the atmosphere change. As we reached the words, "Deliver us from evil, for thine is the kingdom, the power, and the glory"

---

[21] RERC 000248; the names I use are pseudonyms.
[22] Elizabethan English in original.

the feeling of power was immense. The atmosphere was charged with a living presence, impossible to describe. Then everything grew quiet. The air seemed soft and pleasant, as if angel voices were singing, as if a battle had ended, or a great storm had blown itself out. Nathan whispered, "Praise God, Oh what joy." We made our way back to the conference centre. Nathan could not wait until morning to share the news of his deliverance. Quite independently, Nathan told of how he had seen seven black forms emerge from the trees in the wood, and how he felt some power pushing him forward out of my grip."

This case is interesting for the visible role the evil spirits are given; they are "seen" as black shapes interfering with William and Nathan. In this respect they are not true *unobservable* objects, but they can still be theoretical objects inasmuch as their postulation takes place in a theory in which "spirit" and its synonyms or cognate forms are given a denoting role. We are familiar from the sciences with objects that begin their lives in theories as unobservables, but later become observable. One prominent modern theory in which the unobservable objects became observable is genetic theory, which began its life in the work of Gregor Mendel. His "inheritance factors" in peas, mice, and other life forms eventually became genes. Theories postulating unobservable objects in other fields of exact inquiry exhibit comparable variety, so that generalizing about them remains difficult.

By placing the evil spirits in the observable world, their causal (and other) relations to things are not in serious dispute. The spirits are described in this account in relation to William and Nathan, said to be standing in close proximity to each other. By this spatial link (and implied temporal link), which is a relation, not an attribute, the import of "evil spirit" is partly established. As a sidebar here, I observe that at this point in any serious philosophical debate about real existents, the existence of genuine persons with material bodies and the capacity to remember (some) past events is not really in doubt, so David Hume's efforts to make his phenomenalism the foundation of all reality is just not of interest. Of course we can try to reconstruct all reality in accordance with Hume's ontology, including the curious sense experiences reported by William and Nathan (perhaps even Thomas). This reconstruction of the "ordinary" world is now a distraction, for we need to construct these objects and the aberrant objects out of the same "material," which seemingly puts all of the objects on the same footing. Phenomenalists have addressed this issue in their treatment of hallucinated objects, by assigning less constancy and more unpredictability to the aberrant objects, compared to "ordinary" ones, but the ordinary distinction between hallucinated objects and real ones still remains. We have made little, if any, progress. Postulated objects acquire their "ontological weight" by virtue of their relations to things that are not in dispute, which could conceivably include God himself, depending upon the way in which theorizing has gone, although this is not the route I am proposing here. A theoretical object no longer a matter of dispute becomes an addition to a theory by means of which other objects are then added. Speaking generally, we might say that if claims about spirits are never implicated in the undisputed world that we live in, such claims acquire no "ontological grip." In this sense the foundation on which the Theory of Spirits rests is the world that is affirmed by physicalism. This will not please all theists, to be sure, but it appears to me to be enjoined upon us by an empiricist epistemic stance.

The *Rhineland Case* speaks phenomenologically in a very curious way to a cognizant, powerful force acting in and through William, so much so that he felt that the exorcizing words were forced out of his mouth. Nothing in the biblical record comes close to describing any exorcising act from the standpoint of the exorcist, and perhaps such detail is generally unavailable even now. This phenomenological detail provides some insight about the source of the exorcizing words, including some attributes that are needed for such an event. William feels the "mouth-stretching words" phenomenologically, so that insights from the internal phenomena add to the insights from the external phenomena. A "complete account," if such is even imaginable, would bring information from both sources. We might not think that God – the apparent exorcising power – would act with such force upon a person, but I get no sense from this account that William minded at all.

The correspondence with the Research Center indicates that Thomas was contacted by Sir Alister Hardy to give further details of the event, but he declined to do so. Thomas mentioned that he had written a full account of the event at the time it occurred, but had shown it to no one, and did not want to relive it for even a moment. The impression of this whole event on Thomas, who was hardly involved apart from *observing* the events that would have been observable by any bystander, perhaps, was evidently profound. His unwillingness to comment on the event, or to share the report he prepared for himself, is striking. This point is cause for some concern, for it suggests that people might observe much more in RSM experiences than they are willing to divulge. Perhaps some people fear for their safety, possibly even their lives or members of their families, if they speak too freely, which means that substantial detail is lost and might never be acquired. An implication of this feature of (some) exorcism cases is that data that might help to fill out a significant component of the Theory of Spirits is unavailable to the public. Only those implicated in exorcism understand some features of the phenomenological dimension, whose details are needed for theorizing.

1. *Hallucinatory experience*: The fact that William and Nathan are said to have seen the same dark forms meet the requirements for intersubjective observation. Their tactile, haptic, visual, and proprioceptive senses evidently cooperated in providing the detail. That Thomas saw nothing introduces a complication into the description, however. Perhaps his eyes were closed or averted, for he evidently felt a great deal. The kind of feeling here is emotional, and even though this is rarely given value as a causal effect of some indisputable reality, we have to be open to allowing the causal network to be suitably enhanced when dealing with spiritual Orders. These are only dimly known, I surmise, although emotions are often registered as having causal significance in RSM matters. The likelihood of hallucination in this case is low, in my judgment.

2. *Scientific misconduct*: I again trust the competence and integrity of the Alister Hardy Trust in handling reports that have come their way. The fact that William is an Anglican priest also contributes to the likelihood that no misconduct is present. I put the likelihood of misconduct as very low, perhaps nil.

3. *Custody of evidence*: Here again the report is submitted by the one central to the exorcism, so no third party intervenes between the incident and the report, as a possible source of error. Even Thomas's response is curiously corroborative. The custody is very satisfactory.

4. *Semi-experimental experience*: Exorcism in some detectible sense, rather than the form in which a ritual is routinely performed that is not expected to register any distinctive observation, is seemingly frequent enough to be classified as a semi-experimental phenomenon, rather than an anecdotal kind, which I discussed briefly in Chapter 3. These cases are so efficient in advancing the reality of two transcendent orders that less significant cases are apt to be ignored.

5. *Integration of phenomenological features*: The phenomenological features of the experience evidently meshed with those that were intersubjectively observable. A closer scrutiny of this would be helpful in putting to rest any questions about a specific case.

6. *Continuing personhood*: The diabolical powers symbolized by the dark shapes exhibit a curious resistance to the exorcizing authority functioning in and through William. They exhibit some of the attributes we associate with persons, including intentionality and volition, but only glimpses of the destructive minds they seemingly have are in view. Their capacity to understand the exorcizing authority speaks to their intellectual powers. The exorcizing authority in William also exhibits some of the attributes that we know are present in human persons. It is on this basis that we accord to both diabolical and Divine powers the status of minds. Whether they exhibit all the attributes that Locke considered important is impossible to determine, since Locke identified some attributes on the basis of self-awareness. Some variation on Locke's factors is seemingly present among humans, and we would be rash to think that no variations would be found among nonhuman persons. Here Wittgenstein's approach to definition based upon family resemblance is helpful.[23]

Another phenomenological perspective on the "possession" phenomenon is provided by an account also coming from the Alister Hardy collection. I shall identify the writer here as Adeline.[24]

THE CASE OF ADELINE

One evening I had spent a pleasant couple of hours with an aunt and her family in ____ and about ten p.m. was travelling by subway back [to my place]. I was in a pleasantly relaxed frame of mind – my mind idle [and] my eyes shut – when I was quite suddenly "assaulted" by a sense of Evil. I opened my eyes to see if anyone had entered the compartment of the train but it was empty, [except] for a middle-aged man who seemed to be snoozing in the corner diagonally opposite and for a pleasant looking girl who sat opposite. I was filled with an indescribable feeling of mental revulsion and horror, my mind seeming to work like that of a threatened animal as I tried to sense from where the threat came. I felt as if my mind was being threatened by some destructive force and thought it might be associated with the people in the compartment, and determined to leave the train some three stations before I should normally leave and get a tram or walk. I left the train and was aware that the evil was with me. I felt that I couldn't combat it, then argued that I couldn't recoil so completely if it were part of me and that I must pray for help. I started with the Lord's Prayer (I was walking home by

---

[23] Wittgenstein, *Philosophical Investigations*, esp. pp. 65–71.
[24] Account 001476, Religious Experience Research Center (RERC).

this time) and prayed with an intensity that sometimes made me stagger. When I came to the petition, "Deliver us from evil," I "knew" that this was the key word and phrase. I repeated [it]. I had a religious upbringing and remembered a text: "Nothing can separate us from the Love of God," and refused to let my mind think of anything but those two ideas. I went to bed and slept and woke to the horror, though I said then, "It is not with you, it is just the memory that is with you." The strange thing was that one part of my mind seemed to be in this conflict and seemed to direct me, and to reason fairly logically with me, but somehow could not reassure. I stayed in my room for a day and contemplated going [to my parent's] home, as I felt that I was mentally deranged. By the end of three days this horror had departed and the memory gradually became less vivid, but it was one of the moving factors in my life. I have no way of describing this evil force, and never thought there was a similar force till I read of the German concentration camps, and thought that this was the force that planned them.

Adeline's account is devoid of any obvious intersubjectively observable element and could not be decisive on its own, but it is rich with (private) phenomenological "observation." The account is intelligible in spite of the lack of observability of the forces involved, and we might expect to hear more accounts like hers if the diabolical orders for which I am arguing here actually exist. Adeline's account takes on a more definite hue when seen from the possibility that the *Gerasene* or *Rhineland Cases* are real. When we scour the NT for accounts of the circumstances in which those who were exorcized first became aware of their oppression, we quickly realize that no descriptions are given. This category of reality is evidently assumed to be real even in the absence of definitive criteria. One might construe the *Gerasene Exorcism Case* as "decisive" for the claim that two orders of spirit are real. I have already argued that the evidential weight of this incident is extraordinarily great, as great as the photographic tracks of the lambda-baryon particle and other particles in atomic physics. The discovery of this similarity occurred somewhere during my own critical reflections on ontological questions raised by RSM experience.

I was raised in the home of a Protestant minister, but the orthodox Christian beliefs of my Father and Mother seemed devoid of empirical support, especially those speaking of transcendent orders. They construed in spiritual terms things that seemed susceptible to a naturalistic explanation; I eventually put this down to their not having had university education. When I attended university and could "think for myself," I discovered that I had no orthodox beliefs to speak of, although I was never an atheist. Following Rudolf Bultmann, I adopted the perspective of those who "demythologize" the Hebrew and Christian Scriptures.

I did not doubt that someone known as Jesus of Nazareth existed, for example, but considered Christian beliefs about his Deity to be conceptually confused, or merely the component of a conceptual framework that did not serve empirical research. Old Testament figures such as Moses or Abraham were so remote that I hardly accorded basic historicity to them. I was suspicious of the claim that the accuracy of the NT about ordinary events, such as the rulers in various Roman provinces at the time of Jesus mentioned by St Luke, was evidence for Luke's accuracy about extraordinary events alleged, such as Mary's Virginal Conception of Jesus. Considerable time would elapse before I was able to put this suspicion into a form amenable to scrutiny using central concepts of confirming evidence theory.[25] My suspicion of the religious realities featured in NT accounts, as opposed to its accounts of ordinary events, was associated with a suspicion that the ancient world accorded uncritical credence to the idea that the course of nature can be perforated by supernatural powers. Noting that history does not take into account any intervention of God or of the Devil or of demons, Bultmann maintained that these elements should be removed from Christian faith.[26] This alternative to the literalism with which I was raised was very liberating psychologically speaking, and met with my enthusiastic assent.

I was sure that the claim that Jesus was resurrected after his Crucifixion was specious – the texts that purport to describe post-Resurrection encounters seemed too inconsistent, too flawed, to be believable, so the NT offered little by way of evidence. Moreover, the emergence of the Christian Church as a causal effect of the Resurrection seemed very weak as evidence – the *belief* that he was resurrected could provide the causal source. I surmise that the RSM environment in which one is reared cannot be eliminated easily. Such an environment affects one's epistemic stance, a stance that is possibly at variance with other important epistemic outlooks in one's culture. My studies in philosophy at the University of Manitoba celebrated the empiricist outlook of Quine from Harvard, under whom my MA advisor, Roy Vincent, had studied. There I learned the view championed by Wilfrid Sellars that accorded minimal value to the commonsense framework, and somewhere I discovered that Jack Smart conferred even less value upon commonsense. When I went to Australia to do my PhD I chose Adelaide because he was there.

---

[25] See my "Authenticating"; see Larmer, "Reply to Authenticating," p. 121ff, for his reply.
[26] Bultmann, *Jesus Christ and Mythology*, p. 15.

These views about method challenged what remained of the religious views taught by my parents. I did not understand how some impressive intellects could embrace Christian faith, and felt sure that the Theory of Spirits was being used irresponsibly. I thought that all the possible evidence concerning the Resurrection had been collected long ago, which evidence was unimpressive. I did not expect to change my view on the matter for the rest of my life.

My view of what was possible was changed by meeting some people claiming to have seen (or "seen") a being they identified as the Christ. My empirical outlook, though incompletely developed, required that each such item be considered for the implications implicit in them. I heard first hand about four or five of such claims by the time I was twenty-six, and began to be open to the epistemic and ontological possibilities arising from such evidence. I made my peace with the Church, I suppose, and then became a participant in its life, not really knowing how little of its historic teaching I initially embraced. Karl Popper's insistence that we treat claims conjecturally and look actively for evidence that might falsify beliefs, and Carl Hempel's insistence that we might also look for evidence that is confirmatory, influenced me. Charles Saunders Pierce's endorsement of retroduction (or abduction), required for assessing theories postulating unobservable objects, also struck me as insightful. So the empiricism that I adopt is shaped by major motifs in twentieth-century philosophy. Since principles of evidence are themselves subject to falsification and confirmation, my form of empiricism extends to the principles themselves by which empiricism is articulated – this "circularity" seems capable of being challenged by another level of theory. My earlier rejection of the parts of NT narrative claiming that the Christ was seen alive after his death was gradually modified, and with that has come my openness to the conjecture that spirits exist and are causally implicated in some extraordinary events. The empiricism I embrace treats RSM claims purporting to describe actual events as probabilities, which also allows possible legend (or folklore) to be included in Christianity's earliest documents. I also recognize that myths with profound theological motifs can be found in sacred writings, such as in the early chapters of *Genesis*, or the book of *The Revelation of St John*, but I consider myths to be distinguishable from legend or fact.

When I came to think that spirits (of whatever kinds) might be real, I was more troubled by the possibility that evil spirits might exist than that good ones existed who were intent on my well-being. I was dogged by what seemed to be an evil presence that I could not shake. This sense of evil – a cognition having its own particular "feel" – was more pronounced at night than during the day, when my normal duties kept my mind focused on events at hand. I could not identify its onset, and so I could not even conjecture about a possible cause. In any case, knowing the onset of some such malady might not provide a person with enough knowledge to remove it. I considered the possibility that I was experiencing a normal neurosis, but was not sure how to proceed further. After meeting and getting to know Leo Harris in Adelaide I received some practical instruction in 1971 or 1972 about resisting this dogged neurosis, or whatever it was, comparable to what William and Adeline employed. I learned later that this was the preparation Leo gave to those who seemingly needed exorcizing "prayer."

   I do not remember exactly how long I kept up a daily regimen of confronting my fear, but I know that after we purchased our first home in Canada in 1976 I was still working at it. Every night I would be oppressed by fear, and every night I would combat it by "prayer" accompanied by relevant texts, such as "I have given you authority over serpents and scorpions...,"[27] a remark attributed to the Christ. Leo taught that such a text could be appropriated by any Christian, since it was originally said to a wide group of disciples, not just The Twelve. I used to wonder if Leo's "formula" would ever work, and despaired over the prospect of having to fight with fear every day of my life. One day this all changed, however. I remember exactly where I was in our new home when I "grasped the truth," although I do not know the exact day. I was pacing the newly carpeted floor of our living room when I grasped the import of "treading upon serpents and scorpions." I was inadvertently grinding my heels on the floor as though something was being crushed beneath them. I cannot say that my sense perception was *explicitly* tactile or haptic, but it seemed perceptual. I estimate that I had been at this exercise virtually every day for about five or six years. On one specific day I "believed," but not because I chose to believe; up to that point I would say that I hoped. The attacks of fear immediately began to lessen: First I had one every two or three days, then once a week, then once a month, and for many years I had one immediately after I related this account. Perhaps I was not convinced that any spirits were real until this event.

   My experience with self-administered exorcism, if this is what it was, is a typical example of many spiritual phenomena, I conjecture, inasmuch as no intersubjective features were present in it. The events were known to me alone, and although they were extremely significant to me, they do

---

[27] *Luke* 10:18–20.

not provide impressive grounds for thinking that some spiritual Orders of reality were implicated. My grounds for thinking that such Orders *exist* arise from the *Gerasene,* the *Rhineland,* or comparable cases. A rough continuum seems to exist, but most people never encounter an extreme case capable of making an impressive ontological statement. Moreover, once the theory is in place, its aficionados gladly impose its conceptual structure on puzzling or unexplained phenomena. Authoritarian or charismatic social figures who use draconian measures around this topic, especially upon those who are psychologically vulnerable, can cause great havoc. No measures to prevent excesses can be easily found, in my opinion. When the Church exercised all the authority in Western culture, people were in some jeopardy. We might say, in general, that democratic structures need to be in place before theories postulating demonic powers are publically articulated. Also, efforts need to be expended to provide explanations that are naturalistic in character before resorting to ones postulating spiritual Orders, but having substantial democratic structures in place in society will allow competing positions to come into view. Even though I consider my own experience to belong to the low end of the fear-inducing spectrum, the fears were substantial enough for me to treat the whole topic with caution. I realize that personal experience, which might be purely phenomenological, as in my own case, might be given too great a place in (one's) epistemology, but it could also be given too little.

POSTMORTEM EXISTENCE

The possibility that humans might exist in some form after death has exercised the human mind so appreciably that various models of the form this might take have been offered and debated. Here I will survey some notable empirical approaches that do not simply rely on specious arguments, such as the claim that because the soul is simple (without parts), it cannot fall apart.[28] Perhaps these arguments have more merit than I am able to see, for some very notable intellects have adopted them; here I restrict my attention to empirical matters.

RESURRECTION

A view of human immortality (or survival) might include the belief that a human might be resurrected from being a dead corpse. Professor

---

[28] Plato advances a form of it in *Phaedo* 92–95; cf. Augustine, *Trinity,* bk. 6, chap. 6.

John Hick (1922–2012), who taught at the Universities of Cambridge, Princeton, and Cornell during his career, and held chairs at both Claremont Graduate University (US) and The University of Birmingham (UK), asserts that two examples of *resurrections* can be found in Hinduism from the last one hundred years:[29] Sri Yukteswar Giri is said to have appeared after his death (in 1936) to Paramahans Yogananda in Bombay (Mumbai), and Sri Yukteswar is said to have seen his own guru in 1895. These claims as *resurrections* would be spectacular if they were true, and would allow Hinduism to rival Christianity as far as significant postmortem events are concerned. We could generalize Hick's view to suppose that anyone seen as an apparition after death has been resurrected, as Hick evidently does; their number would be impossible to estimate, I surmise.

I do not doubt that these gurus saw (or "saw") their own gurus, but Hick is surely wrong to view these as instances of *resurrection*. Resurrections share with postmortem apparitions the feature of having a deceased being appear to an onlooker in a form similar to that in which they were known in life. However, a defensible claim to resurrection also involves having a corpse *disappear or cease to exist*. If we were to observe a resurrection take place before our eyes we would presumably see a corpse become a living being, so that after the event was over no corpse would exist at all. A skeptic might understandably wonder if the person had really been dead, for "dead men do not rise," supposedly. Seeing an apparition understandably causes its observer to conjecture that postmortem existence in some form is possible, but if the two gurus were resurrected, we might legitimately demand evidence that their bodies had disappeared. Hick is surely wrong to assert the reality of resurrection merely on the basis of apparitions. Actual apparitions naturally raise questions about the nature of postmortem existence, but resurrection is not a probable outcome on those grounds alone. These remarks have a bearing on the Christian claim that the Christ appeared on earth, and that he was resurrected several days after his death.

The conditions necessary for a resurrection include (a) that a given person is indisputably dead, (b) generally, that a postmortem apparition of that person be seen by someone or other, and (c) that the corpse of the dead person no longer exists, since the corpse has become a living being. When we review the unbelievably large literature around the resurrection of Jesus, we discover that disputes swirled around for some time

---

[29] Hick, *Disputed Questions*, p. 42; cf. Yogananda, *Autobiography*.

concerning the question of his actual death,[30] although most scholars now concede his death.[31] Christic apparitions obviously satisfy the second condition mentioned earlier, although probabilities again enter the picture; NT evidence on this topic is complicated. The disappearance of the corpse of the Christ is a fascinating problem, and much has been written arguing that the textual evidence from the NT is *sufficient* to defend the claim that his body could not be found because it had disappeared. I cannot see textual evidence as doing so by itself, however, especially in view of the voluminous criticism of the NT texts, much of which calls into question their historicity.

A curious piece of evidence relevant to the Resurrection has emerged in the last three decades from examinations of the Shroud of Turin, *quite apart from the identity of the Man exhibited on it*. Three laboratories were given samples of this cloth in 1988 in order to carbon-date it. The slightly different specific findings from the laboratories in Tucson, Zurich, and Oxford were not publicized in the announcement that summarized their work, probably because news sources are reluctant to impose too many numbers upon an information-saturated public. The medieval date given to the Shroud (1260–1390) was disappointing to those who thought it was ancient in origin, and linked in some way to the Christ. A careful review of the specific findings from the three laboratories is of interest, for one can hardly argue that incompetence, fraud, or deception occurred. The C_{14} findings from the three laboratories exhibit statistically significant differences, some statisticians say,[32] for even in cloth samples a few centimeters apart a difference in C_{14} is detectable. Since carbon dates depend upon the ratio of C_{14} to ordinary carbon, C_{12}, and consequently upon the number of neutrons (not protons) in the nuclei of these atoms, the variation in neutrons suggests that a *neutron-flux* accounts for the differences.

Physicist and historian of physics, Thaddeus Trenn (1937–2013),[33] introduces the term *weak dematerialization* to describe a conjecture

---

[30] See the recent questioning of crucifixion in Samuelsson, *Crucifixion in Antiquity*.
[31] See Evans and Wright, *Jesus, the Final Days*, for a discussion of the conservative consensus.
[32] See Walsh, "Radiocarbon Tests Reconsidered," http://web.archive.org/web/20040422010105/, www.shroud.com/nature.htm, and http://web.archive.org/web/20040428023751/ (accessed May 18, 2018); cf. Rucker, "The Role of Radiation in Image Formation on the Shroud of Turin," www.academia.edu/28946606/Role_of_Radiation_in_Image_Formation_on_the_Shroud_of_Turin (accessed October 11, 2022).
[33] Trenn, "The Shroud of Turin," p. 131.

offering to account for the mysterious fluctuations. He supposes that the additional C_{14} (besides that already present in the original Shroud cloth, deriving from flax used to make linen) arises from the dematerialization of the atoms of the body that once lay in the Shroud. In order for dematerialization to occur, the Strong Nuclear Force binding the nuclei of the atoms of the Man featured in the Shroud was overcome, thereby *releasing* the subatomic particles (including neutrons) forming the atoms involved. To accomplish this, according to Trenn, energy would need to *be supplied to* the body of the Man, energy sufficient to replace the binding energy found in an object weighing about eighty kilograms (the estimated weight of the Man). This is a calculable amount, roughly that found in "twenty-nine atomic bombs." Moreover, since the mass of a man of 80 kg (≈176 lb) would take up about 2.8 cubic feet of space, this amounts to about 10 atomic bombs in a cubic foot.

Trenn is here envisaging sufficient energy coming *from outside the body* to overcome the Strong Force binding the atomic nuclei forming the atoms of his body. Various effects from such a conjectured dematerialization might be expected, including the production of a gaseous flux of neutrons and protons.[34] The protons would chemically bind (explosively) with oxygen to form water, and some of the neutrons would strike nitrogen (N_{14}) atoms in the linen of the Shroud, converting these atoms into C_{14}. The result would be variation in concentrations of radiocarbon, the highest amounts found in the center of the cloth along its entire length, where the body earlier lay. Trenn's conjecture is testable, and consequently scientific. Determining whether C_{14} distributions are uniform on the Shroud could be tested by placing photographic film upon the Shroud laid out flat, encasing both in sheets of lead in total darkness, and then reviewing the results a day or so later.[35] This test could provide startling new evidence for the conjecture that the image was caused by a Man who "broke apart at the subatomic level." However, this test could also falsify Trenn's conjecture, making us wonder again whether another conjecture might be found supporting the claim that a body disappeared in a way required by a resurrection that no one witnessed. If the Shroud image is that of the Christ, it offers some evidential support for a Resurrection claim that is otherwise deficient; if the Shroud image is of some other person, it reveals the evidence that Christianity needs but does not have, suggesting that someone else underwent this extraordinary end to his life.

---

[34] Trenn, "Sketch and Highlights of Resurrection Model". Private correspondence (2007).
[35] Trenn, "The Shroud of Turin: Resetting the Carbon-14 Clock," p. 129.

A curious implication of this conjectured weak dematerialization can possibly be seen in the blood which has evidently oozed from the wounds of the Man onto the Shroud, such as at the Man's wrists. No fraying of the cloth fibers containing blood is seen, confirming the conjecture that something dematerialized the body of the Man in the Shroud, including his blood, but did not touch that blood already soaked into the Shroud. This discriminating yet intensely powerful Mind exhibits power far exceeding the strong Nuclear Force, but the claim features testability. The Creator God might be implicated, especially insofar as manipulation of the building blocks of matter is in evidence, but nothing in the conjectured events requires omnipotence. Given the ongoing apparitions of a being continuing to be identified as the Christ, and given the possibility that his corpse disappeared, the Resurrection of Jesus becomes a testable notion. Although apparitions of Mary continue to have great significance in the Christian Church, the claim that her body and soul were taken into heavenly glory seemingly has no object as a by-product of her alleged Assumption to corroborate it, comparable to the Shroud. Evidential support for the Assumption is uncertain. Philosophy offers its practitioners a remarkable degree of freedom, often (relatively) free from the influence of governments, universities, grant-councils, foundations, seminaries, and churches – at least this is how I experience it in my homeland of Canada.[36] I applaud the Catholic Church's imposition of (apparently) austere conditions on anyone claiming that a miracle has occurred. If a miracle is simply an event in which a nonhuman spirit can be implicated, then I have no difficulty with the claim. However, claims that natural laws have been overridden are another matter, and require special epistemic attention.

MARIAN APPARITIONS

In extending my critical reflections on apparitions to Mary, the Blessed Virgin, I wish to examine the apparition at Knock, Ireland, on August 21, 1879. The figures of the Blessed Virgin Mary, her husband St Joseph, St John the Evangelist, and a lamb on a plain altar appeared over the gable of the village chapel, enveloped in a bright light.[37] The official

---

[36] Cf. the remark in Corte, *Who Is the Devil?* (Kindle, Locations 66–68). "This definition is a dogmatic one, which all Christians are obliged to accept. All must subscribe to it not only outwardly but inwardly, by a genuine act of faith."

[37] See the basic information provided at www.miraclehunter.com/marian_apparitions/approved_apparitions/knock/index.html (accessed October 11, 2022).

eyewitnesses include three men, six women, two teenage boys and a girl, and two children, who observed the spectacle for as many as two hours in the pouring rain. Within a year some three hundred cures were reported at the site.[38] The event was investigated and approved, following the strict measures adopted by the Roman Catholic Church for investigating such claims. This apparition provides grounds for postmortem survival, at least for the humans featured in them, but it does not address the peculiar nature of this kind of human life, or the general likelihood of postmortem survival. The healings said to have occurred in conjunction with Marian apparitions, not only at Knock but also at Fatima, Lourdes, and Medjugorje, are seemingly causally connected – the presence of the healings (and other peculiar phenomena) are either a causal effect or concomitant of the apparitions.

More details about the nature of the apparition at Knock suggest that the variations described are consistent with the kind of evidence typically given about an observed event from a variety of witnesses. It was seen both before the sun had fully set and also just after it was set,[39] ruling out some obvious play of light on the chapel gable. Although rain poured in substantial amounts on the apparition, the figures did not appear wet; moreover, the silvery glow they exhibited did not diminish during this downpour.[40] Some of the witnesses saw the figures so clearly that they could see eyeballs, including the iris and the pupil, although the boy, Patrick Hill, who reported this, did not know the exact names for the parts of the eye.[41] Patrick lived in Claremorris, which is about nine kilometers from Knock, and was bringing peat home from a nearby bog. He dropped in to see his aunt who lived in Knock, when Dominick Beirne (also spelled Byrne) came into the house and excitedly reported that miraculous lights and beautiful visions were seen at the chapel in Knock. He and three others, including a small boy, John Curry, went to see the spectacle. In John MacPhilpin's recounting of the testimony from fifteen witnesses, he describes Patrick's account as the fullest. The small boy, John Curry, gave substantially the same testimony as the other witnesses, but much abbreviated; he reported that he saw "beautiful images, the Blessed Virgin and St. Joseph."[42]

---

[38] See www.marypages.com/Knock1.htm (accessed October 11, 2022).
[39] MacPhilpin, *The Apparitions at Knock*, chap. 4.
[40] Ibid., chap. 5.
[41] Ibid.
[42] Ibid.

Patrick reported seeing a full-blown rose just under the crown worn by the Blessed Virgin, but no one else did. He said he saw angels, their faces veiled, fluttering around the Lamb, but other witnesses say they saw lights, not angels. He reports seeing a cross behind the Lamb, and perpendicular to the altar, but not upon the Lamb or touching it. Others offer conflicting testimony on exactly how the cross was positioned in relation to the Lamb. Patrick reported that he observed the extraordinary spectacle for an hour and a half, during which time he was drenched by the pouring rain. He got so close to the figure considered to be St John, who wore a bishop's miter, that he could see the lines and the letters from the book that St John seemed to be speaking from: "He appeared as if he were preaching, but I heard no voice." The witnesses were consistent in saying that the figures appeared lifelike, but since they said nothing, something about the whole vista gave the sense that they were not alive in the sense that we associate with living humans who breathe, act, speak, move, and so on.

Bridget Trench, also from Knock, was in the house of Judith Campbell when Mary Byrne came in and reported that a remarkable sight was to be seen at the chapel. When Bridget arrived at the spot where the three figures were visible she threw herself upon her knees. She reports "I went in immediately to kiss, as I thought, the feet of the Blessed Virgin, but I felt nothing in the embrace but the wall [of the chapel], and I wondered why I could not feel with my hands the figures which I had so plainly and so distinctly seen." The three motionless figures that she saw were statue-like and "seemed raised about two feet above the ground." She later reported that although rain was falling very heavily "no rain fell where the figures were. I felt the ground carefully with my hands and it was perfectly dry. The wind was blowing from the south, right against the gable of the chapel, but no rain fell on that portion of the gable or chapel in which the figures were." She stayed about an hour to observe and reverence the mystery to which she was privy.

An Ecclesiastical Commission of inquiry was struck by the Archbishop of Tuam on October 8, 1879, which concluded that no natural causes of the events could be plausibly offered; fraud was also ruled out.[43] The Archbishop did not rule in favor or against the apparition. A second Commission was struck in 1936, and the surviving witnesses confirmed the evidence they had given in 1879. Over time the Church came to

---

[43] "Knock Shrine," Wikipedia, https://en.wikipedia.org/wiki/Knock_Shrine (accessed November 23, 2017).

view the event as an authentic apparition of Mary, which climaxed with a Papal visit to Knock in 1979.[44] We can evaluate this event in terms of its evidential value, much as I did above with other cases. The relevant categories are similar to ones used above, but the case has its own peculiarities.

1. *Hallucinatory experience*: Having fifteen people report similar observations about the extraordinary sight rules out hallucination. Also, one would think that if hallucination were operative, a witness such as Patrick might have begun to hallucinate at his aunt's house, just when he heard that an extraordinary event was taking place. Assigning the experience of mass hallucinations to just the spot where the witnesses congregated involves in incalculable improbability and is also too convenient a method of dismissing these witnesses. I consider the absence of hallucination to have a *very high probability*. This estimate includes a factor arising from an estimate of human *propensities* to hallucinate, which is a probability interpretation that does not satisfy the Probability Calculus.[45]
2. *Misconduct (scientific or otherwise)*: The fact that various personnel of the Catholic clergy were involved in the interviews of those who allegedly saw the apparition, where the Catholic Church itself seems to treat apparitions with aloofness, requires that accounts meet a sizeable burden of proof. Fraud was ruled out, leaving the witnesses in a favorable position on having reported reliably. The fact that a second Commission was struck some fifty-seven years after the event means that those reporting their experiences of nearly six decades earlier were able to evaluate the original experiences with some detachment. The simplicity of some of those who reported is mentioned by John MacPhilpin, and I suppose this includes having little education in matters that generally undermine the believability of RSM claims. Perhaps those that believe RSM claims, after having dismissed them, might exhibit comparable dispassionateness. I deem the probability of proper conduct in the handling of evidence to be *very high*.
3. *Custody of evidence*: The witnesses were evidently examined within two months of the incident, so the eye-witness testimony was still fresh in memory, I surmise. Moreover, having a committee

---

[44] "The Apparition at Knock," https://theotokos.org.uk/the-apparition-at-knock/ (accessed November 25, 2017).
[45] See Salmon et al., *Introduction*, chap. 2.

of clergy to examine the experiences of the laity allows the clergy to offer an assessment without having clergy influence the assessment. One of the witnesses went to the parish priest's house to tell him what she had seen, in an effort to arouse his interest, but he evidently showed none. He could have been an influential ally, had he gone over to see for himself, but he did not.

4. *Integrated experience*: The experience of Bridget Trench calls for some comment, since she fully expected, it appears, to have an experience in which her visual sensation was integrated with her tactile and vestibular sensation. She did not deliberately attempt a reality check, apparently, given her account of the matter, but was surprised when the usual integration of experience was not forthcoming. The accounts from the fifteen witnesses generally give the impression that something was peculiar about the figures that appeared. They are described as lifelike, but they neither moved appreciably nor spoke. Judith Campbell reports that she came within a foot of them. They did move back toward the chapel when people came quite near, but they evidently did not "walk." Moreover, being raised above the ground gave them an air of unreality. Bridget also checked the ground near the apparition in order to determine whether it was wet. It had not appeared wet, and indeed was found not to be. This is, in effect, a second reality check of her visual powers, and they were functioning as they should.

5. *Continuing Personhood*: No obvious method of establishing continuing personhood with the biblical notables is possible. Perhaps the real purpose behind the apparition is to call attention to the values advanced by the Christ, which are represented, to varying degrees of success, no doubt, by the institution he is credited with having created.

6. *Implications for ontology*: I assume that Bridget was the only one of the fifteen witnesses who attempted to embrace and kiss the feet of the one she took to be the Blessed Mother. The fact that she was unable to do so speaks to the peculiar character of the figure that appeared to Bridget. If no one else had commented on the peculiar character of the figures that appeared, we might conclude that Bridget's experience was hallucinatory. In view of the common observations among the visionaries, I surmise that the visionaries at Knock were privy to a form of reality that is obscure, but related to human beings that earlier existed. The sizeable number of witnesses suggests that they indeed saw something (not merely "saw"

something), capable of reflecting photons of light (or generating them). This incident is sufficiently like innumerably many reports of apparitions of the dead, and warrants consideration on that count alone.

7. *Conceptual Framework*: I have chosen this account of Marian apparitions because it is approved by the Church, because it involves a sizeable number of witnesses, and because it comes from a time and place with which Western thought is familiar. I expressed some concern earlier with interpretive frameworks that include "marvels and miracles" adduced to provide support for religious or spiritual interpretations of the cosmos. These sometimes appear to be imposed on phenomena, even in twentieth-century Melanesia perhaps, where, according to anthropologist Bronislaw Malinowski, the causal agents responsible for human conception were considered to be *baloma* (spirits), not conventional sexual intercourse.[46] This position is seemingly not the consequence of careful and critical observation. Rather, a "spiritual" framework appears to have been presupposed for the elucidation of data needing explanation – we might understandably wonder how animal husbandry could flourish in Melanesia. The Marian apparition in 1879 in Knock does not appear to involve imposing a conceptual structure (or paradigm) upon an event so that it has been given a RSM significance, where it actually had none. We know enough about British culture to know that Ireland was free to shed its ancient beliefs and legends, and to adopt modern biological knowledge. Melanesia's situation is different, seemingly, since its prevailing view of something as fundamental as human conception was out of step with basic biological knowledge. Modernity's intellectual forebears also explained phenomena by a generous appeal to the efficacy of spiritual agents.

I am impressed with the evidence from Knock, and consider the reported event to be authentic.

NEAR-DEATH EXPERIENCES (NDES)

I surmise that the importance of NDEs for the twentieth century (and beyond) cannot be easily overestimated. RSM views of the cosmos seemed

---

[46] Malinowski, *Magic, Science and Religion*, p. 220ff.

on the brink of being eliminated completely, at least in Western thought, influenced, as it was, by Marxism, positivism, and naturalism, but the NDE has given pause to drawing this far-reaching conclusion. The exact nature of NDE might not be known, but it portends something weighty and substantial. It might not have great ontological weight, but it has significant psychological force. Philosopher and physician Raymond Moody is credited with having coined the acronym "NDE," and his description of a "typical NDE" is a suitable starting point for considering the question whether it has much to teach us about ontological claims. The features Moody identifies are the following:[47]

1. Hearing pronouncement of "death"
2. Hearing an uncomfortable noise
3. Feeling that one is moving through a long dark tunnel
4. Finding oneself outside one's own body, but capable of seeing one's own body in the normal environment
5. Emotional upheaval over resuscitation attempts
6. Awareness of new body
7. Awareness of strange properties of the new body
8. Awareness of "spirits" of other already-dead people
9. Inability to communicate with the living, although often attempted
10. Encounter with being of light
11. Evaluation of one's life, and playback of major events
12. Approach of a barrier incapable of being crossed
13. Required to return to normal life
14. Reluctance to return
15. Feelings of intense joy and peace
16. Reunited with physical body
17. Reluctance to share experience
18. Ineffability of experience
19. Profound impact of experience on life
20. New views of death

Moody observes that no single experience seems to have all of above properties; also that no single property is found in all experiences, that some NDEs have no experiences of the above kind in them at all, and that the order of events varies. As a class of experience, it continues to offer new insights. Writing in 2017, Jeffrey Long, a medical doctor who has collected personal accounts from over 4,000 patients deemed dead or

---

[47] Moody, *Life*, passim.

near dead, writes "Although no two near-death experiences are identical, it is remarkable that in thousands of reports there are consistent patterns of elements. This fact is part of what gives us confidence in their veracity."[48] His summary of the typical content of an NDE includes elements[49] that highly resemble the summary offered by Moody.

On the surface, the epistemic weight of NDEs seems negligible, since the content of a NDE is known only to the person having undergone it. On the other hand, NDEs might be capable of filling in other kinds of knowledge related to dying and death, giving us a fuller picture of a reality that might be missed had it not been for NDEs undermining the overconfident outlook of naturalism. While I do not see NDEs on their own as providing "decisive cases" for spiritual realities, once sufficient grounds are adduced for credible claims for the Divine and diabolical spiritual orders, the bar of evidence concerning postmortem human survival has been either reduced or left intact; it certainly has not been raised. My strategy in this book has been to leave postmortem human life as a challenge to be evaluated in light of other evidence for spirits.

One of the features of NDEs that continues to evoke conjectures about the state of being experienced in an NDE is the later recall of phenomena that could not be generally known, such as the discovery that a sibling has died during the time a subject undergoes an NDE, or even novel phenomena that seemingly require a vantage point outside the body of the subject, such as reports of shoes being "seen" from inside a hospital when they are only visible from a vantage point outside the hospital. In another place I recount the experience of one of my students – I shall call him "Adam," a pseudonym of course – who reported an NDE in a hospital to which he was taken after losing one of his legs when a train ran over it. He reports that he saw his body stretched out on a hospital bed, but the point of view was beyond the walls of the room in which his body was located, and above the ceiling of that part of the hospital. This kind of perceptual memory is perhaps quite common, and Moody reported similar cases already in 1975. The reliability factor in this report given to me by my student is not apt to enjoy the high level I accorded to A. J. Ayer's NDE account in Chapter 2. I actually consider my student's account to be highly reliable, knowing that his account of the experience was not made an object of public speculation and that it has remained consistent over a thirty-year period. Here we encounter our curious capacity to view

---

[48] Long, *God and the Afterlife*, p. 11. Dan Klassen drew this to my attention.
[49] Ibid., p. 11.

some claim at a "distanced" perspective, and simultaneously to view it from the personal perspective without which life could not be effectively lived. One of the impressions that RSM experience gives is that such experience is primarily personal rather than public – as though the cosmos is created with a feature to it that does not yield its insights unless the public, scientific perspective is held in abeyance. This is an uncomfortable position for those for whom "scientific method" is all we have when it comes to knowledge, and remains disquieting for me. However, this other perspective seems to be forced upon me.

The "scientific perspective," so-called, supposes that I should view the NDE that my student reported as hallucinatory. My earlier remarks about hallucinations being generated by stress, or sexual deprivation, or excessive fasting, or incessant prayer all hold water for me here – none of them have plausibility. These psychological efforts to explain aberrant perceptions are at best a very poor approximation of the places to look for causes. Much more impressive is the view of the Perceptual Release Theory, which supposes that memories of perceptions, feelings, cognitions, and more, get jumbled up and dropped into conscious experience in much the way they are dropped into unconscious experience where they are experienced as dreams. This *Theory* supposes that at some time in Adam's past he had a perceptual view of a hospital room and a body on a stretcher with his head closest to the wall while the torso and legs were stretched out into the room; also the sense of looking at his own body from a vantage point behind the location of his head and higher than the ceiling of his room; as well as the feeling of being resuscitated by an emergency team so that the apparently lifeless body was revived; and so on. We can understand the memory of being in a hospital, of being on a stretcher, and of being resuscitated (both perceptual and the feeling), since these are events that happened to him – to his body, we might say – but what about the other perceptions? Exactly how did he cobble together "memories" that included the unique perspective of his room where his body lay, of being outside that room and above the ceiling? The defender of the Theory just insists "Oh, we will find out where this came from in due course; don't trouble us with our conjecture of hallucination." To which my reply is "Well, Adam's disembodied perceptual view involving 'a-something-we-know-not-exactly-what', conventionally known as the human spirit, is not absurd, and does explain something in his collective memory upon which the other conjectures cannot improve. Maybe it will in time, in which case the Theory of Spirits will be successfully supplanted."

6

The Future of Religious Experience

In Chapter 2, I identified four key questions to the critical scrutiny of a Theory of Spirits, the fourth being "Is the Theory indispensable to a complete view of the cosmos?" In order to interact with this question I will briefly look at an interesting and possibly important phenomenon taking place even now in the nation of Japan.

THE FUKUSHIMA PHENOMENA

In March 2011, an earthquake having a magnitude of 9 on the Richter Scale struck the northeast part of the Island of Honshu, Japan's main island. Although the earthquake was not a surprise, for seismologists had been predicting one, the immensity of the tsunami that followed was a surprise. The effects of it continue to be keenly felt, with perhaps as many as 50,000 people still displaced from their homes as recently as 2017.[1] To complicate the issues facing Japan, the Fukushima Daiichi Nuclear Power Plant was inundated by the tsunami, causing its cooling system to fail, which resulted in a nuclear meltdown and the discharge of radioactive materials. Japan has suffered much more devastating earthquakes than this one, but the associated tsunami unexpectedly killed more than fifteen thousand people, with several thousand still unaccounted for as of September 2017.[2] A striking concomitant of all this disaster continues to be registered in the RSM beliefs and practices of the Japanese people, including the "ghosts" getting rides from taxis, which I will comment on further below.

Richard Lloyd Parry, Asia editor of *The London Times*, reports meeting a priest in the north of Japan who (allegedly) exorcised the spirits of people who had drowned in the tsunami at Okuma, on the east coast of Japan. Parry writes:

---

[1] Oskin, "Japan Earthquake," *Live Science*, September 13, 2017.
[2] Ibid.

"Reverend Kaneda's first case of possession came to him after less than a fortnight [after the tsumani]. He was chief priest at a Zen temple in the inland town of Kurihara. The earthquake on 11 March 2011 was the most violent that he, or anyone he knew, had ever experienced. ... Nearly twenty thousand people had died at a stroke. In the space of a month, Kaneda performed funeral services for two hundred of them. ... Amid this numbness and horror, Kaneda received a visit from a man he knew, a local builder whom I will call Takeshi Ono. ... [who] had been at work on a house when the earthquake struck. He clung to the ground for as long as it lasted; even his lorry shook as if it was about to topple over.

"Ten days after the disaster, Ono, his wife and his widowed mother drove over the mountains to see for themselves. They left in the morning in good spirits, stopped on the way to go shopping, and reached the coast in time for lunch. As the road descended towards the coast, their jaunty mood began to evaporate. Suddenly, before they understood where they were, they had entered the tsunami zone. ... There was no advance warning, no marginal area of incremental damage. The wave had come in with full force, spent itself and stopped at a point as clearly defined as the reach of a high tide. Above it, nothing had been touched; below it, everything was changed. No still photograph was capable of describing it. Even television images failed to encompass the panoramic quality of the disaster, the sense within the plain of destruction, of being surrounded by it on all sides. ...

"Ono, his wife and his mother sat down for dinner as usual that evening, [and] ... afterwards, and for no obvious reason, he began calling friends on his mobile phone. 'I'd just ring and say, "Hi, how are you?" – that kind of thing,' he told me. 'It wasn't that I had much to say. I don't know why, but I was starting to feel very lonely.' His wife had already left the house when he woke the next morning. Ono had no particular work of his own, and passed an idle day at home. His mother bustled in and out, but she seemed mysteriously upset, even angry. When his wife got back from her office, she was similarly tense. ...

"And so his wife and mother described the events of the night before, after the round of needy phone calls. How he [Ono] had jumped down on all fours and begun licking the tatami mats and futon, and squirmed on them like a beast. How at first they had nervously laughed at his tomfoolery, but then been silenced when he began snarling: 'You must die. You must die. Everyone must die. Everything must die and be lost.' In front of the house was an unsown field, and Ono had run out into it and rolled over and over in the mud, as if he was being tumbled by a wave, shouting: 'There, over there! They're all over there – look!' Then he had stood up and walked out into the field, calling, 'I'm coming to you. I'm coming over to that side,' before his wife physically wrestled him back into the house. The writhing and bellowing went on all night until, around five in the morning, Ono cried out, 'There's something on top of me,' collapsed, and fell asleep. 'My wife and my mother were so anxious and upset,' he said. 'Of course I told them how sorry I was. But I had no memory of what I did or why.'

"It went on for three nights. The next evening, as darkness fell, he saw figures walking past the house: parents and children, a group of young friends, a grandfather and a child. 'They were covered in mud,' he said. 'They were no more than twenty feet away, and they stared at me, but I wasn't afraid. I just thought, "Why are they in those muddy things? Why don't they change their clothes? Perhaps their washing machine's broken." They were like people I might have known once, or seen before somewhere. The scene was flickering, like a film. But I felt perfectly normal, and I thought that they were just ordinary people.' The next day, Ono was lethargic and inert. At night, he would lie down, sleep heavily for ten minutes, then wake up as lively and refreshed as if eight hours had passed. He staggered when he walked, glared at his wife and mother and even waved a knife. 'Drop dead!' he would snarl. 'Everyone else is dead, so die!'

"After three days of pleading by his family, he went to Reverend Kaneda at the temple. 'His eyes were dull,' Kaneda said. 'Like a person with depression after taking their medication. I knew at a glance that something was wrong.' Ono recounted the visit to the coast, and his wife and mother described his behaviour in the days since. 'The Reverend was looking hard at me as I spoke,' Ono said, 'and in part of my mind I was saying, "Don't look at me like that, you bastard. I hate your guts! Why are you looking at me?"' "Kaneda took Ono by the hand and led him into the main hall of the temple. 'He told me to sit down. I was not myself. I still remember that strong feeling of resistance. But part of me was also relieved – I wanted to be helped, and to believe in the priest. The part of me that was still me wanted to be saved.' Kaneda beat the temple drum as he chanted the Heart Sutra. ... Ono's wife told him that he pressed his hands together in prayer and that as the priest's recitation continued, they rose high above his head as if being pulled from above. The priest splashed him with holy water, and then suddenly he returned to his senses and found himself with wet hair and shirt, filled with a sensation of tranquillity and release. 'My head was light,' he said. 'In a moment, the thing that had been there had gone. I felt fine physically, but my nose was blocked, as if I'd come down with a heavy cold.'

"Kaneda spoke to him sternly; they both understood what had happened. 'Ono told me that he'd walked along the beach in that devastated area, eating an ice cream,' the priest said. 'He even put up a sign in the car in the windscreen saying 'Disaster Relief', so that no one would stop him. He went there flippantly, without giving it any thought at all. I told him: "You fool. If you go to a place where many people have died, you must go with a feeling of respect. That's common sense. You have suffered a kind of punishment for what you did. Something got hold of you, perhaps the dead who cannot accept yet that they are dead. They have been trying to express their regret and their resentment through you." Kaneda smiled as he remembered it. 'Mr Bean!' he said. 'He's so innocent and open. That's another reason they were able to possess him.' Ono recognised all this, and more. It wasn't just the spirits of men and women that had possessed him, he saw now, but also animals – cats and dogs and other beasts which had drowned with their masters. He thanked the priest, and drove home. His nose was streaming as if with catarrh, but what came out was not mucus, but a bright pink jelly like nothing he had seen before."[3]

We could analyze this account using the criteria in Chapter 5, I suppose, where what I described as decisive cases came into view. How well it

[3] Parry, "Ghosts."

would fare is unclear. Certainly the source in Richard Parry, an editor for *The London Times*, provides very significant credence to what he researched, given the status of this newspaper in the world. The apparent concurrence of Ono, his wife, and Rev. Kaneda contribute to its authority as an account of actual incidents.

The reality of postmortem existence (in some form or other) comes into clear view with the account that Ono and his family gave of his experience, as well as with the research into "ghost" riders, creating questions about the extent to which such data is available from Earth's locales in which naturalism has stifled the voice of "naked religion," not particularly constrained by faith traditions in which interest in the departed has significantly evaporated. Perhaps postmortem encounters are much more numerous than naturalism concedes, such as the one offered by Perry and his friends; by the friends of my brother-in-law who reported that something was producing disturbances on their property, which all disappeared when a funeral was provided for the man reporting that his murder had not been avenged; by my cousin who saw his mother in his hotel room moments before the nearby hospital informed him that his mother had just died; and by innumerable accounts found more in popular culture than in academic culture. Perhaps naturalism in the West – through education, through academic books and journals, through research supported by educational religious institutions, through influential newspapers whose editors are schooled by naturalism, and so on – is managing to keep its adherents and sympathizers ignorant of phenomena that speak of postmortem survival, including NDEs that speak to this part of "The Theory of Spirits"?

The reprimand of Ono given by Rev. Kaneda concerning the conditions in which his life became so porous by other spirits is troubling, for Western culture, including its forms of the Christian Church, that may have made itself vulnerable to (largely unrecognized) dark powers that intend the total destruction of that which is enhancing of and wholesome in human life.[4] Ono displayed a casual, irreverent attitude toward the dead, for which he was recompensed by being possessed (seemingly) by having his porousness exploited. We might wonder whether Ono

---

[4] The account here from Richard Lloyd brought to mind an incident about which I had almost forgotten. I once attended a funeral in which the undertaker handed out multicolored felt markers to those standing around the coffin so they could write some parting remark on the coffin just before it was lowered into the ground. He made the whole event flippant and lighthearted, removing the traditional solemnity that committal of a corpse into the ground has historically had (in the West).

was hallucinating, of course, and also wonder whether elements of the prevailing religious belief system among traditional Japanese people contribute to the interpretation given to it. However, Rev. Kaneda said that many Christian, Shinto, and Buddhist priests were performing exorcisms, so a larger RSM perspective seems in order.

Knowledge of these recent phenomena of "possession" in northern Japan seems to have been triggered by an article published in 2016 in a journal about "the ghost problem."[5] After this article was published some researchers at Tohoku University began to catalog the stories. Yuka Kudo, a major in sociology at Tohoku Gakuin jocular University, interviewed one hundred taxi drivers for her graduation thesis, and found seven drivers who had "phantom passengers," that is, drivers whose passengers had "disappeared." The drivers reported that although their meters had been started, their passengers became unpaid fares – "ghosts" who generally appeared as young people.[6] "One of the drivers told Ms. Kudo that a woman climbed into his taxi near Ishinomaki Station just a few months after the disaster. She asked him to go to the Minamihama district, to which the driver said there was nothing left standing there because of the Fukushima tsunami. The driver recounted that the woman asked, 'Have I died?' and, when he turned to look, his taxi was empty."[7] This account appears to be typical of those deriving from this place of devastation, which indicates, at the very least, that the belief in postmortem survival is based on evidence. Even though those who report having seen mysterious beings connected in some way with the tsunami of 2011 cannot say exactly what it is that they encountered, these phenomena bolster traditional beliefs that people somehow "survive" bodily death and generally have more epistemic weight than NDEs.

In Figure 2.3, I sketch a view of the social sciences in which the attributes, behaviors, and interactions of (human) persons come into view. I construe religion as one of these sciences, although in obvious dependence upon many fields of inquiry, perhaps once simply identified as Psychology, Sociology, Anthropology, History, Linguistics, Economics, etc. These social sciences have expanded exponentially as university departments and private corporations have sponsored research on persons, both individually and collectively, and on social structures, whether "natural" or contrived. The relative wealth of governments and

---

[5] Takahashi, "The Ghosts of Tsunami."
[6] Ryall, "Taxi drivers in tsunami disaster zone."
[7] *Ibid.*

benefactors since World War II has allowed information to be gleaned on a vast array of topics not available prior to the twentieth century. The commonsense framework in which everyday life is lived – once the dominant framework for understanding human attributes and relationships – has given way substantially to perspectives bearing scant resemblance to their originals. The relatively simpler concepts in the commonsense framework, out of which complex studies have evolved, look comparatively anemic and inadequate as sources of profound insights. This contrast is undeniably clear when we look at commonsense views of nature and their modern counterparts in the physical sciences. The question with religion, and spirituality in general, is whether their concepts, also found in the commonsense framework, have the capacity to resist the inevitable changes that close, critical studies bring? Will RSM views of aspects of life with fairly obvious reliance on concepts readily recognizable as spiritual or religious be replaced with more sophisticated and better researched concepts than those now associated with the RSM outlook?

Including RSM studies in the panoply of exact studies would bring about a change at the level of paradigms, perhaps, not simply at the level of theories considered worthy of careful and critical study. I have been speaking freely about The Theory of Spirits, but my remarks might extend beyond a theory to a paradigm. My understanding of naturalism is that it is quite indifferent about the number and complexity of social sciences, perhaps now collected under established headings, or under some variation that offers no offense to physicalism's predilections. If RSM studies were to be admitted into this domain without excising the Theory of Spirits, or any comparable or equivalent conceptual structure, physicalism's confidence that in letting physics be the foundation of the natural sciences and in allowing psychology to be the foundation of the social sciences, naturalism has yielded its hegemony over some significant intellectual issues. The Theory of Spirits would be seen as problematic whether it is a paradigm (conceptual framework) or a theory. I am reluctant to insist that the Theory of Spirits be interpreted as a *paradigm*, for paradigms are often viewed as arbitrary choices, or at least ones that might be devoid of significant rational defense. I reject this construal of both paradigms and the Theory of Spirits, but cannot take the space to defend this claim about paradigms. I am attempting to articulate this Theory of Spirits clearly enough that if it is false, it is *fairly clearly seen* to be false. I add the qualifier here because theories postulating unobservables are not straightforward.

One of the obvious benefits of higher education is that those who acquire it are exposed to competing interpretations and conceptual frameworks of the cosmos, or significant portions of it, which demands evaluation of these competing views. Education tends to confront people not only with different theories, but also with different conceptual frameworks (paradigms) in which those theories are embedded. Here conceptual frameworks that are *imposed* on theories and phenomena explained by them are apt to be identified as such – this is an unempirical move evidently designed to preserve some portion of belief systems, which only calls the move into question. Naturalism is an immensely powerful framework, for good or for ill, and anyone interacting with RSM experiences in places where naturalism is ascendant might also be conversant with traditional conceptual frameworks, such as the one that Ono exhibited. Retaining the traditional framework, in the face of naturalism's efforts, gives tradition more epistemic weight than it would have it if did not have to compete for consideration. Just as a theory that competes successfully for consideration against others is thereby rendered more plausible than its competitors, a similar phenomenon at the level of paradigms might be detected. Here the idea articulated by Karl Popper about the greater relative value of theories that have withstood falsification is apparent, and no reason exists that I can see for withholding a similar epistemic principle concerning paradigms that compete for credibility.

SPIRIT POSSESSION AND ATTACHMENT

The interpretation that Ono gave of his bizarre and frightening behaviors, including possession by pets, perhaps of those who died at Fukishima, is astounding. When people exhibit the behaviors of animals, such as Ono did, who "had jumped down on all fours and begun licking the tatami mats and futon, and squirmed on them like a beast," perhaps the conjecture that spirits of animals exist, and can inhabit a human being's body, begins to be plausible. Of course we would want assurance that such people are not simply acting, which is not a trivial matter to assess, and may take much observation. Comparable beliefs about the spirits of beasts possessing humans can be found around the world, including claims about shape-shifters in (local) Indigenous North American cultures, as well among the cultural groups examined by the first (acknowledged) anthropologist, Edward B. Tylor (1832–1917), who observes that the "Hindus settled in Chota-Nagpur and Singbhum firmly believe that the Mundas[8] have powers of witchcraft, whereby they can transform

---

[8] This is a tribal group from south-east India.

themselves into tigers and other beasts of prey to devour their enemies, and can witch away the lives of man and beast."[9] These claims about possession by animal spirits must be subject to the constraints I have placed around "decisive cases," in my opinion, in the absence of which we can justifiably minimize their value for theorizing about ontological matters.

The data coming recently from north-eastern Japan take us substantially into the question of postmortem existence. Postmortem beliefs about human beings are one thing, and beliefs about "possession" of people by animal spirits are another. I will not offer an assessment of the latter, since I am unsure that an adequate database exists lending credence to the conjecture. Such data would have an obvious bearing on reincarnation claims, about which I also wish to keep an open mind.

In a fascinating study by Frederick Smith on possession by deities and spirits in the literature and culture of South Asia, he identifies several forms of possession and attachment. These give the impression that the human self is porous, or susceptible to influence, even possession, by some other agency, the identity of which is not always clear. Smith describes a tradition according to which actors who lose self-control and became too strongly identified with, say, a bloodthirsty heroine, might become possessed: "a clear lack of distinction [exists] between spirit or deity possession, intense absorption in emotion, and acting." He cites instances gathered by Sarah Caldwell from Kerala in which actors who accidentally killed another themselves died of grief during the performance.[10] C. D. Wallis, in a doctoral dissertation titled "To Enter, to be entered, to merge: The role of religious experience in the traditions of Tantric Shaivism," observes that "the selfhood revealed by the Tantric materials [unlike Brahamical texts] is, as we have noted, not only mutable and fluid but also porous and permeable: it can overlap and intermingle with other beings, powers, and energies."[11] In this respect the notion of self may seem more porous than the standard view in Western thought, but a review of possession in Western literature also calls a fixed view into question.

Smith says that possession is traumatic "in just the way that disease or enlightenment can be" ... "[I]t is an experience of alterity, a fundamental,

---

[9] Tylor, *Primitive Culture*, p. 114.
[10] Smith, *Self Possessed*, p. 353, citing Caldwell, "Bhagavati: Ball of Fire."
[11] C. D. Wallis (2014). *UC Berkeley*. ProQuest ID: Wallis_berkeley_0028E_14665. Merritt ID: ark:/13030/m5zp79nv, https://escholarship.org/uc/item/4p0666qj (accessed October 11, 2022).

even unrecognizable strangeness, within the individual. It is the outsider within the complex individual, with his or her narrative of identity, who evaluates and comes to terms with the multivocality within."[12] Smith observes that the Indian Constitution preserves the ambiguity of the concept standing for an individual, so that possession is more readily possible than in conceptual and linguistic contexts in which the individual is well defined.[13] Smith reports that a long tradition exists of seeing possession as an aspect of "a women's religion," rather than "a man's religion," which is "supposedly more intellectualized and ritually formulated."[14] In oracular possession, however, this imbalance is corrected, and women give expression to ideas with which men can relate. In keeping with his analytic interests, Smith distinguishes various kinds of possession, which includes a psychological event, a social or sociopolitical event, a kind of shamanism, and "a 'real' incursion of spirits or deities to be taken at face value."[15] Smith does not shy away from making what I would describe as provisional ascriptions of ontic reality. The exact criteria by which these states can be distinguished, presumably by an observer, are not offered.

Smith observes that from a vast literary source, "possession [was] induced in prepubescent youths."[16] Smith conjectures about the practice, wondering if youths were used to try to obtain information about future events, or events occurring in another place, because they were regarded as pure and morally neutral. Much of this possession is viewed as innocent, but destructive spirits known as "childsnatchers" are also known to exist, capable of possessing children, even fetuses.[17] Inducing Deity possession in children is known from Chinese practices, but it is also found in South Asia, the area that Smith is particularly interested in. A child is taken, bathed, anointed with fragrances, and clothed in pure white garments; spells are said while the child's hair is plaited, then the child's hands are filled with flowers; next incense is crushed and scattered, then rice is scattered in the vicinity of the child, then more spells are said, and when the child trembles then the possession is complete.[18] I once witnessed violent trembling in a Pentecostal Church, where prayers had just been said over a young man who wished to be "filled with the

---

[12] Smith, *Self Possessed*, p. 587.
[13] Ibid., p. 588.
[14] Ibid., p. 70.
[15] Ibid., p. 78.
[16] Ibid., p. 448.
[17] Ibid., p. 445.
[18] Ibid., pp. 435–36.

Holy Spirit." The young man began to speak in what sounded like a possible language to me, but I understood nothing of what he said; he trembled so fiercely that his words came out in staccato. One of the older men who prayed for the young man had spent a number of years in Africa, including South Africa. He said that he recognized what was being said. I was quite frightened by what I observed, but was comforted by the fact that this older man was unfazed by the events of that evening. He had become a high-school teacher in our city, which gave me some confidence that he might have looked at religious events (at some time earlier) with some detachment.

Although Smith identifies South Asia as his object of particular interest, his work has implications for a wider context. He offers some insights on the literature of other areas of Asia and leaves the unmistakable conclusion that studies into the RSM experience of an area are aided by knowledge of texts that offer a history of that experience. Smith also recognizes that first-hand acquaintance of ongoing RSM experience requires the relevant linguistic and cultural knowledge. I approach this topic assuming that the Occidental cases that I have featured in previous chapters would be matched by ones deriving from the Orient. This too is a conjecture that is subject to possible confirmation or disconfirmation.

In keeping with the argument of Chapter 5 over decisive cases, I wish to limit my affirmations to (a) the existence of Divine beings intent on our well-being, and of (b) evil spirits who are intent on our undoing, and of (c) the uniqueness of human beings as either having or being spirits. These are the three existential orders with which I am particularly concerned, especially the first two, not for the countless other beings variously construed as real in different parts of the world, such as the spirits of animals. The three orders admit of evidence that varies substantially with the kind of experience adduced. Perhaps most of the cases that are evidentially efficacious in the mind of some experiencer, or observer, are well below an evidential limit that we can describe as decisive. However, prior beliefs about the experiences of others, in addition to many indefinable factors found within a social stratum or community, might be innumerable, but the *rationality* of such beliefs depend upon the kinds of features I have been throughout this book, especially in the Chapters 4 and 5. The phenomena that have suggested "possession" to observers, or possibly to participants in "possession," are so extensive that they constitute the basis for many books. I cannot claim great expertise, although it is obviously related to my central interests; I have been focused in my own thinking on the subject on the ontological questions that are raised by experience, in particular, which RSM experiences among the innumerable allegations should be seriously considered.

I view ontology as central to the main thrust of philosophy in the Greco-Roman-Christian tradition (Western tradition). It functions, in my view, like each of the other major fields of philosophy (identified in Figure 2.2), and we can see seminal similarities in their structures.[19] Perhaps Logic gives us as clear an outline as any other area, so I will start with it. The philosophic study of deductive logic begins with a review of all the inferences made by people deemed to be valid (truth-preserving). Then the critical phase occurs, when the claims of validity are called into question, and mechanisms (such as The Propositional Calculus) are introduced that offer to distinguish valid from invalid inferences. This critical phase is itself subjected to every critique we can consider, such as reviewing The Propositional Calculus for consistency – a logical concept – in an effort to prevent any inference from receiving commendation that is not truth-preserving. We cannot guarantee that no circular reasoning is present, but if general rules of inference cohere with – another logical concept – the particular inferences very widely deemed to be valid, a system is in place. Deductive logic is an important place from which we choose to begin, for anyone calling into question The Propositional Calculus, or the inferences it permits, must either make a claim for which no reasoning is offered or makes one that is dependent on reasons (logic). If no reasons are offered we are faced with bare-faced violence, and if reasons are given they will require logic. If the logic is said to be other than that exhibited in The Propositional Calculus, some defense for that logic (such as the Hegelian-Marxist, or a three-valued, or an infinite-valued logic) will need to be offered, which requires appeal to some rules of inference. Managing to evade The Propositional Calculus is a very tall order.

The "justifications" of inductive logic or epistemology exhibit a similar structure. We canvass all the instances of confirming evidence (induction) that are adduced, both individual and rule structured, such as the ones I considered in Chapter 3. We then canvass them for logical consistency, assuming that deductive logic is among the structured portions of philosophy that are already justified. If we find inconsistent cases, as Hempel seemed to find in various combinations of principles, each considered reasonable in itself, then some decisions must be made about the nature of confirming evidence. We will consider every rule of induction, and every supposed instance of induction, and try to ensure that no instance

---

[19] I was influenced on this topic many years ago by Goodman, *Fact, Fiction, and Forecast*.

that withstands critical scrutiny is eliminated, and that every rule avoids approving an indefensible instance. In the rough parity between rules and instances the structure of inductive logic comes into view. I submit that a similar justificatory effort is found in epistemology, ethics, aesthetics, general value theory, and ontology. Perhaps my claim about aesthetics might seem to be the most difficult to argue, but I will not try to do that here, since ontology is of chief interest.

We must be cognizant of the effects that language has on the phenomena described. Terms that another language uses that are untranslatable into our language of choice can be understood by construing them as denoting things, attributes, or relations to other things whose existence is not in dispute. By learning the language around the term in question, it too acquires meaning, although it might remain untranslated. We can easily bring to our own attention the terms that are given none. Perhaps it goes without saying that my sentiments are much more with modernity than post-modernity, but that is a matter for a very long discussion, especially inasmuch as I think that post-modernity has brought significant issues to light. My intellectual background is Western, and the religious influences in my life are primarily Christian. I was influenced for a time by naturalism, which is tantamount to a religion since it quite readily takes a (negative) view on the reality of spirits. My conversion to Christian faith occurred during a forty-year period (ca. 1968–2008) during which time I came to some (probabilistic) conclusions that are largely ontological. Since every theorist has ideas embedded in some grand narrative, whose parts are only known in fragments to their possessors, I prefer to let my reader know about my own (limited but significant) perspective. We may aspire to view the universe *sub specie aeternitatis*, but we do not know exactly when this is achieved, since this is a philosophic problem about philosophy itself, hence so remote from general inquiry that those who attempt it lose most of their audience. We might secure this perspective more often than we ever know.

IS THE THEORY OF SPIRITS DISPENSABLE?

The question whether the Theory of Spirits is dispensable is a question about its probable future viability. The question has to do with importance of the theory, and its likelihood to either escape any effort at reducing it unscathed or to escape in a recognizable form. Most of the items symbolized in Figure 2.3 are theoretically open to modification, as more data about the cosmos is obtained. Commonsense claims are characteristically subject to change, since this is the portion of the view of the cosmos that is being replaced by the sciences, all aided by mathematics, in order to give us a quantitative understanding, not just a qualitative one. The replacement of common sense can result in certain theories disappearing, because they are too flawed to be modified. The Theory of Phlogiston belongs in this category, inasmuch as it postulated a substance, phlogiston, supposedly found in everything combustible, and driven out by heat. This Theory has suffered the expected fate of the Theory of Spirits among those who identify themselves as physicalists or naturalists. Dan O'Brien, philosopher at the University of Birmingham, makes a remark that is representative of common philosophic opinion: "Certainly, at one end [of the spectrum], ontologies such as those concerning demons or phlogiston should be eliminated."[20] The other end of the spectrum for O'Brien is a *reduction* of "that ghostly substance thought to inhabit human bodies" by way of the Identity Theory – although this way of putting the contrast overlooks the numerous variations that have been proposed by theorists sympathetic to materialism.[21] Those for whom neurophysiological *identities* will take the place of specific mental states (or processes) will find some merit in offering descriptions using the familiar mental terms. We could describe the end result as involving two conceptual frameworks, one mental and the other neurophysiological, and since both are capable of asserting true properties or relations, the mental framework would continue to have value. The Identity version of the future of mind–body discussion preserves truth, hence significance.

The interesting question about the Theory of Spirits is whether some option comparable to the Identity Theory is feasible. The prevailing view among materialists seems to be that the likely reduction for the Theory of Spirits is some version of elimination. Attention is sometimes drawn to the replacement of the theory that accounts for psychopathic behavior in terms of the demons that assail people. For example, in *Speaking of the Devil* psychotherapist Carl Goldberg asserts that he can explain malevolent behavior more convincingly than any demon hypothesis by conjecturing the existence of shame, contempt, rationalization, justification, inability or unwillingness to self-examine, and magical thinking.[22] This assertion construes this part of the Theory of Spirits as having been supplanted by a version that makes reference to mental states, and on

---

[20] O'Brien, Review of *"The Emergence of Consciousness."*
[21] Stoljar, "Physicalism."
[22] Goldberg, *Speaking with the Devil*, pp. xii–xiii.

the supposition that the kinds of mental states he offers can be reduced, his proposal is naturalistic. If Eliminative Materialism asserts the most plausible future for mental states, Goldberg's theory would disappear in favor of some neurophysiological account of behaviors once said to be caused by demonic spirits. In the approach I am taking in this book I do not construe matter and spirit as substances that exclude one another by definition. Spirit gets its ontological status by virtue of being placed in causal contexts where evidence for causal interactions includes relations with objects whose existence is not in doubt, including material ones. I do not try to rule on the ultimate "stuff" comprising spirits; I do not try to rule on the scope of "ontology," but am arguing that it needs to be expanded from the narrow perspective seen in naturalism.

In order to consider the impact that reduction of the Theory of Mental States might have on events in which spirits are said to be implicated, I will look at the experiences that Pauline Langlois reported to me as part of my study of Christic visions (reported above as *Case 2* in Chapter 2). She reported that a man she took to be the Christ appeared to her as she lay in bed contemplating suicide, then touched her with his hand to comfort her. She finally threw restraint aside, reached out her hand and touched his side, which felt solid to her touch. He stayed there for some time and then just faded from view. I will look at the events central to Pauline's experience as we now understand them. She evidently had *memories* of significant events that she considered to be spiritual in character. These memories are obvious instances of mental states, which, according to the Identity Theory, consist of neural events whose neurophysiological structure is now coming into view. These memories are of events the least controversial of which are the memories of lying in bed, of wanting to take her own life, and of worrying about the care her young daughter if Pauline were to die. These memories are not all of sensations but still of rather ordinary matters. The more difficult part is the memory of sensing a presence in her room even though she saw nothing at first. I take it that a physicalist interpretation of the cosmos, specifically the Identity Theory, might baulk at the source of this memory, for to admit such phenomena as felt presences, in the absence of conventional sensations, is to begin to concede assertions typically made by the Theory of Spirits. We can hardly view the memory of sensing a presence as concocted, since the sense of presence is a well-known phenomenon. The source of the sensed presence is the main question here. The Identity Theory evidently wishes to provide a physicalist explanation of all psychological phenomena in terms of physical objects, their properties and their relations to other physical things. This is the point at which the Identity Theory will contribute to an understanding of the claims made by the Theory of Spirits, for the Identity Theory will offer an explanation of the unique form of sense of presence reported by Pauline in physicalist terms. It may provide a causal account either by locating the origin wholly within the neural resources of Pauline herself, in which case her experience of this sense of presence is hallucinatory, or it will provide an explanation that refers to some object not considered by physicalists to be part of the cosmos at all – a development that would mark the end of physicalism. Similar remarks are relevant to the sensations she remembers having had, including the sensation of being touched, seemingly by the one whose presence she felt without seeing or tactilely feeling anything. She then remembers extending her hand and gingerly touching the man's side. Again, the reductionists among us expect the Identity Theory to have such competence in determining the causes of such mental states as being touched by or touching another that the problem of the origins of Pauline's memory of both will be solved – Pauline either hallucinated these experiences pertaining to tactile touching or she was actually touched by some mysterious object (being). In this way the efforts of the Identity Theory will shed light on what are now mysteries.

Physicalism asserts that *all* of the mental will eventually be explainable by physicalism, and it is for this reason that RSM experiences will eventually end up in its laboratories for analysis. Experience of this kind is often ignored, for naturalistic theorists seem to assume that it will easily resolve into neural structures now under investigation. This might be far from the truth. The analytic work predicted to be a part of the coming reduction will be helpful to the whole domain of RSM experience, for it will address the question of how sensation arises. With ordinary objects laboratory analysts will readily identify the way in which neural structures change from alterations no more significant than changing the (ordinary) color or shape of (ordinary) objects that are set before a (ordinary) viewer, with (ordinary) sensory abilities. This process might eventually end in every mental state found in some observer being describable using the language of neurophysiology, not that of (ordinary) mentalism. However, the question of whence the neural states (once mental states) arise will presumably be answered along with the description of those neural states. The efforts of physicalism will eventually shed light on RSM experience. RSM is not vulnerable now to being overtaken by physicalism's efforts, for little effort is being expended to document the nature of RSM experience in sufficient detail to give direction to physicalism's efforts; it could be vulnerable in the future, however. We could concede to naturalism that it will effectively reduce the ordinary mental states, such as those found in Ryle's *The Concept of Mind*. This would not touch the domain of RSM experience for a description of it, comparable to Ryle's description of ordinary mental states does not yet exist. The cataloguing of RSM experience has hardly begun. My work on Christic visions strongly suggested that comparable phenomena had occurred in various places in the world, but very little was known of them, so completely had Christic vision been ignored.

Empiricist philosophers once confined their attention to "immediate perceptions" that were experienced by a subject, as though we might consider these without considering the objects that gave rise to one kind of perception rather than another. Philosophers once considered their task to "show that an external world exists," that is, a world external to a perceiver; in fact, since the perceiver was supposedly a construct, attention was given to the little bits of immediate perception, as though we might "construct" the brown table in the corner and even the perceiver from immediate perceptions, and assert that only perceptions exist. This was a miserable time in philosophy, and philosophers made their vocations look foolish and extravagant in a world where real mysteries exist. The rise and success of physical atomism has given us back "the ordinary world," and now the challenge is how we might "construct" everything from the micro-constituents of (physical) atoms. The question how we might manage mental states takes on a new look, certainly much more promising than the one that traditional empiricism offered. Physicalism might of course discover that Pauline had sensations, not merely "sensations," of a man, perhaps a man whose properties are obscure. We could call him a spirit, of course, to stay with the tradition suggesting that spirits might not be comprised of conventional matter. No injury would be done to RSM experience if physicalism were to find that its constructs could barely describe the being she touched. However, physicalism cannot claim that it already knows all there is to know about the inner cosmos, and the Theory of Spirits will endure until the Theory of Mental States is reduced, if that ever happens.

THE FUTURE FOR RSM EXPERIENCE

The remark in Parry's account that Buddhist, Shinto, and Christian priests were all involved in exorcism is an important one, for it offers evidence concerning behavioral disorders that overcame people to such an extent that they or their families have sought exorcism. Some might think that their particular (form of) faith "has the corner on" exorcism, but such accounts of rituals from around the world suggest that this is not so. The exorcism phenomena said to be occurring in Fukushima, involving priests of three religions, speak to widespread beliefs concerning both diabolical forces and Divine ones. The (possible) insights from all these traditions suggest that the problems that are deemed to be ameliorated by exorcism are not so esoteric as to be unrecognizable. While Christian exorcists might think that their tradition is the most insightful, we need to be cautious. Christian faith considers Jesus of Nazareth to be "the true Christ," whose insights into the human condition exceed those of every other human, and while this claim has a probability above zero, it is not so well established that we can endorse it without evidence. I take it that when Rev. Kaneda exorcised Ono, if that is what indeed happened, Rev. Kaneda made no reference to the Christ or the authority that he is said to have given his followers. We could find some Christian exorcists to be less successful than their counterparts in Shinto or Buddhist faiths. While I personally think that Jesus is "the Christ," I have recently come to think of Hebrew-Christian faith in a slightly different light than those who are triumphalist about it.

I was brought up to think that Hebrew-Christian faith was superior to every other faith, and that they were in competition with each other. Perhaps I was too focused on questions of truth, which would be normal for a philosopher, and not enough on questions of love, which have the capacity to touch every person in the world, no matter how philosophical. I have begun to think that the Christ would be less about proving himself right than proving himself helpful, if he were somewhere near at hand. The Hebrew-Roman historian, Josephus (ca. 37 ≈ 100 CE), attributes knowledge in the Hebrew tradition of how to conduct exorcisms to their King Solomon, claiming that he saw Solomon's methods used in his own day by a man named Eleazar,[23] in front of Vespasian, the Roman emperor. This ritual was supposed to cause the demoniac to fall to the ground, whereupon the demon was instructed to overturn a basin of water some distance away, in order to prove to onlookers that it had indeed left. So the Hebrews incorporated some physical effect left by an unobserved (assumed) being, thereby giving some credence to the reality of the postulated being. This effect is not proof, of course, but it would be evidence. Neither ancient nor modern peoples, which I assume the

---

[23] Josephus, *Antiquities*, bk. 8, chap. 2, Para 5. Cf. Perkins, "Greater than Solomon."

Japanese to be, are wholly irresponsible in their handling of interpretations of RSM experiences. Some curious remarks in the NT synoptic Gospels claim that the Christ's ability to perform exorcism was greater than people had previously observed.[24] In an important sense, he perhaps represents a climax in the ability to exorcize, as though all the comparable efforts the world over find their highpoint in him. This is what we might expect the Christ to do, without diminishing human efforts that are not as impressive, but still directed to the wretched oppressions people have not even been aware of, except most inchoately, as Ono, who knew that he should not mock the dead.

In several other areas the Christ expresses a climax in human efforts to find and pacify, perhaps, God or the gods. We know that all over the earth people have offered sacrifices to atone for their errors, to entreat the gods for help with their lives, their families, and their children, to enhance their ability to find enough food, and so on. In some ancient cultures, perhaps even in many, people go to extraordinary lengths to ensure that their entreaties might be heard, even to the point of giving their children as living sacrifices in a ritual whose actual effects, if any, could only poorly be matched with their efforts. The ancient Hebrews knew about this and were instructed not to do the same as others were doing: "You shall not give any of your offspring to offer them to Molech, nor shall you profane the name of your God; I am the LORD."[25] This gives expression to inherent dignity and value in all humanity, including the children. We could perhaps say that the ultimate insight concerning sacrifice is that said of the Lamb of God, who takes away the sin of the world. Christians are not in one mind about how this should be finally interpreted, and have focused a great deal on differences from one another in beliefs. One other area in which the nations of the world are insightful has to do with recognition of "the Great Spirit" who created all things; such views are common among North American Natives and also across Africa. The Christ perhaps takes this to a deeper level in speaking of a Father whose name is holy, and whose will is good. Also, the belief that peace might be sought and found, to the satisfaction of the one pursuing, is a prevailing value in various religious traditions. The Christ offers peace, although how it compares with that encountered in other religious traditions, or even independently of specific traditions, is unclear. One of the pursuits that Thomas Merton will be most remembered for is his

---

[24] See *Matthew* 9:33, and *Luke* 4:36.
[25] *Leviticus* 18:21.

exploration of the mysticism pursued by his Trappist community and the peace for which Zen Buddhism is known.

Religion strikes me as capable of the foulest evils that humanity has ever invented, and perhaps this goes along with the thought that religion might also bring us our most lasting and noble goods – a Platonic note, of course, often expressed by Socrates. Perhaps I am most conscious of the flagrant wrongs of Christianity – the faith that is supposed to present all that which in finest in the Christ – because I live in the West. Perhaps all religions are comparably corrupted, but the perspective from which this is most authoritatively seen might come from other religious traditions. Religion seems to be most susceptible to diabolical distortions when it is used for personal aggrandizement – and this might apply across the board, including what we see in Western expressions of Christendom. It also applies to the use of children to obtain forecasts of future events, as Frederick Smith has documented.

The future of RSM experience lies with the research of those who are most familiar with a culture and its RSM traditions. No single person has a comprehensive enough view of all the diversity that is present in a culture or to the nuances of meaning in descriptions of RSM experience. This fact was brought home to me in researching Christic visions and apparitions. I found a possible subject, and after asking her some standard initial questions and then getting her responses I realized that I did not have enough French and that she did not have enough English for each of us to understand the other fully, at least at the level where nuances are vital. I personally cannot imagine that I have the capacity to enter adequately into the phenomena reported in Fukushima, but people with language skills in Japanese could provide an interpretation of what those who report encounters with ghosts are saying. Adequate studies of RSM experience are not in place. When I think of the domains sometimes advanced to more-or-less describe the scope of Christendom – Roman Catholic, Eastern Orthodox, Anglican, Lutheran, Calvinist, Baptist, Pentecostal – I am hard pressed to direct students to inquiries about RSM experience in some particular Christian tradition. A particular tradition needs to be identified, since possible biases need to be noted, as well as the impact of such biases on the review of specific kinds of RSM experience, for example, Roman Catholics may be found to be more sympathetic than Protestants to Visions of Mary, and such a bias might be discovered in evaluation of Marian visions. The requisite detailed study of RSM experience either needs to be much more widely publicized, if it has been done, or needs to be undertaken. If I am right in thinking that this is the domain out of ontological claims emerge, then the viability of religion is dependent upon such studies. We conduct detailed studies in every conceivable domain (of experience), so we might expect that a similar database is needed for religion to remain plausible, whatever the form this might take. I construe the description of RSM experience to have begun especially with the work of William James and Alister Hardy, described in Chapter 1. Other authors have also pointed the directions for more inquiries.

In view of the likelihood that some accounts that form part of the history of some religious tradition resemble accounts in that tradition, we do well to identify the kinds of RSM experience that appear to occur often enough to form a semi-experimental bodies of data. If visions of angels appear to be frequent enough in the Church of the Latter Day Saints to form a semi-experimental body of cases, we would do well to collect RSM experiences seriously around this heading. We cannot tell in advance of very detailed studies what data we actually have, from which plausible reasoning might begin. It goes without saying, perhaps, that the original (or favored) language of the one having had a vision needs to be the language in which data are collected. This places a constraint on visions of angels which come to us from antiquity, or the medieval world. We cannot assert without argument that one description is translatable (or not) into another language. A position on this matter would be consideration of specific cases, to see how they fare under translation. A similar caution applies to accounts from antiquity or the medieval era – a particular language can undergo enough changes in meaning to make equation of one account with another from a different century problematic. Historians who are concerned about accounts deriving at particular stages of inquiry I am envisaging here, along with linguistic specialists, are needed to appraise the historicity, or otherwise, of accounts deriving (or appearing to) from a particular era.

Theorists having familiarity with competing paradigms and competing theories would also be important among those attempting to evaluate the overall evidential value of particular evidence claims. This desideratum was already made in remarks earlier in this chapter and arises quite naturally from the kinds of features of reports and the theories offered for them made in Chapter 3. Religion already appears to be among the most interdisciplinary studies found just from a review of the features of it identified in six of the seven fields of inquiry mentioned by Ninian Smart earlier (excluding experience).[26] The features of critical (but

---

[26] See the Preface of this book, p. vii.

sympathetic) philosophical inquiry that I am attempting to incorporate here are fundamental to epistemology, whose delineation is not complete. The modern age has developed some (competing) views of what this *must* look like for advancing the description of the world on which we have substantial agreement. Some of these features are found in the evidential principles that I discussed in Chapter 3. But disagreements about such principles abound and continue to present challenges for epistemology. Only in some ideal world do principles vital to Religion, including RSM experience, appear to be open to assessment. We almost live in such an ideal world now, perhaps, where research is openly conducted in public universities, and researchers do not have pressure exerted upon them to draw specific conclusions, although I expect that we would not find full agreement on these criteria being met even in such a country as Canada. I am thinking primarily about the degree of freedom to discuss cases and allegations that have a bearing on the question whether spirits exist.

Both naturalism and supernaturalism, as competing ideologies, can exist in forms and circumstances that exclude each other. The ascendancy of the Christian Church has at times prevented the articulation of naturalism by those opposing religion, for instance, by the Christian Church in European countries whose Christian governments prevented or opposed naturalism within universities such as the control exhibited in European universities during the seventeenth to nineteenth centuries. In like manner, those with political power in Socialist countries exercised their ideological power to allow the advancement of atheism, and allowed Christian (and other religious) thought to be suppressed. We live in a time in which atheism is allowed significant expression, and the status of religion as either a rational or an irrational perspective is allowed to be debated. The freedom of expression is articulated in various ways in countries that have articulated the right to freedom of religion, which generally means that activities deemed to be religious are apt to be reviewed by civil courts that attempt to determine whether those activities fall into the parameters and constraints created by legislation. The "decisive cases" that I am discussing in this book seemingly provide rational grounds for advancing religious claims, so that in some particular circumstances religious claims are rational; of course religious claims might also be found to be irrational much of the time. The discussion of rationality itself is part of this study, which means that the foundation with which a particular "science" is conducted is also in question. The precise import of "rationality" cannot go ahead of specific cases, and specific cases cannot be plausibly considered outside their "natural" context.

The freedom to examine conceptual frameworks, and propose new ones or variations on old ones, is a significant indicator that evidence is being allowed to take its place in our deepest deliberations. Whether we can trace or identify the fields where evidence is rational or irrational is a leading question and can stifle further discussion. A sizeable tradition has emerged that considers foundational principles of evidence to be beyond evidence itself – a point where a priori perspectives are said to emerge. I cannot explain my own predilection for the view that questions about evidence are never exhausted, but this might itself be a function of my early university studies in science and mathematics that might have produced the confidence that various measures for reconstructing the studies needed to illuminate the structure of knowledge can be found – not imposed, we might hope – and that the resulting introduction of exact concepts will not misrepresent some field of inquiry. I will confess that the universe at times seems amenable to exact inquiry using defined concepts that are put in place of their "natural" counterparts, whereas at other times its intricacies seem just outside our reach.

The two estimates of key values, namely, the reliability of an evidence report, and the probability that an event has occurred meeting its description, are matters on which we can achieve some agreement, I suggest, although it means that we consider RSM evidence reports in a particular way, and with specific constraints, such as

1. Have one small committee assess the reliability of an evidence report, and another assess the probability that the alleged event occurred much as described (perhaps independently of one another), and then change the tasks for the two committees.
2. Include in the committee addressing the reliability of an account people who are familiar with the language used in reporting, as well as any biases likely to be included in this reporting, including biases about ontological commitments.
3. Allow close questioning of those giving RSM reports; this activity can be psychologically intimidating, and some measures must be in place to mitigate this. Perhaps one way of mitigating intimidation is by allowing a friend of the person providing a first-hand account to be present during questioning. This committee should also include a well-educated advocate for the one reporting the RSM experience.
4. Include researchers who are familiar with paradigms, and the possibility that paradigm shifts are involved in description. Researchers

with various degrees of familiarity with the structures exhibited in theories are ideal candidates for inclusion on the committees

The evaluation of RSM experience for claims about what is real is in its infancy, I surmise. I have attempted to disentangle the problem of the reliability of an account from the problem of the epistemic weight of that account. My proposals here are open to further criticism and refinement, of course. In these and other ways RSM experience will increasingly be seen to have significance for the question: What is real?

Bibliography

Alston, William. *Perceiving God: The Epistemology of Religious Experience.* Ithaca, NY: Cornell University Press, 1991.

Aquinas. "Summa Theologica," *Encyclopedia Britannica.* Translated by Fathers of the English Dominican Province and revised by Daniel J. Sullivan. Chicago: The University of Chicago Press, 1952.

Aristotle. "Metaphysics," translated by W. D. Ross and "De Anima," in Richard McKeon (ed.), *The Basic Works of Aristotle.* Translated by J. A. Smith. New York: Random House, 1966.

Augustine of Hippo. *On the Quantity of the Soul: The Measure of the Soul* (Latin text with English translation). Translated by Francis E. Tourscher. Philadelphia: B. Herder, 1933.

Augustine of Hippo. "On the Trinity," in Philip Schaff (ed.), *A Select Library of the Nicene and Post-Nicene Fathers of the Christian Church*, Vol. 3. Translated by A. W. Haddan. Grand Rapids, MI: William B. Eerdmans, 1956.

Augustine of Hippo. *The Literal Meaning of Genesis.* Translated by John Hammond Taylor. New York: Newman Press, 1982.

Ayer, Sir A. J. *Language, Truth, and Logic.* 2nd ed. New York: Dover Publications, 1946.

Baillie, John. *The Sense of the Presence of God: Gifford Lectures, 1961–2.* New York: Charles Scribner's Sons, 1962.

Bergmann, Jenni. "The Significant Other: A Literary History of Elves," Ph.D. Dissertation, University of Cardiff, 2011.

Blom, Jan Dirk. *A Dictionary of Hallucinations.* New York: Springer Science and Business Media, 2010.

Bord, Janet. *Fairies: Real Encounters with Little People.* New York: Dell, 1997.

Brasic, James R. "Hallucinations," *Perceptual and Motor Skills*, 86 (1998): 851–77.

Braude, Stephen. *The Limits of Influence: Psychokinesis and the Philosophy of Science.* London: Routledge and Kegan Paul, 1986.

Bultmann, Rudolf. *Jesus Christ and Mythology.* New York: Charles Scribner's Sons, 1958.

Burnet, John. "The Socratic Doctrine of the Soul," *British Academy Proceedings*, 8 (1915–16): 235–59.
Caldwell, Sarah. "Bhagavati: Ball of Fire," in John Stratton Hawley and Donna Marie Wulff (eds.), *Devi: Goddesses of India*. Berkeley, CA: University of California Press, 1996.
Calvin, John. *The Institutes of the Christian Religion*. Translated by Henry Beveridge for the Calvin Translation Society. Grand Rapids, MI: Christian Classics Ethereal Library, 1845. www.ccel.org/ccel/calvin/institutes.pdf (accessed June 27, 2018).
Carnap, Rudolf. *Logical Foundations of Probability*. Chicago: The University of Chicago Press, 1950.
Carroll, Michael P. *The Cult of the Virgin Mary: Psychological Origins*. Princeton: Princeton University Press, 1986.
Chakravartty, Anjan. *A Metaphysics for Scientific Realism: Knowing the Unobservable*. Cambridge: Cambridge University Press, 2007.
Chalmers, David. "Australasian philosophy family tree," *david chalmers* (blog). http://consc.net/tree.html (accessed May 13, 2017).
Churchland, Patricia. "Reductionism and Antireductionism in Functionalist Theories of Mind," in Brian Beakley and Peter Ludlow (eds.), *The Philosophy of Mind*, pp. 59–68. Cambridge, MA: The MIT Press, 1992.
Churchland, Patricia and Terence J. Sejenowski. "Neural Representation and Neural Computation," in William G. Lycan (ed.), *Mind and Cognition: A Reader*, pp. 224–52. Oxford: Blackwell, 1990.
Close, Frank, Michael Marten, and Christine Sutton. *The Particle Explosion*. Oxford: Oxford University Press, 1994.
Cornford, Francis. *Before and after Socrates*. Cambridge: Cambridge University Press, 1932.
Cornford, Francis. *From Religion to Philosophy: A Study in the Origins of Western Speculation*. New York: Dover Publications, 2004.
Corte, Nicolas. *Who Is the Devil?* Translated by D. K. Pryce. Sophia Institute Press, 2013. Kindle edition [Originally published in 1956.]
David, Anthony and Geraldo Busatto. "The Hallucination: A Disorder of Brain and Mind," in Maria A. Ron and Anthony S. David (eds.), *Disorders of Brain and Mind*, pp. 336–62. Cambridge: Cambridge University Press, 1998.
Davis, Carolyn Franks. *The Evidential Force of Religious Experience*. Oxford: Oxford University Press, 1989.
Dennett, Daniel C. "The Self as a Center of Narrative Gravity," in Frank S. Kessel, Pamela Cole, and Dale L. Johnson (eds.), *Self and Consciousness: Multiple Perspectives*, pp. 103–15. Hillsdale, NJ: Erlbaum, 1992.
Dionysius the Areopagite. *The Mystical Theology and the Celestial Hierarchies*. 2nd ed. Surrey, England: The Shrine of Wisdom, 1965.
Edmonds, Bruce. "Simplicity Is Not Truth-Indicative," in Carlos Gershenson, Diederik Aerts, and Bruce Edmonds (eds.), *Worldviews, Science, and Us: Philosophy and Complexity*, pp. 65–80. Singapore: World Scientific, 2007.
Evans, Craig A. and N. T. Wright. *Jesus, the Final Days: What Really Happened*, in Troy A. Miller (ed.). Louisville, KT: Westminster John Knox Press, 2009.

Fang, Ferric C., R. Grant Steen, and Arturo Casadevall. "Misconduct Accounts for the Majority of Retracted Scientific Publications," *Proceedings of the National Academy of Sciences*, 109(42) (2012): 17028–33. https://doi.org/10.1073/pnas.1212247109 (accessed October 11, 2022).

Fee, Gordon. *God's Empowering Presence: The Holy Spirit in the Letters of Paul*. Peabody, MA: Hendrickson, 1994.

Feigl, Herbert. "The 'Orthodox' View of Theories: Remarks in Defense as well as Critique," in Michael Rudner and Stephen Winokur (eds.), *Minnesota Studies in the Philosophy of Science: Analysis of Theories and Methods of Physics and Psychology*, Vol. 4, pp. 3–16. Minneapolis: University of Minnesota Press, 1970.

Findlay, J. N. *Meinong's Theory of Facts and Values*. Oxford: Oxford University Press, 1963.

Fischer, Roland. "Cartography of Inner Space," in R. K. Siegel and L. J. West (eds.), *Hallucinations: Behavior, Experience and Theory*, pp. 197–239. New York: Wiley, 1975.

Flew, A., R. M. Hare, and B. Mitchell. *Theology and Falsification: A Symposium*. www.stephenhicks.org/wp-content/uploads/2015/06/FlewHareMitchell-What-Faith-Is.pdf (accessed June 26, 2018).

Freud, Sigmund. "The Interpretation of Dreams," *Encyclopedia Britannica*. Chicago: The University of Chicago Press, 1952.

Fulford, K. W. M. *Moral Theory and Medical Practice*. New York: Cambridge University Press, 1991.

Gellman, Jerome. "Mysticism," in Edward N. Zalta (ed.), *The Stanford Encyclopedia of Philosophy*. Stanford, CA: Stanford University Press, 2017 (Spring edition). https://plato.stanford.edu/archives/spr2017/entries/mysticism/ (accessed October 11, 2022).

Gershenson, Daniel E. and Daniel A. Greenberg. *Anaxagoras and the Birth of Scientific Method*. New York: Blaisdell, 1964.

Godwin, Malcolm. *Angels: An Endangered Species*. New York: Simon & Schuster, 1990.

Goldberg, Carl. *Speaking with the Devil: Exploring Senseless Acts of Evil*. Harmondsworth, Middlesex: Penguin Books, 1996.

Goodman, Nelson. *Fact, Fiction, and Forecast*. Cambridge, MA: Harvard University Press, 1955.

Green, Celia and Charles McCreery. *Apparitions*. London: Hamish Hamilton, 1975.

Greyson, B. "Western Scientific Approaches to Near-Death Experiences," *Humanities*, 4(4) (2015): 775–96. https://doi.org/10.3390/h4040775.

Griffin, David. *Parapsychology, Philosophy, and Spirituality: A Postmodern Exploration*. New York: The State University of New York Press, 1997.

Guiley, Rosemary E. *Encyclopedia of Ghosts and Spirits*. New York: Facts on File, 2009.

Hanson, Norwood Russell. *Patterns of Discovery: An Inquiry into the Conceptual Foundations of Science*. Cambridge: Cambridge University Press, 1958.

Hardy, Alister. *The Spiritual Nature of Man: A Study of Contemporary Religious Experience*. Oxford: Oxford University Press, 1979.

Harris, Peter. "Can 'Creation' Be a Metaphysical Concept?," in William Sweet, (ed.), *God and Argument - Dieu et L'Argumentation Philosophique*. Ottawa: University of Ottawa Press, 1999.

Heathcote-James, Emma. *Seeing Angels: True Contemporary Accounts of Hundreds of Angelic Experiences*. London: John Blake, 2002.

Hempel, Carl G. *Philosophy of Natural Science*. Upper Saddle River, NJ: Prentice Hall, 1966.

Hempel, Carl G. "Problems and Changes in the Empiricist Criterion of Meaning," *Revue Internationale de Philosophie*, 4 (1950): 41–63.

Hempel, Carl G. "Studies in the Logic of Confirmation," in *Aspects of Scientific Explanation and Other Essays in the Philosophy of Science*. New York: The Free Press, 1967: 245–290.

Herbermann, Charles, et al. (eds). *The Catholic Encyclopedia*. Fifteen volumes. New York: Robert Appleton, 1912.

Hick, John. *Disputed Questions in Theology and the Philosophy of Religion*. New Haven, CT: Yale University Press, 1993.

Holy Bible. *Revised Standard Version. Oxford Annotated, with Apocrypha*. New York: Oxford University Press, 1965.

Hooker, Clifford. "Towards a General Theory of Reduction," *Dialogue: Canadian Philosophical Review*, 20 (1981): 38–59, 201–36, and 496–529.

Horowitz, M. J. "Hallucinations: An Information-Processing Approach," in R. K. Siegel and L. J. West (eds.), *Hallucinations: Behavior, Experience and Theory*, pp. 163–95. New York: Wiley, 1975.

Hume, David. *Philosophical Essays Concerning Human Understanding*. London: A. Millar, 1777.

Jain, Mishrilal and Kamal M. Jain. "The Science of Yoga: A Study in Perspective," *Perspectives in Biology and Medicine*, 17 (1973): 99–102.

James, William. *Varieties of Religious Experience: A Study in Human Nature*. New York: Book-of-the-Month Club, 1997 [Originally published in 1902].

James, William. "The Will to Believe," in *The Will to Believe and Other Essays in Popular Philosophy*. New York: Dover Publications, 1956 [Originally published in 1896].

St. John of the Cross. *The Ascent of Mount Carmel*. Eastford, CT: Martino Fine Books, 2016.

Josephus, Flavius. "The Antiquities of the Jews," in *The Life and Works of Flavius Josephus*. Translated by William Whiston. Philadelphia: John C. Winston, n.d.

Julian, Jaynes. *The Origins of Consciousness in the Breakdown of the Bicameral Mind*. Toronto: University of Toronto Press, 1976.

Jung, Carl. *Memories, Dreams, Reflections*. Recorded and edited by Aniela Jaffé. Translated by Richard and Clara Winston. London: Collins and Routledge & Kegan Paul, 1963.

Kant, Immanuel. *Anthropology from a Pragmatic Point of View*. New York: Cambridge University Press, 2006. [Originally published in 1798].

Kant, Immanuel. *Groundwork of the Metaphysics of Morals*. Translated by Allen W. Wood. Binghamton, NY: Yale University, 2022. [Originally published in 1785].

Kenney, John Peter. *The Mysticism of Saint Augustine: Re-reading the Confessions*. New York: Routledge, 2005.

Kramer, Heinrich and James Sprenger. *Malleus Maleficarum*. Translated by Montague Summers. New York: Dover, 1971.
Kuhn, Thomas S. *The Structure of Scientific Revolutions*. Chicago: The University of Chicago Press, 1970.
Lakatos, Imre. "History of Science and Its Rational Reconstructions: PSA," *Proceedings of the Biennial Meeting of the Philosophy of Science Association*, 8 (1970): 91–136.
Larmer, Robert. (ed.). *Questions of Miracle*. Montreal and Kingston: McGill-Queen's University Press, 1996.
Larmer, Robert. *The Legitimacy of Miracle*. Plymouth, UK: Lexington Books, 2014.
Levi-Strauss, Claude. *The Savage Mind*. Translated by George Weidenfield and Nicholson Ltd. Chicago: The University of Chicago Press, 1966.
Lewis, C. S. *The Discarded Image: An Introduction to Medieval and Renaissance Literature*. Cambridge: Cambridge University Press, 1964.
Lewis, David K. "An Argument for the Identity Theory," *Journal of Philosophy*, 63 (1966): 17–25.
Lewis, David K. "How to Define Theoretical Terms," *Journal of Philosophy*, 47 (1970): 427–46.
Lewis, David K. "Psychophysical and Theoretical Identifications," *Australasian Journal of Philosophy*, 50 (1972): 249–58.
Long, Jeffrey. *God and the Afterlife: The Groundbreaking New Evidence for God and Near-Death Experience*. New York, NY: HarperCollins, 2017. Kindle edition.
MacPhilpin, John. *The Apparitions and Miracles at Knock*. PJ Kennedy, 1904.
Malinowski, Bronislaw. *Magic, Science and Religion, and Other Essays*. Garden City, NY: Doubleday, 1954.
Mariña, Jacqueline. "Friedrich Schleiermacher and Rudolf Otto," in John Corrigan (ed.), *The Oxford Handbook of Religion and Emotion*, pp. 457–73. Oxford: Oxford University Press, 2007.
Mascall, Eric. *He Who Is: A Study in Traditional Theism*. London: Longman, Green and Co., 1943.
Maurice, Frederick D. *Lectures on the Ecclesiastical History of the First and Second Centuries*. Cambridge: Macmillan, 1854.
Mayr, Ernst. "The Autonomy of Biology: The Position of Biology among the Sciences," *The Quarterly Review of Biology*, 71 (1996): 97–106.
McKirihan, Richard D. *Philosophy Before Socrates: An Introduction with Texts and Commentary*. Indianapolis: Hackett Publishing, 1994.
Miller, Alexander. "Realism," in Edward N. Zalta (ed.), *The Stanford Encyclopedia of Philosophy*. Stanford, CA: Stanford University Press, 2016 (Winter edition). https://plato.stanford.edu/archives/win2016/entries/realism/ (accessed October 11, 2022).
Mishrilal, Jain and Kamal M. Jain. "The Science of Yoga: A Study in Perspective," *Perspectives in Biology and Medicine*, 17 Autumn (1973): 99–102.
Mobbs, Dean and Watt, Caroline. "There Is Nothing Paranormal about near-Death Experiences: How Neuroscience Can Explain Seeing Bright Lights, Meeting the Dead, or Being Convinced You Are One of Them," *Trends in Cognitive Sciences*, 15(10) (2011): 447–49. https://doi.org/10.1016/j.tics.2011.07.01

Molinari, Paul. *Julian of Norwich: The Teachings of a 14th Century English Mystic*. London: Longman, Green & Co., 1958.
Moody, Raymond. *Life after Life*. Covington, GA: Mockingbird Books, 1975.
Mounce, H. O. *Metaphysics and the End of Philosophy*. London and New York: Continuum, 2007.
Nadler, Steven. *Occasionalism: Causation among the Cartesians*. Oxford and New York: Oxford University Press, 2011.
Nambu, Y. *Quarks: Frontiers in Elementary Particle Physics*. Translated by Kwōku. Philadelphia, PA: World Scientific, 1985.
Nielsen, Kai. *Philosophy and Atheism: In Defense of Atheism*. Buffalo, NY: Prometheus Books, 1985.
O'Brien, Dan. "Review of *The Emergence of Consciousness*," *Human Nature Review*, 2 (2002): 249–52. www.human-nature.com/nibbs/02/obrien.html (accessed January 13, 2018).
Oskin, Becky. "Japan Earthquake & Tsunami of 2011: Facts and Information," *Live Science*, September 13, 2017.
Otto, Rudolf. *The Idea of the Holy: An Inquiry into the Non-rational Factor in the Idea of the Divine and Its Relation to the Rational*, 2nd ed. Translated by John W. Harvey. Oxford: Oxford University Press, 1950 [Das Heilige, 1917].
Pals, Daniel. *Nine Theories of Religion*. Oxford: Oxford University Press, 2015.
Papineau, David. "Naturalism," in Edward N. Zalta (ed.), *The Stanford Encyclopedia of Philosophy*. Stanford, CA: Stanford University Press, 2016 (Winter edition). https://plato.stanford.edu/archives/win2016/entries/naturalism/ (accessed October 11, 2022).
Parry, Richard Lloyd. "Ghosts of the Tsunami," *London Review of Books*, 36 (3), 2014: 13–17.
Passmore, John. *A Hundred Years of Philosophy*. New York: Pelican Book Company, 1978.
Perkins, Larry. "Greater than Solomon (Matthew 12: 42)," *Trinity Journal* (new series) 19 (1998): 207–17.
Pilch, John J. "Visions in Revelation and Alternate Consciousness: A Perspective from Cultural Anthropology," *Listening: Journal of Religion and Culture*, 28 (1993): 231–44.
Pilch, John J. "The Transfiguration of Jesus: An Experience of Alternate Reality," in Philip F. Esler (ed.), *Modelling Early Christianity: Social-Scientific Studies of the New Testament in its Context*, pp. 47–64. London and New York: Routledge, 1995.
Pilch, John J. "Appearances of the Risen Jesus in Cultural Context: Experiences of Alternate Reality," *Biblical Theology Bulletin*, 28 (1998): 52–60.
Plantinga, Alvin. *Warranted Christian Belief*. Oxford: Oxford University Press, 2000.
Plato. *The Dialogues of Plato*. Translated by B. Jowett. New York: Random House, 1937.
Pope Pius XII. *Munificentissimus Deus*. http://w2.vatican.va/content/pius-xii/en/apost_constitutions/documents/hf_p-xii_apc_19501101_munificentissimus-deus.html (accessed July 22, 2018).

Popper, Sir Karl. *The Logic of Scientific Discovery*. 2nd ed. London: Hutchinson, 1968.

Postel, Danny. "High Flyer: Richard Rorty Obituary," *New Humanist*, Thursday, July 5, 2007.

Poulain, Augustin François. *The Graces of Interior Prayer: A Treatise on Mystical Theology*, 6th ed. Translated by Leonora L. Yorke Smith. London: Kegan Paul Trench Trubner, 1921.

Putnam, Hilary. "Dreaming and Depth Grammar," in R. J. Butler (ed.), *Analytical Philosophy: First Series*, pp. 211–35. New York: Barnes & Noble, 1960.

Quine, W. V. O. *From a Logical Point of View*, 2nd ed. New York: Harper & Row, 1963.

Quine, W. V. O. *Word and Object*. Cambridge, MA: Massachusetts Institute of Technology Press, 1964.

Quine, W. V. O. and Sam Ullian. *The Web of Belief*, 2nd ed. New York: McGraw-Hill, 1978. http://socialistica.lenin.ru/analytic/txt/q/quine_1.htm (accessed June 26, 2018).

Ramsey, William. "Eliminative Materialism," in Edward N. Zalta (ed.), *The Stanford Encyclopedia of Philosophy*. Stanford, CA: Stanford University Press, 2016 (Winter edition). https://plato.stanford.edu/archives/win2016/entries/materialism-eliminative/ (accessed June 23, 2018).

Rebello, Lara. *International Business Times UK*, updated news report, January 6, 2017.

Rohde, Erwin. *Psyche: The Cult of Souls and Belief in Immortality among the Greeks*. Translated by W. B. Hillis. New York: Harper & Row, 1966.

Rorty, Richard (ed.). *The Linguistic Turn: Essays in Philosophical Method*. Chicago: The University of Chicago Press, 1967.

Rorty, Richard. "Mind–Body Identity, Privacy, and Categories," in David M. Rosenthal (ed.), *Materialism and the Mind-Body Problem*, pp. 174–99. Englewood Cliffs, NJ: Prentice-Hall, 1971.

Rorty, Richard. "Some Inconsistencies in James's Varieties," in Wayne Proudfoot (ed.), *William James and a Science of Religions: Re-experiencing the Varieties of Religious Experiences*. New York: Columbia University Press, 2004, pp. 86–97.

Rorty, Richard and Gianni Vattimo. *The Future of Religion*. Edited by Santiago Zabala. Translated by William McCuaig. New York: Columbia University Press, 2005.

Russell, Bertrand. "The Philosophy of Logical Atomism (1918)," in David Pears (ed.), *The Philosophy of Logical Atomism*, pp. 1–125. Peru, IL: Open Court, 1998.

Russell, Bertrand. "Logical Atomism (1924)," in David Pears (ed.), *The Philosophy of Logical Atomism*, pp. 126–150. Peru, IL: Open Court, 1998.

Ryall, Julian. "Taxi drivers in tsunami disaster zone report 'ghost passengers'," *The Telegraph*, January 21, 2016.

Ryle, Gilbert. *The Concept of Mind*. London: Hutchinson, 1949.

Salmon, Merrilee H., John Earman, Clark Glymour, James G. Lennox, Peter Machemer, J. E. McGuire, John D. Norton, Wesley Salmon, and Kenneth F. Schaffner (eds.), *Introduction to the Philosophy of Science*. Englewood Cliffs, NJ: Prentice Hall, 1992.

Samuelsson, Gunnar. *Crucifixion in Antiquity – An Inquiry into the Background of the New Testament Terminology of Crucifixion.* Tübingen: Mohr Siebeck, 2011.

Schroter-Kunhardt, M. "A Review of Near Death Experiences," *Society for Scientific Explanation,* 7 (1993): 219–39. www.noufors.com/Documents/Books,%20Manuals%20and%20Published%20Papers/Specialty%20UFO%20Publications/Journal%20of%20Scientific%20Exploration/jse_07_full.pdf (accessed April 28, 2018).

Searle, John. *The Rediscovery of the Mind.* Cambridge, MA: Massachusetts Institute of Technology Press, 1992.

Sellars, Wilfrid. *Science, Perception and Reality.* London: Routledge & Kegan Paul, 1963.

Sellars, Wilfrid. *Empiricism and the Philosophy of Mind.* Cambridge, MA: Harvard University Press, 1997.

Shapere, Dudley. "The Concept of Observation in Science and Philosophy," *Philosophy of Science,* 49 (1982): 485–526.

Sidgewick, H. A., A. Johnson, F. W. H. Myers, F. Podmore, and E. M. Sidgwick. Report on the Census of Hallucinations. *Proceedings of the Society for Psychical Research,* 10 (1894): 25–422.

Skinner, B. F. "Behaviorism at Fifty," in T. W. Wann (ed.), *Behaviourism and Phenomenology: Contrasting Bases for Modern Psychology,* pp. 79–97. Chicago: The University of Chicago Press, 1964.

Smart, J. J. C. "Sensations and Brain Processes," *Philosophical Review,* 68 (1959): 141–56.

Smart, J. J. C. "Conflicting Views about Explanation," in R. S. Cohen and M. W. Wartofsky (eds.), *Boston Studies in the Philosophy of Science.* Vol. II, pp. 157–69. New York: Humanities Press, 1965.

Smart, Ninian. *The World's Religions,* 2nd ed. Cambridge: Cambridge University Press, 1998.

Smith, Frederick M. *The Self Possessed: Deity and Spirit Possession in South Asian Literature and Civilization.* New York: Columbia University Press, 2006.

Smith, Quentin. "The Metaphilosophy of Naturalism," *Philo,* 4 (2001): 195–215.

Smith, Quentin. "Time Was Created by a Timeless Point: An Atheist Explanation of Spacetime," in Gregory E. Ganssle and David M. Woodruff (eds.), *God and Time: Essays on the Divine Nature,* pp. 95–128. New York: Oxford University Press, 2002.

Spanos, Nicholas P., Deborah M. Flynn, and Natalie J. Gabora. "Suggested Negative Visual Hallucinations in Hypnotic Subjects: When No Means Yes," *British Journal of Experimental and Clinical Hypnosis,* 6 (1989): 63–67.

Spinoza, Baruch. *Ethics.* www.gutenberg.org/files/3800/3800-h/3800-h.htm (accessed August 3, 2018).

Steiger, Brad and Sherry Hansen Steiger (eds.). *The Gale Encyclopedia of the Unusual and Unexplained,* Farmington Hills, MI: Thomson-Gale, 2004. Eds. art. 'Guardian Angels.' pp. 211–14.

Stoljar, Daniel. "Physicalism," in Edward N. Zalta (ed.), *The Stanford Encyclopedia of Philosophy.* Stanford, CA: Stanford University Press, 2017 (Winter edition). https://plato.stanford.edu/archives/win2017/entries/physicalism/ (accessed January 14, 2018).

Strawson, Galen. *Locke on Personal Identity: Consciousness and Concernment*. Princeton, NJ and Oxford, UK: Princeton University Press, 2011.
Swinburne, Richard. *Epistemic Justification*. Oxford: Clarendon Press, 2001.
Swinburne, Richard. "Chapter 13: The Argument from Religious Experience," in *The Existence of God*, 2nd ed. Oxford: Clarendon Press. 2004.
Takahashi, Hara. "The Ghosts of Tsunami Dead and *Kokoro no kea* in Japan's Religious Landscape," *Journal of Religion in Japan*, 5 (2016): 176–98.
Taves, Ann. *Religious Experience Reconsidered: A Building-Block Approach to the Study of Religion and Other Special Things*. Princeton and Oxford: Princeton University Press, 2009.
Taylor, A. E. *Socrates: The Man and His Thought*. Garden City, NY: Doubleday, 1953.
Taylor, Charles. *A Secular Age*. Cambridge, MA: Harvard University Press, 2007.
St. Teresa of Avila, *The Life of St. Teresa of Jesus*. Translated by David Lewis. London: Thomas Baker, 1904.
St. Teresa of Avila. *Interior Castle*. Translated by K. Kavanaugh and O. Rodriguez. London: SPCK, 1979 [Original published in 1588].
Thornton, Stephen. "Karl Popper," in Edward N. Zalta (ed.), *The Stanford Encyclopedia of Philosophy*. Stanford, CA: Stanford University Press, 2017 (Summer edition). https://plato.stanford.edu/archives/sum2017/entries/popper/ (accessed October 11, 2022).
Tranzillo, Jeffrey. "German Bishops Employ Lutheran Subjectivism for Marriage Agenda." www.crisismagazine.com/2018/german-bishops-employ-lutheran-subjectivism-marriage-agenda (accessed May 25, 2018).
Trenn, Thaddeus. "The Shroud of Turin: Resetting the Carbon-14 Clock," in Jitse M. van der Meer (ed.), *Facets of Faith and Science. Volume 3: The Role of Beliefs in the Natural Sciences*, pp. 119–33. Lanham, MD: University Press of America, 1996.
Trenn, Thaddeus. "The Shroud of Turin: A Parable for Modern Times?" *Journal of Interdisciplinary Studies*, 9 (1997): 121–40, 127.
Trenn, Thaddeus. "Sketch and Highlights of Resurrection Model" (2007). Private correspondence.
Trethowan, Dom Illtyd. *Certainty: Philosophical and Theological*. Westminster: Dacre Press, 1948.
Tylor, E. B. *Primitive Culture: Researches into the Development of Mythology, Philosophy, Religion, Language, Art, and Custom*, 4th ed. London: Murray, 1920 [Originally published in 1871]. https://archive.org/stream/primitivecul ture01tylouoft/primitiveculture01tylouoft_djvu.txt
Underhill, Evelyn. *Mysticism: A Study in the Nature and Development of Man's Spiritual Consciousness*, 12th ed. London: Methuen, 1930. [Revised edition].
Waismann, Friedrich. *Wittgenstein and the Vienna Circle*. Oxford: Blackwell, 1979.
Walsh, Bryan J. "The 1988 Shroud of Turin Radiocarbon Tests Reconsidered" (in two parts). http://web.archive.org/web/20040422010105/http://members.aol.com:80/ turin99/radiocarbon-a.htm and http://web.archive.org/web/20040428023751/ http://members.aol.com:80/turin99/radiocarbon-b.htm (accessed May 18, 2018).
West, Louis J. "A General Theory of Hallucinations and Dreams," in L. J. West (ed.), *Hallucinations*, pp. 275–91. New York: Grune & Stratton, 1962.

West, Louis J. "A Clinical and Theoretical Overview of Hallucinatory Phenomena," in R. K. Siegel and L. J. West (eds.), *Hallucinations: Behavior, Experience and Theory*, pp. 287–311. New York: Wiley, 1975.

Whitehead, Alfred North. *Process and Reality: An Essay in Cosmology*. New York: The Free Press, 1978.

Wiebe, Phillip H. "Hempel and Instantial Confirmation," *Philosophy Research Archives*, 2 (1976).

Wiebe, Phillip H. "Authenticating Biblical Reports of Miracles," *The Journal of Philosophical Research*, 18 (1993): 309–25. Reprinted with changes in Robert A. Larmer (ed.), *Questions of Miracle*, pp. 101–20. Montreal & Kingston: McGill-Queen's University Press, 1996.

Wiebe, Phillip H. *Visions of Jesus: Direct Encounters from the New Testament to Today*. Oxford: Oxford University Press, 1997.

Wiebe, Phillip H. "Finite Spirits as Theoretical Entities," *Religious Studies*, 40 (2004a): 341–50.

Wiebe, Phillip H. *God and Other Spirits: Intimations of Transcendence in Christian Experience*. Oxford: Oxford University Press, 2004b.

Wiebe, Phillip H. "Degrees of Hallucinatoriness and Christic Visions," *Archiv für Religionspsychologie*, 24 (2004c): 201–22.

Wiebe, Phillip H. "Deliverance and Exorcism in Philosophical Perspective," in William K. Kay and Robin Parry (eds.), *Exorcism and Deliverance: Multidisciplinary Studies*, pp. 156–80. London: Paternoster, 2011.

Wiebe, Phillip H. *Visions and Appearances of Jesus*. Abilene, TX: Abilene Christian University Press (Leafwood Press), 2014.

Wittgenstein, Ludwig. *Tractatus Logico-Philosophicus*. Translated by D. F. Pears and B. F. McGuinness. New York: Humanities Press, 1961 [Originally published in 1921].

Wittgenstein, Ludwig. *Philosophical Investigations*. Edited by G. E. M. Anscombe and R. Rhees. Translated by G. E. M. Anscombe. Oxford: Blackwell, 1953.

World Health Organization. "Chapter V: Mental and behavioural disorders," *International Statistical Classification of Diseases and Related Health Problems 10th Revision (ICD-10)*, pp. 281–346. Geneva: World Health Organization. https://apps.who.int/iris/bitstream/handle/10665/246208/9789241549165-V1-eng.pdf (accessed October 12, 2022).

Xenophon. *Memorabilia: Reflections of Socrates*. Translated by H. G. Dakyns. www.gutenberg.org/files/1177/1177-h/1177-h.htm (accessed June 18, 2018).

Yandell, Keith. *The Epistemology of Religious Experience*. New York: Cambridge University Press, 1993.

Yogananda, Paramhansa. *Autobiography of a Yogi*. www.gutenberg.org/files/7452/7452-h/7452-h.htm (accessed June 23, 2018).

Zaehner, R. C. *Concordant Discord: The Interdependence of Faiths. Being the Gifford Lectures on Natural Religion delivered at St. Andrews in 1967–1969*. Oxford: Clarendon Press, 1970.

Zaleski, Carol. *Otherworld Journeys: Accounts of Near-Death Experience in Medieval and Modern Times*. Oxford: Oxford University Press, 1987.

Index

Abbotsford Visitor, 43, 71, 89
abduction, 57, 79, 162
Abraham, 80, 81, 154, 161
Acts of the Apostles, 8, 19
affective prayer, 15
afterlife, 5, 37, 52
Aftonbladet, 40
Agabus, 6
agnosticism, 109, 139, 143
Alister Hardy collection, 159
Alister Hardy Research Centre, 147, 154
Alister Hardy Trust, 158
American Psychiatric Association, 23
Ananias and Sapphira, 6
Anaximander, 58
angel, 11, 26, 31, 44, 80, 85, 90–95, 101, 137, 138, 141, 152–154, 196
    encounter, 45, 151, 153–154
    Gabriel, 85, 141, 154
Anselm (Saint), 80, 81
anthropon, 61
apostolic authority, 7
apparition, 4, 5, 7, 20, 40, 41, 59, 86–90, 110–113, 117, 118, 122, 123, 126–128, 134, 135, 141, 142, 144, 146–148, 150, 152–154, 165, 166, 168–173, 195
    Christic, 118, 136, 166
    doppelgänger, 20
    Marian, 118, 168–173
    of Christ, 41, 135, 168
    of mythical figures, 20
    of religious figures, 20
    of the dead, 20, 59, 111, 112, 144, 165, 173
    of the living, 111
Aquinas, Thomas, 51, 52, 80–82
Archbishop of Tuam, 170
Aristotelian way, 60
Aristotle, 52, 60, 79
ascription, 82, 185
atheism, 37, 52, 83, 109, 139, 197
atheist, 37, 52, 93, 125
Athenian court, 59
Athenian stranger, 2
Athens, plague upon, 5
atomic physics, 35, 48, 49, 53, 160
Augustine (Saint), 8–11, 16, 20, 61, 122, 129–131, 136
Augustinian categories, 8, 14
Australian fallacy, 65
automatisms and automatic writing, 20
Ayer, Alfred J., 36, 41, 43, 52, 53

baloma see spirits
baptism in the Spirit, 7
Beaven, Robert, 46
behaviorism, 63
Beirne, Dominick, 169
belief systems, 34, 183
benevolent super-beings, 71
Bergmann, Jenni, 93
Berkeley Lab, 53
Berkeley, George, 50, 55
Bezanson, Helen, 112
Biblical scholarship, 8

bilocation, 20
biological evolution, 39
blessing of divine madness, 3
bliss or serenity, 27
body-soul dualism, 111
born again, 17
Boutle, Mathilde, 135
Brahamical texts, 184
Braude, Stephen, 99
bridegroom, 13, 16
British Humanist Association, 52
Buddha, 27
Buddhism, Zen, 195
Bultmann, Rudolf, 160, 161
Bunyan, John, 18
Burnaby "Evil Spirit", The, 41, 71, 89, 102
Burnet, John, 2, 58, 59
Busatto, Geraldo, 119
buying honour, 3
Byrne, Dominick *see* Beirne, Dominick
Byrne, Mary, 170

Caldwell, Sarah, 184
Calvin, John, 131
Campbell, Judith, 170, 172
Carnap, Rudolf, 49, 98
Cartesian dualism, 63
Cartesian philosophy, 62
cartography of inner space, 23
Case of Adeline, The, 159
catatonia, 24
Catholic
  Church, 119, 168, 169, 171
  clergy, 171
  doctrine, 134, 135
  faith, 129
  theologians, 125
  tradition, 135, 136
Catholic Encyclopedia, The, 32, 134
Celestial Hierarchies, 137
Census on Hallucinations, 111
centaurs, 137
chaitanya, 25
Chakravartty, Anjan, 35
charm the Gods, 5
chitta, 25
Christian, 1, 14, 18, 127, 128, 134, 135, 137, 138, 163, 188, 194
  beliefs, 105, 126, 160, 161
  charismata, 7

Church, 6, 161, 168, 180, 197
exorcism, 181, 192
exorcists, 193
faith, 2, 25, 131, 161, 162, 188, 193
folklore, 162
governments, 197
Greco-Roman, 187
paranormal phenomena, 46
perspective, 28
scriptures, 11, 160
theism, 42, 105, 109, 110
theology, 6
tradition, 1, 12, 15, 44, 195
views, 7
worship, 7
Christianity, 27, 33, 61, 109, 125, 139, 154, 162, 165, 167, 195
Christina (Princess of Sweden), 40
Christine, Lucie, 135
Churchill, Winston, 46
clairvoyance, 20, 29
Cleopas, 125
cloud chambers, 49, 53
cognitive disorder, 105
commonsense, 37, 38, 55, 66–69, 76, 98, 114, 122, 123, 161, 182, 188
Concept of Mind, The, 65, 192
concepts of abstraction and compounding, 50
conceptual framework, 31, 38, 39, 70, 78, 98, 101, 102, 161, 173, 182, 183, 189, 198
conceptual structure, 39, 40, 164, 173, 182
conjure the dead, 5
conscious awareness, 11
continua, 23, 25
converse consequence principle, 94
conversion, 18, 19, 136, 139, 188
Cornford, Francis, 2, 59
corpus, 8
Cratylus, 3
Crito, 3, 4, 59, 60
Crombie, I. M., 38
Curry, John, 169
custody of evidence, 150, 152, 158, 171

Daily Mail, 45, 46
Daniel, 141
Darwin, Charles, 55
David, Anthony, 119

Index

Davis, Caroline Franks, 26, 27, 31, 32, 103
death omen, 20
death process, 29
deathbed visions, 20
decretum absolutum, 87
deduction of truths, 15
deductive logic, 95, 187
deductivist model, 56, 57
deifying union, 16
deities, 185
demands of a lover, 3
dematerialization, 166–168
demon, 21, 73, 155, 189, 193
demonic, 6, 22, 32, 73, 137
　obsession, 21
　possession *see* possession
　powers, 102, 129, 132, 138, 164
　spirit *see* spirits: demonic
deprivation, 113, 114, 176
Descartes, 63, 65, 117
devil, the, 14, 132, 161
devils, 110, 129
Dharna, 24
Dhyan, 24
diabolical, 7, 10
　agents, 77
　distortions, 195
　encounters, 26
　forces, 22, 193
　influence, 78, 131
　locutions, 132
　powers, 33, 100, 154, 159
　super-beings, 71
　see also orders: diabolical
　see also spirits: diabolical
Diotoma of Mantineia, 5
discerning of spirits, 6, 46
dispositions, 15, 65
divination, 7, 10, 20
Divine, 7, 12, 17, 26, 27
　action, 16
　beings, 6, 34, 186
　encounters with, 117
　forces, 193
　imaginary visions, 14
　influence, 16, 33, 78, 92
　insight, 140
　locutions, 132
　object, 16
　powers, 154, 159

source, 6
wisdom, 6
see also orders: Divine
see also spirits: divine
Divine–human interaction, 12
diviner, 3, 5, 6
Division of Evidence, 99
double-aspect view, 63
Doyle, Arthur Conan, 45–47, 92
Drottningholm phantoms, 40, 86, 87
Duke of Brunswick, 32
dwarfs, 137
Dyck, Barry, 115

Ecclesiastical Commission of inquiry, 170
ecstasy, 3, 4, 7, 14, 25, 27
ecstatic union, 16
EEG waves, 25
efficacious sacrifice, 5
Egyptian priests, 33
Einstein, Albert, 53, 98
Eleazar, 193
electrifying energy, 153
elevations, 132
Eliminative Materialism, 190
eliminativism, 66
eliminativists, 69
Elizabeth II (Queen), 149
elves, 92–94, 137, 138
Emmerich, Catherine, 16
emotion, 23, 65, 88, 184
Empedocles, 58
empiricism, 36, 38, 145, 162, 192
empiricists, 36, 75, 83, 145, 157, 161, 192
enchantments, 5
Encyclopedia of Ghosts and Spirits, The, 20
Entailment Principle, 95
Ephesians, 126
Epimenides, 5
epiphenomenalism, 63
epistemology, 62, 68, 92, 103–105, 122, 123, 164, 187, 188, 197
ergotropic arousal, 23
extra-sensory perception (ESP), 29
espousals, 13
Esquirol, Jean, 121
Euclidean geometry, 56
evidential principles, 197
Exodus 3, 80

exorcism, 5, 7, 20, 30, 72, 74–76, 154, 155, 158, 163, 181, 192–194
  Buddhist, 181, 192, 193
  Gerasene *see* Gerasene Exorcism Case
  Philippi, 7
  Shinto, 181, 192, 193
experience
  Christian, 5, 12, 28, 127, 128, 195
  Christic, 32, 103, 112, 113, 117–118, 129, 131, 190, 192, 195
  conversion, 18, 19
  dream, 154, 176
  extraordinary, 11, 134
  hallucinatory, 25, 108, 117–119, 122, 145, 149, 152, 158, 171, 172, 181, 191
  imaginary, 130
  integrated, 172
  interpretive, 26
  mystical, 1, 8, 12, 13, 15, 27, 28, 113
  mysticism, 27
  near-death (NDE), 5, 28, 29, 52, 53, 92, 173–175, 181
  numinous, 27
  of alterity, 184
  of reality, 11, 66, 138
  of the dying, 20
  ordinary, 10, 11, 26
  perceptual, 15, 124
  perceptual-emotive-cognitive, 12
  pervades the order of, 76
  phenomenological, 28, 31–33, 91, 107, 110, 128, 132, 153, 158, 164
  quasi-sensory, 26
  redemption to another universe, 18
  regenerative, 26
  religious, 1, 8, 17, 19, 26, 29, 30, 103, 108, 113, 124, 184
  revelatory, 26
  RSM *see* RSM: experience
  semiconscious, 59
  semi-experimental, 150, 152, 158, 196
  sensory, 45, 111, 121, 151, 156, 172
  spiritual, 1, 7, 8, 29, 30, 63, 91
  visionary, 11, 41, 105, 125–129, 134, 136
  see also continua
Extreme Illuminates Obscure, 100
Ezekiel, 141

fairies, 93, 137, 138
fakir, 22
familiars, 78
faunes, 137
Feast of Pentecost, 5
Fee, Gordon, 7
Feigl, Herbert, 47–50
Fischer, Roland, 23–25
Flew, Antony, 38, 39
folk psychology, 61, 63, 66, 91
folk religion, 61, 91, 154
Freud, Sigmund, 56, 87, 122
Fulford, K. W. M., 118, 119
functionalism, 66

Geller, Uri, 21
Genesis, 81, 154, 162
Gentiles, 6
Gerasene Exorcism Case, 74–76, 78, 83, 86, 100–102, 106, 160
Ghost in the Machine, The, 65
ghost problem, the, 181
ghosts, 40, 41, 43, 51, 99, 100, 111, 177, 181, 195
Gifford Lectures, 16, 27, 35
gifts of healing, 6
gifts of the Spirit, 5, 11, 46
Giri, Yukteswar, 165
giving of the Spirit, 5
glossolalia, 7, 9
gnomes, 137
God, 3–6, 8, 9, 12, 13, 16, 17, 26, 27, 37, 41–44, 51, 52, 67, 68, 73, 75–78, 80–83, 87–89, 105, 113, 125, 126, 128, 132, 138–140, 154, 156, 157, 160, 161, 168, 194
  active pursuit of, 12
  definition of, 51, 82, 83
  gift of, 11
  His Majesty, 13
  incapable of deceit, 4
  Light is, 11
  locutions from, 132
  Love of, 14, 160
  minds of poets, 3
  Spirit of, 17
  word of, 13
God and Other Spirits, 43
God is in the soul, 16
Goldberg, Carl, 189, 190
Good Spirit, the, 41, 42
Gospel of St Luke, The, 72, 85, 136
gravitational force, 48
Great Spirit, 194

Index

Greco-Roman-Hebrew view, 137
Greek antiquity, 5, 138
Green, Celia, 111
grounding event, 133
Guardian, The, 40
guardians of space, 53
Guiley, Rosemary, 20, 31

hallucination, 19, 23, 42, 44, 86, 108, 111, 112, 117–119, 121, 122, 126, 127, 130, 144, 145, 149, 158, 171, 172, 176, 191
hallucinatory psychosis, 34
hallucinatory states, 23, 25
Hanson, Norwood Russell, 101
Hardy, Alister, 29, 143, 147, 149, 150, 157–159, 196
Hardy's schema, 29
Hare, R. M., 38
harmony view, 63
Harris, Leo, 74, 163
Hathaway, Marian, 125
Heathcote-James, Emma, 30, 31, 44, 91, 151–153
Hebrew, 139, 194
  Feast of the Pentecost, 5
  Bible, 81, 114, 154
  literature, 5
  tradition, 193
Hebrew-Christian
  Bible, 8, 136
  faith, 109, 138, 193
  influences, 140
  scriptures, 6, 11, 92, 160
  tradition, 42, 128, 137
Heinrich Institoris, 129
Hempel, Carl, 47, 49, 95, 96, 98, 162, 187
Heraclitus, 58
heretics, 129
Hertfordshire Angel Case, The, 151, 154
Hick, John, 165
Higgs, Peter, 97, 98
Hill, Patrick, 169
Hindu Samadhi, 18
Hinduism, 28, 165
Holy Communion, 14
Holy Spirit, 5–7, 89, 186
Homer, 4
human
  actions, 51, 64, 71, 87
  affairs, 4
  attributes, 62, 76, 81, 159, 181, 182

behavior, 20, 63, 66, 86, 181
capacity, 84
conception, 173
existence, 107
imagination *see* imagination
immortality, 137, 164
insights, 11, 140, 193
medium, 21
mind, 9, 17, 61, 64, 71, 75, 78, 107, 141, 164
perception, 8, 9
power, 30, 33, 41, 76, 129
soul, 3, 10, 58, 62, 63, 93, 137
spirit, 9–13, 52, 58, 61–64, 93, 132, 176, 183
survival, 53, 110, 146, 169, 175
wisdom, 6
see also experience: human
Hume, David, 38, 50, 107, 108, 117, 156
Humean, 145
hyperacuity, 21
hypnosis, 18, 21, 90

Idea of the Holy, The, 27
idealism, 63
Identity Theory, 34, 65, 66, 189–191
imagination, 8–11, 39, 65, 113, 129, 130
imaginative vision *see* vision: imaginative
impaired cognition, 24
impiety, 3, 4
incantations, 5
incubi, 129
Indian Constitution, 185
induction, 57, 95, 98, 187
inductive logic, 95, 187, 188
inferior corporeal object, 10
infinite regress, 62
inheritance factors, 55, 133, 156
Inner Experience, 14
Innocent VIII (Pope), 129
institutional religion, 17
intellect, 8, 9, 11, 65, 131
intellectual status of religion, 36
intelligibility, 36, 37, 39, 40–42, 50, 66, 70, 72, 76, 82
Interior Castle, The, 12, 130
International Association for Near-Death Studies, 28
intuition, 15, 94, 128, 130
Ionian philosophers, 59
Isaac, 80, 81, 154

Jackson, Hughlings, 121
Jacob, 80, 81, 154
Jaffé, Aniela, 87
James, William, 16–20, 26, 84, 196
Jaynes, Julian, 114
Jeremiah, 88
Jerusalem, 6, 136
Jesus Christ, 6, 7, 19, 32, 41, 46, 72, 73, 75–77, 92, 102, 112, 113, 115–118, 120, 124–129, 131, 134–136, 139, 140, 154, 155, 161–163, 165–168, 172, 190, 193, 194, 195
   Ascension, 136
   corpse of, 136, 166, 168
   Crucifixion, 125, 161
   depiction of, 46, 92, 167
   disciples, 6, 7, 125
   exorcism, 72, 75, 102
   physical appearance, 112, 113, 115, 120, 124, 125, 127–129, 131, 134
   post-Resurrection, 26, 124, 161
   Resurrection, 136, 161, 165, 168
   Risen, 7, 19, 125
   Virginal Conception of, 161
Jewish vagabonds, 7
John (Evangelist), 6, 8, 124, 168, 170
John Occhipinti Case, 119
Joseph, 32, 33, 168, 169
Josephus, 193
Journal for Near-Death Studies, 28
judicial system, 108, 110
Julian of Norwich, 130
Jung, Carl, 56, 87, 88

Kant, Immanuel, 87, 88
kinetic energy, 49
Knowing How and Knowing That, 65
knowledge from the gods, 4
Kramer, Heinrich, 129
Kudo, Yuka, 181
Kuhn, Thomas, 39, 101

Lakatos, Imre, 39, 102, 103
Lamb of God, 194
Langlois, Pauline, 41, 89, 120, 190
Larmer, Robert, 121
Law of Indiscernibles, 58
law of universal gravitation, 94, 95
laws of pendula and inclined planes, 94
laws of nature, 52, 56, 98, 99, 133
law of the pendulum, 94, 95

Laws, The, 2, 5
Legion, 73, 75, 77
legislators, 4
Leibniz, Gottfried, 33, 58
levitation, 16, 21, 26, 31–33, 132, 133
Lewis, C. S., 137
Lewis, David, 36, 50
Life after Life, 28
light from heaven, 19
Light, The (painting), 46
light of infused contemplation, the, 135
LIGO, 98
Lincoln College Case, 143, 148, 149
   Perry, 144–147, 150, 180
Linguistic Turn, The, 38
Link, Jim, 127
Locke, John, 50, 153, 159
Logical Atomism, 10
London Times, The, 44, 152, 177, 180
Long, Jeffrey, 174
longaevi, 137, 138
Lord's Prayer, the, 155, 159
Luke (Evangelist), 5–7, 19, 72, 73, 85, 125, 136, 141

MacPhilpin, John, 169, 171
Malinowski, Bronislaw, 173
Malleus Maleficarum (The Witch Hammer), 129
Mansions, 12, 15
   fourth, 12
   seventh, 14
   sixth, 13
Marian Hathaway Case, 125
Mark (Evangelist), 73, 124, 125
Marxism, 174
Marxism-Leninism, 136
Mary, 85, 135–136, 168–171, 195
Mascall, Eric, 81
materialism, 63, 189, 190
materialization, 21
Matthew (Evangelist), 73, 136
Mayr, Ernst, 79
McCreery, Charles, 111
meditation, 15, 24, 25
meditative prayer, 13, 14
Mendel, Gregor, 55, 133, 156
mental illness, 73
mental state, 34, 37, 38, 59, 61–66, 69, 189–192

mentalism, 37, 191
mentalist terms, 110
Merton, Thomas, 14, 194
meta-philosophy, 70
metaphysical, 2, 18, 70, 137
metaphysics, 35
Michelson, Albert, 40
Midgley, Carol, 44, 91, 151
Mill, John Stuart, 57, 84, 89, 153
Mind–Body Identity, Privacy, and Categories, 34
mind-cures, 17
mingling with another spirit, 10
miracle, 6, 17, 32, 33, 85, 116, 121, 133, 151, 168, 173
mirror writing, 21
Mitchell, Basil, 38
modernity, 10, 69, 84, 85, 107, 108, 122, 138, 142, 152, 173, 188
Molech, 194
Molinari, Paul, 130
monastic vocations, 14
Moody, Raymond, 28, 29, 174, 175
Morley, Edward, 40
Morning Star, the, 55
Moses, 33, 80, 82, 161
moving coffins, 21
Muhammad, 154
multilocation, 134, 135
Munificentissimus Deus, 135
Muse, 3
mutatis mutandis, 61
Myth of Er, 5
mysteries in the Spirit, 9
mystic union, 16
mystical rapture, 24, 25
mystical state, 15, 18
mysticism, 14, 15, 27, 28, 130, 138, 195
mystics, 8, 135

naked religion, 180
natural selection, 55
naturalism, 37, 70, 84, 110, 135, 140, 174, 175, 180, 182, 183, 188, 190, 192, 197
naturalistic theories of psychology, 63
necromancy, 21
neologisms, 50
neural states, 191
neurophysiology, 37, 191
neutrino, 53, 54, 67

New Testament (NT), 6–8, 72, 77, 124, 125, 127, 135–137, 160–162, 166, 194
Newton, Isaac, 39
Newtonian physics, 56, 116
Newtonian severance of space and time, 53
Nielsen, Kai, 42, 43, 66, 67, 76, 77
Nordic cultures, 93
nous, 9
nymphs, 3, 137

O'Brien, Dan, 189
Occhipinti, John, 119
Ockham's Razor, 138
Old Testament (OT), 6, 161
once-born, 17
ontologies, 62, 189
ontology, 35, 62, 89, 138, 156, 172, 187, 188, 190
oracle, 3
orders
  cosmic, 153
  Created, 128
  diabolical, 73, 137, 160, 175, 186
  Divine, 73, 88, 137, 175, 186
  human, 79, 186
  of reality, 31, 74, 92, 107, 108, 138
  natural, 6, 46, 82, 85, 93, 111, 138
  spiritual, 1, 33, 74, 78, 93, 122, 139, 158, 160, 164, 175, 186
  temporal, 55
  transcendent, 121, 128, 158, 160
ordinary language philosophy, 65
ordinary world, 45, 156, 192
Orthodox View of Theories, The, 50
Otto, Rudolf, 27
Ouija board, 21

Pals, Daniel, 34
pans, 137
paradigms, 39, 70, 101, 182, 183, 196, 198
parallelism, 63
parasympathetic, 24
Parry, Richard Lloyd, 177, 180, 192
particle
  baryon, 54, 75
  Baryon-II, 106
  Higgs boson, 97, 98
  lambda-baryon, 53, 54, 67, 75, 76, 106, 160
  subatomic, 49, 75, 76, 167
  waves, 48, 49, 53, 68

Pascal's Wager, 140
Paul (Apostle), 5–7, 9, 12, 18–20, 46, 61–63, 136
Pauline passage, 10
Peirce, Charles Saunders, 57, 79, 162
Pentecost, 5, 7
Pentecostal Church, 112, 185
perception-meditation continuum, 25
Perceptual Release Theory, 114, 121, 176
personhood, 148, 150, 153, 159, 172
Peter (Apostle), 6, 125
Phaedrus, 3
phantom passengers, 181
phenomenalists, 55, 156
phenomenological features, 107, 133, 153, 158
Philo: A Journal for Philosophy, 67
Philosophical Investigations, 65, 66
philosophy of science, 48, 51
phlogiston, 56, 96, 97, 189
Phlogiston Theory, 96, 97
photisms, 19
Phthia, 4
physical processes, 65
physicalism, 63, 69, 157, 182, 191, 192
Pierce, Charles Saunders, 79, 162
Pio di Pietrelcina (Saint), 20, 135
Pius XII (Pope), 135
pixies, 137
place of strong emotions, The, 17
Planchette, 21
Plantinga, Alvin, 104, 105
Plato, 2, 5, 12, 60
  Dialogues, 2
  scholars, 59
Platonic understanding, 129
Platonic-Catholic perspective, 134
pneuma, 9, 10, 58, 61
Popper, Karl, 47, 96–99, 103, 162, 183
positivism, 38, 43, 47, 49, 50, 56, 66, 104, 174
positivists, 36, 76
possession, 3, 22, 159, 181, 183–186
  by animal spirits, 183, 184
  by a devil, 10, 11
  by deities, 184, 185
  demonic, 21, 34, 73
  oracular, 185
possession or inspiration, 3
post-Cartesian, 63
postmortem

encounters, 150, 180
existence, 55, 143–145, 164, 165, 180, 184
judgments, 61
survival, 53, 142, 146, 150, 169, 175, 180, 181
Poulain, Augustin, 14–16, 31
prayer of quiet, 16
prayer of recollection, 12
prayer of simplicity, 16
prayer of union, 13, 16
precognition, 29
prescient dream, 3, 59
presence, 5, 16, 78, 83, 112, 156, 190, 191
pre-Socratics, 58, 60
Principle of Ad-hocness, 97
Principle of Clarity Precision, 101
Principle of Conservativism, 85
Principle of Credulity, 103, 124, 142
Principle of Cumulative Effect, 103
principle of fairness, 140
Principle of Modest Hypotheses, 100
Principle of modesty, 101
Principle of Naturalism, 84
Principle of Positive Instances, 95
Principle of Refutability, 97
Principle of Research Programs, 102
Principle of Simplicity, 85, 138
Principle of Testimony, 104, 124
Principle of Theory-laden Data, 101
private shrines, 4
probability calculus, 171
Process Theory, 35
progression of revelation, 9
prophecy, 3, 6
prophet, 3, 5, 6, 88, 114
Prophetic dreams, 21
Propositional Calculus, 187
Protestant Church, 136
Protestant Reformation, 134
Protestantism, 18
Proteus, 5
proto-scientific, 101
pseudo-Dionysius, 137
psuche, 58, 59
Psyche: The Cult of Souls and Belief in Immortality among the Greeks, 59
psychical phenomena, 19, 20
psychokinesis, 21
psychopathology, 123
Putnam, Hilary, 63

pygmies, 137
Pyrrhonic skepticism of Sextus
  Empiricus, 117

Quine, W. V. O., 36, 100–102, 108, 161
Qur'an, 141, 154

Rahner, Karl, 135
rapture, 13, 24, 25, 132
Rationalist Press Association, 52
realities, 11, 15, 66, 134, 142, 161, 175
realm of the dead, 77
recitation, 15, 179
redemption to another universe, 18
reductionist positions, 66
reformed epistemology, 122, 123
religious
  categories, 78
  language, 38, 66
  reality, 35, 75, 161
  statements, 38
  traditions, 27, 42, 45, 140, 181, 194, 195, 196
  see also experience: religious
Religious Studies, 89
reports of ghosts, 99
repositories of the dead, 4
Republic (Plato), 5
research programs, 39, 102
resurrection, 164, 165, 167
  see also Jesus Christ: Resurrection
retrocognition, 21
retroduction, 79, 162
Revelation of St John, The, 124, 162
Rhineland Case, The, 154, 157, 160
Rhineland Keswick Convention, 155
Rohde, Erwin, 59
Rorty, Richard, 34, 35, 37, 38, 41, 63
RSM
  belief, 142, 177
  claims, 152, 162, 171, 199
  environment, 161
  evidence, 23, 38, 107, 198
  experience, 1, 2, 5, 6, 8, 12, 15–20, 23, 25, 26, 30, 31, 45, 59, 65, 73, 91, 92, 98, 103, 105, 107–110, 112, 114, 116, 118, 122, 128, 132, 139–141, 145, 146, 150, 157, 160, 173, 176, 183, 186, 187, 191, 192, 194–199
  matters, 2, 103, 158
  perspective, 181

phenomena, 78, 105
sensibilities, 137
studies, 15, 108, 110, 182, 195
traditions, 139, 140, 195
views, 173, 182
Rules of Deduction, 79
Russell, Bertrand, 10, 60
Rutherford, Ernest, 49
Ryle, Gilbert, 65, 192

sacraments, 12
saintliness, 19
Samadhi, 18, 24, 25
Satan, 6, 138
satyrs, 137
Saul, 19, 136
schizophrenia, 23, 24
Schlick, Moritz, 47
scientific attitude, 138
scientific misconduct, 149, 152, 158
séance, 21
Searle, John, 36, 41
self, 18, 25, 27, 30, 56, 61, 184
  actualization, 30
  administered exorcism, 163
  awareness, 61, 62, 159
  concern, 153
  conscious, 153
  control, 184
  deprecation, 64
  examine, 189
  existent, 42, 67, 76, 82
  identification, 82
  knowing mind, 61
  knowledge, 61, 65
Sellars, Wilfrid, 63, 64, 161
semirealism, 35
Semmelweiss, 133
Sensation and Observation, 65
sense
  of being "born anew", 17
  of divinity, 17
  of Evil, 159, 162
  of God, 17, 113
  of oneness, 27
  of reincarnation, 22
  perception, 15, 20, 61, 111, 136, 145, 163
sensory automatism, 19
sensus divinitatis, 17, 105, 131
SETI, 85

Shamanism, 22, 185
Shroud of Turin, 166
Siberia, explorers of, 22
sightings, 110
sign, the, 3
Silvia (Queen of Sweden), 40
sinning against the gods, 3
Skinner, B. F., 110
Smart, J. J. C. (Jack), 34, 36, 63, 65, 161
Smart, Ninian, 196
Smith, Frederick, 22, 184–186, 195
Smith, Quentin, 67
Socrates, 2–4, 6, 58–60, 64, 195
Socratic, 52
    categories, 11
    concept of soul, 2
    view, 60, 61
soil of experience, 49
soil of observation, 49
Solomon, 193
somatomotor, 24
somatosensory modalities, 15
soul
    after death, 21, 111
    concept of, 2, 9, 10, 12, 13, 58–63, 164
    Divine influence, 11, 13, 14, 16
    evil, 4
    eyes of, 129
    good, 4, 11
    illuminated, 11, 131
    immortal, 61, 63, 137
    in ecstasy, 4
    intellectual, 11, 15
    interior of, 14
    loss, 22
    isolated, 27
    of the dead, 4, 5
    picture shown to the, 135
    power, 10, 135
    prophetic, 3
    rapture, 13, 132, 168
    rational, 8
    see also Human: soul
    see also Theory of Soul–Mind–Spirit
soul–body interaction, 63
South Place Ethical Society, 52
space-time, 53, 55, 75, 91, 112, 128, 133, 148, 149
spatial link, 156
spatiotemporal–causal world, 133
speaking in tongues, 7, 10, 29

Speaking of the Devil, 186
Special Consequence Condition, 95
Special Consequence Principle, 94
Spencer, Kathleen, 46, 84, 92
Spinoza, Baruch, 81, 83
spirit painting, 45, 46, 92
spirit photography, 46
Spirit-baptism, 18
spirits
    attachment, 22, 78, 184, 185
    beings, 34, 85, 93, 94
    belief, 70, 86, 88, 93, 112, 134, 188, 194
    childsnatchers, 185
    claims about, 64, 72–74, 79, 80, 86, 87, 98–103, 106–110, 118, 133, 157, 160, 162, 168, 175, 192, 197
    definition of, 47, 51, 52, 62, 63, 70, 71, 73, 75, 77, 82, 84, 85, 96, 141, 146, 190, 192
    demonic, 6, 21, 73, 78, 138, 155, 190
    diabolical, 79
    divine, 6, 34, 45, 78, 79, 90, 101, 138, 141, 186
    encounters with, 45, 52, 71, 90
    evil, 7, 10, 21, 35, 41, 42, 43, 73, 76, 77, 78, 88, 89, 102, 156, 162, 186
    finite spirits, 43, 87
    good, 10, 11, 41, 42
    influence, 20–22, 27, 46, 92, 133, 173
    of animals, 179, 183, 184, 186
    of divination, 7, 10, 20, 87
    of God, 5, 7, 11, 17, 41, 42, 89, 186
    of the dead, 20–22, 28, 55, 112, 138, 144, 174, 175, 177, 179
    séance, 21
    totem, 22
    writing, 20, 21
    see also spirit painting
    see also Theory of Spirits
spiritual
    espousal, 13
    framework, 173
    marriage, 14, 16
    realities, 11, 134, 142, 175
    revelation, 139
    traditions, 45
    world, 41
Spiritual Journal, 135
spiritus, 8
spooky stuff, 63

Index

spouse, 13
Sprenger, James, 129
St Matthew's Gospel, 136
standard introspection, 15
Stanford Encyclopedia of Philosophy, 15, 70
state of unconsciousness, 3
states of affairs, 15
states of consciousness, 11, 14, 18, 26
Stephen (Saint), 8, 136
Stevenson, Ian, 22
stone throwing, 22
subatomic physics, 48, 53
subliminal door, 18
succubi, 129
Sunday Telegraph, The, 52
supernatural, 12, 21, 22, 34, 47, 84, 119, 134, 161
supernaturalism, 86, 197
supernaturalistic, 115
Swinburne, Richard, 25–27, 124
Symposium on Theology and Falsification, 38

Tantric Shaivism, 184
Taves, Ann, 1
Taylor, A. E., 2, 11, 59
telepathy, 22, 29
teleportation, 22
Teresa (Saint), 8, 12–16, 20, 128–134, 136, 139
Thales, 58
theism, 37, 43, 53, 61, 66, 77, 82, 83, 109, 128, 139
  see also Christian: theism
theistic philosophers, 109
theists, 37, 67, 109, 157
Theorems, 79
theoretical entities, 47–51, 55–58, 63, 66
Theoretical Model, 29
Theory of a Luminescent Ether, 39
Theory of Angels, 94
Theory of Demons, 34
Theory of Dream Intrusion, 121
Theory of Elves, 93–95
Theory of Gravitational Attraction, 94
Theory of Human Personality, 35
Theory of Mental States, 66, 190, 192
Theory of Mind, 34, 37, 38, 69, 86
  see also mental states
Theory of Phlogiston, 189

Theory of Relativity, 53
Theory of Soul–Mind–Spirit, 62
Theory of Spirits, 34–43, 45, 47, 50–52, 57–58, 61, 64, 66, 69, 70, 72, 73, 75, 78, 79, 84, 93–95, 99–101, 103, 104, 106, 133, 138, 141, 142, 157, 158, 162, 176, 177, 180, 182, 188–192
Theory of Subatomic Structures, 35
Theory of Theism, 53, 82
Thetis, 5
To Enter, to be entered, to merge, 184
Tolstoy, Leo, 18
totemism, 22
tower pattern, 48
Tractatus Logico-Philosophicus, 65
trance-state, 23
transcendence, 67
transcendent, 10, 11, 42, 43, 67, 77, 121, 128, 154, 158, 160
Treasurer's House, The, 100
Trench, Bridget, 170, 172
Trenn, Thaddeus, 39, 166, 167
Trethowan, Dom Illtyd, 132
trolls, 137
trophotropic arousal, 24
true wisdom, 13
Twelve, The, 163
Twenty Cases Suggestive of Reincarnation, 22
twice-born, 17
Tylor, Edward B, 183

UFO, 86
UK Angel Encounter, 44, 90, 151
Ullian, Sam, 100, 101
ultimate realities, 66
unconscious life, 18, 59
unconscious, the, 56
Underhill, Evelyn, 130
unitive life, 12

Vancouver Sun, The, 45
Varieties of Religious Experience, The, 17
Venus, 55
verificationist criterion, 43
Vespasian, 193
vide infra, 25
Vienna Circle, 47, 66
Vincent, Roy, 161
virtues, 11

vision
  Christic, 8, 31, 103, 112, 117, 131, 134, 190, 192, 195
  corporeal, 9, 122, 129–131
  extraordinary, 10, 32
  imaginative, 10, 11, 14, 129–131
  intellectual, 9, 14, 129–131
  Marian, 125, 195
  mystical, 113
  noncorporeal, 11
  of angels, 78, 196
  of Christ, 41, 115, 118, 120, 124, 129, 135, 154
  of Mary, 118, 195
  picture shown to the soul, 135
  religious, 113, 114, 117, 124, 169
  sensory or quasi-sensory, 26, 29
  spiritual, 9–11, 14, 32
  veridical, 126
  waking, 4
visions and apparitions, 7
Visions of Jesus: Direct Encounters from the New Testament to Today, 41, 77, 112

Waismann, Friedrich, 66
waking dreams, 23
Wallis, C. D., 184
Watts, Fraser, 123
Web of Belief, The, 100
Wesley, John, 26
West, Louis, 121

Western
  civilization, 2, 61, 140
  culture, 1, 17, 58, 61, 71, 83, 91, 93, 108, 134, 164, 180
  discussion of experience, 8
  history, 2, 5, 12
  interpretation of visionary experience, 129
  literature, 184
  thought, 2, 34, 56, 61, 104, 146, 173, 174, 184
  tradition, 62, 104, 187
Wheeler, Robin, 32
Whitehead, Alfred North, 35
Whitman, Walt, 27
Will, The, 65
witch, 78, 88, 129, 184
witchcraft, 5, 88, 129, 183
without a body, 42, 43, 67
Wittgenstein, Ludwig, 38, 47, 65, 66, 123
wizard, 5, 78
word of knowledge, the, 6
word of wisdom, the, 6
working of miracles, The, 6

Xenophon, 2

Yogananda, Paramahans, 165

Zaehner, Robert, 27
Zazen, 24

For EU product safety concerns, contact us at Calle de José Abascal, 56–1°,
28003 Madrid, Spain or eugpsr@cambridge.org.

www.ingramcontent.com/pod-product-compliance
Ingram Content Group UK Ltd.
Pitfield, Milton Keynes, MK11 3LW, UK
UKHW041920120825
461732UK00004B/4